AMERICAN SOLDIER AT
13 YEARS OLD
WW II

SERVED IN KOREA AND VIETNAM WARS

To Marieke

You're a good Patriotic
American.

Best Regards
James R. Clark

TRAFFORD

Note for Librarians: a cataloguing record for this book that includes Dewey Decimal Classification and US Library of Congress numbers is available from the Library and Archives of Canada. The complete cataloguing record can be obtained from their online database at: www.collectionscanada.ca/amicus/index-e.html

ISBN 1-4120-5938-0

Printed in Victoria, BC, Canada

Printed on paper with minimum 30% recycled fibre.
Trafford's print shop runs on "green energy" from solar, wind and other environmentally-friendly power sources.

TRAFFORD

Offices in Canada, USA, Ireland and UK

This book was published *on-demand* in cooperation with Trafford Publishing. On-demand publishing is a unique process and service of making a book available for retail sale to the public taking advantage of on-demand manufacturing and Internet marketing. On-demand publishing includes promotions, retail sales, manufacturing, order fulfilment, accounting and collecting royalties on behalf of the author.

Book sales for North America and international:

Trafford Publishing, 6E–2333 Government St.,

Victoria, BC v8t 4p4 CANADA

phone 250 383 6864 (toll-free 1 888 232 4444)

fax 250 383 6804; email to orders@trafford.com

Book sales in Europe:

Trafford Publishing (uk) Limited, 9 Park End Street, 2nd Floor

Oxford, UK OX1 1HH UNITED KINGDOM

phone 44 (0)1865 722 113 (local rate 0845 230 9601)

facsimile 44 (0)1865 722 868; info.uk@trafford.com

Order online at:

trafford.com/05-0839

10 9 8 7 6 5 4

AMERICAN SOLDIER AT AGE 13, WW II

GOD AND SOLDIERS ALL MEN ADORE.
BUT WHEN WAR IS OVER AND ALL THINGS RIGHTED,
GOD IS NEGLECTED AND SOLDIERS SLIGHTED.

ACKNOWLEDGMENTS

I would like to extend my thanks to the many people who gave me the encouragement to write my autobiography. First, to my sisters, Jean Wyke, Jane Savage, Maxine Mc Leroy, Donna Healy, and Marguerite Smith. Growing up with all my sisters, remembering and cherishing all our yesterdays together, I find fulfillment within me. Also, thanks to my daughter, Micki and her husband, John Sterbick, my niece, Betty Jane, and her husband, Bill Cooper, my wife, Dorothy Clark, my editor, Deanna Mason and Rebecca Lopez of Graham, Washington whose research for a school project on the Nazi war criminals was very helpful.

Thank you

DEDICATION

This book is dedicated to my only granddaughter, Evan Arianna Odette Sterbick, and to my wife, Dorothy, who helped me fight off my habit of procrastination and gave me the confidence to finish this book.

PREFACE

At the age of thirteen I served in the United States Army during World War II. I lied about my age to the local Draft Board, was inducted, went through basic training and served for a year before it became known by my superior officers that I was only fourteen years old.

I grew up in a large family during hard times. The depression was just coming to an end. My father was an alcoholic, but my mother was determined to keep the family of seven children together and she brought us up as good Americans, and to have a sense of patriotism for our country. Those were hard times, but we were lucky too because we had Franklin D. Roosevelt as our president. Young men were running to draft boards to join one of the services. Older citizens were volunteering their services to the Red Cross or giving blood to the blood banks. People accepted shortages and doing without. We all wanted to win the war and back up our servicemen.

This book is about those early years of my life and my service in the military, from World War II to Korea, and then to Vietnam. I will never forget the strong patriotism that all Americans felt during the war with Germany and Japan. I served in the Army for about a year and was discharged when I was fourteen. After my discharge I was inducted into the American Legion in 1944 as the nation's youngest Legionnaire.

As a civilian I began to realize how much I missed military life. I had made up my mind while serving that I wanted to be a career soldier. But after that first year, I knew that I would have to wait until I was seventeen years old. I'm glad I made the service my career, and I'm happy to have had the opportunity to serve with so many patriotic and brave men, from World War II, Korea, and Vietnam.

I've been asked whether I would do it all over again if I could. There are two things I would change. First, I would stay at home and finish high school and then go into the service. The other thing I'd change is that I would not go back to Vietnam as a civilian while the war was still raging. I found out the hard way that the enemy is just as willing to kill American civilians as they were to kill American soldiers. I have no regrets about my military service. My exposure to war will be forever in my memories. But there are times when the joy of life replaces despair and the scars of war, and in those times of joy we go on with our lives.

CONTENTS

1

GROWING UP IN HARD TIMES OF THE DEPRESSION

I grew up poor and on welfare with a father and a mother, one brother and five sisters. We moved a lot from one state to another. My father was an ironworker who followed big contracting jobs when bridges, dams and steel mills were being built. My mother told us that my father was on a crew that did the high climbing jobs. When a job was finished in one state, my father would leave his family and travel alone to find another job. Then he would send for all of us to join him. When he found work, we would travel by bus. We did a lot of traveling and living in first one state and then another.

This was in the 1930's. The United States was trying to recover from the depression. My family was always poor no matter how much money my father made on a job. He was addicted to alcohol and lived for just one thing, the whisky bottle. I remember how angry my mother would be when my father came home from work on pay day. He would always cash his paycheck at the tavern near the work place where a lot of his fellow workers would also stop to have a drink.

My father did not know how to manage money. By the time he arrived at home on pay day, he was almost broke, after having bought everyone in the tavern drinks, and after having paid back all his fellow workers all the money he had borrowed between pay days so that he could buy whisky. My father was not a family man. He was not a caring man. He was always drunk. He didn't like dogs or cats. He didn't like the boys in the family either. I learned at an early age to stay out of his way. If I didn't I got his big hand across my face, or he would kick me. He always said, "Shut up, boy. Children are to be seen and not heard."

My father would use a long and wide razor strap. When he started hitting me, he would hit hard. The razor strap was what barbers used to sharpen their straight razors. I remember my mother's crying when he would slap her. I was so sad because of the way he would treat her. The only person who would stand up to my father and his mean ways was my older sister, Jean.

I remember one night when my father came home and in a bad mood. That night my mother wasn't at home. That made him even angrier. He sat at the kitchen table drinking his whisky. All of us kids were in another room. We all knew that it was better to stay out of his way when he was drinking and in a bad mood. My father yelled for us to come out to the kitchen where he was. Jean told him that we were going to stay in the room where we were hiding. My father could see that Jean was firm on standing up to him, so he backed off. Then he went back into the kitchen and to his whisky bottle.

My mother and sister, Donna, told me in later years about an incident when my father held my nine-month old baby sister, Donna, by one ankle and dangled her out the window of our eighth-floor apartment. He threatened to drop her to the ground unless my mother gave him the only two dollars that she had. She had no choice but to give him the money.

My father was not a man who would stay and support his family. He would not take responsibility for a family as the other fathers who lived around us were doing. My father moved us to Grafton, West Virginia and into a basement apartment. Then he left and went looking for work in Pennsylvania. My mother went to work in a small restaurant so that we could always have food on the table. She knew that my father couldn't be depended on to take care of his family.

In Grafton my mother made good friends with another family with children our age. We all liked visiting that family. They were hillbillies and quite musically inclined. On Saturday nights we would join in with them and sing old country songs. There was an old man there they called, "Pappy." That was for grandfather. We all called him "Pappy" too. He had a female German Police dog that had puppies. Pappy didn't have a car and he walked everywhere he went. I would see him walking past where we lived with his big dog and all the little puppies following along behind.

One day I asked him how much he wanted for one of the puppies. He said, "Five dollars." I was about seven years old at the time. I wanted a dog of my own, and I pestered my mother until she gave in and bought me one. The next time Pappy came by with all the puppies, I got to pick out the one I wanted. It was a male dog and I named him, "Vonnie." This was my first responsibility, and the dog and I became the very best of pals. I know the dog loved me as much as I loved him.

After living in Grafton for some time my father sent for us to move to

Curry Hollow, Pennsylvania. He had a job as an ironworker building a steel mill. He wrote to my mother telling her that he had built a house for us. When we arrived in Curry Hollow we found that he had built a three-room, tar-paper shack. The house had board sidings, and the outsides were covered with black tar-paper. There were wooden floors, no carpeting, and no insulation. There was no toilet. We had a handmade outhouse up on a hillside behind the house. There was no running water or electricity. After the first year we had electricity. Water had to be carried from a natural spring that was quite a distance from our shack. There were woods and hills all around us. My dog and I liked that. We could run wild in the woods together. My father didn't like my puppy, so I made sure that I kept the dog out of his way.

We all learned to take a bath in a galvanized iron tub that was brought into the house on Saturday nights. That was bath night. And that was the night my brother and I had to make many trips back and forth from the shack to the community spring where everyone had to carry their own drinking water and bath water. My brother and I carried two buckets each. The spring was about three hundred yards from our shack.

There was a creek not too far from the shack. It was a strong running creek with clear water, and in summer we would strip down to our underwear and stack up round river rocks from the bottom of the creek to build up a dam so that we could slow down the flow of the water. This would give us our own swimming pool. The only bad thing about damming up the creek to cool off in was that people who lived in shacks upstream used the creek to throw their garbage in. Some even had their outhouses in the middle of the creek.

The outhouses were resting on two cut-down trees with each end of the trees resting on each bank of the creek, and the outhouses resting in the middle of the logs. The water was always cold in the creek when we wanted to swim and play in the dammed up creek. We had to throw out all the garbage that had floated down. There were times when used condoms would float down the creek. Some of the younger kids who didn't know what they were would blow them up like balloons.

There were about eight or nine families who lived in this neighborhood of tar-paper shacks close to ours, but there were about fifteen or twenty more families who lived up the dirt road from our neighborhood. Of all the families who lived in Curry Hollow, only about five of the families owned a car.

If somebody had to go to the doctor, we would ask a neighbor with a car to take us, or we would have to walk down the dirt road from our shack to the main road, which was about a mile. This was where the bus stop was to go to town. The bus would run about once an hour during the day. To get to the bus stop we would walk down the dirt road and under a railroad overpass.

There was no school bus for us kids to take to school. School was about two miles away. There was a shortcut to walk to school that was a mile shorter, but that was through the cemetery up on a hill. You had to go up a steep hill and through some woods to get to the cemetery. Not many of us would take the shortcut because we were afraid. Some of us did take the shortcut. Some of us boys would try to get a head start on the rest of the kids when school was let out. We would run to get to the cemetery and then hide behind a headstone. When kids would get close to the headstone, we would jump out and scare them so bad the hair would stand straight up on their heads. The boys would run like a race horse and the girls would stand still and scream.

My older brother, Bob, quit school and went to work with my father as a steel worker. It wasn't long before he started drinking along with my father. When my brother went to work I was the only one left to do all the chores like chopping wood and carrying water. The only heat we had in the shack was a potbelly stove that was in the middle of the floor of our small kitchen. This was the same stove that my mother used for cooking. In the winter, on cold mornings, all us kids would gather round the warm stove to keep warm while we got dressed for school.

It was my job to keep the stove in wood. Sometimes on the weekends some of the neighbor boys and I would go down to the railroad tracks and pick up chunks of coal that had fallen off the open coal train cars. If we were lucky, when we got to the train tracks there would be a train stopped there for some reason. This would give us time to climb up on the train and throw or kick coal off the top of the coal train. We all carried a big burlap bag to put the coal in. Sometimes we would make three or four trips carrying coal from the railroad tracks to home. Coal in the stove would burn longer than wood.

Another of my chores was taking care of the chickens. We didn't know about, or have the convenience of going to the supermarket and buying a chicken that was cleaned and packaged. When I was eight years old it was left up to me to chop off the head of the chicken and then dip it into hot water. Then my sisters and I would pull off all the feathers. I learned how to remove the heart, liver and gizzard. These were saved for cooking. We were poor, but my mother always saw to it that we had food. There was always a pot of beans on the stove, or a pot of chicken and dumplings. We had no refrigerator. We had a second-hand icebox, and we had kerosene lamps for light in our shack.

My older sister, Jean, had found a job and left home before we moved into the tar-paper shack in Curry Hollow. I know that she must have been happy to get away from our father. With Jean away from home that left five of us kids still there. I was the second to the youngest in the family. My oldest sister, Jane, who was still in her teens, was now the one who was responsible for looking after things when my mother had to be away from home for any reason. And now that my brother, Bob, had a paying job, that left me to be the only one to carry the water.

On wash day I had to carry the water from the spring, rain, snow or shine. I didn't look forward to Saturday afternoons when my mother washed all our clothes. She did the washing in the same galvanized iron tub that we bathed in. She used an Irish washboard. I saw her washing our clothes with that washboard until her knuckles would bleed. My sisters would help my mother with the washing by wringing out the wet clothes by hand, and then hanging them up to dry, outside in good weather and inside in bad weather.

I remember the day when one of our good neighbors who were moving to the big city of McKeesport gave my mother a manually operated clothes wringer and a washer drum to hold water. This was a luxury washing machine in those days. We didn't have any other luxuries at that time. No one had ever heard of or seen a TV. We didn't have a radio because there was no electricity for a long time. We couldn't go to the movies because my parents couldn't afford it, and it was a long way to any town that had movies.

What did we do for entertainment? Well, on Friday and Saturday nights our family, except for my father, would all go up the dirt road to the house of friends of ours from Grafton, West Virginia. There would be banjo, mandolin, guitar, and violin playing and singing. They had kids the same ages as we were. We had a good time singing old country songs and old gospel songs.

My father never went to these gatherings of the families. Alone, he could drink all he wanted to, and he didn't have to hide the bottle from my mother. On Sundays we went to a little white church that was just within walking distance from our shack. My mother would make sure that we all went, except my father. He always had some place else to go, like to the tavern in Dravosburg about three miles away from Curry Hollow.

I liked going to church because we would sing some good gospel songs. My mother would give us each a nickel to put in the basket at church. The seating in the church was on homemade long wooden benches, and for heat there was a potbelly stove. The older men would get to church ahead of the rest of the congregation so they could build a fire in the stove.

We didn't get to go to church every Sunday because the preacher was a traveling preacher. And on some Sundays he wouldn't show up. He was the only one with a key to the church. There was one thing about going to church that I didn't like, and that was getting saved.

I didn't like going up to the altar to be saved because the preacher would put his big hand on the top of my head and push down hard driving my chin into my chest. Then he would say, "Jesus, save this boy and make him sin no more." Then, with his hand still pressing down on my head, he would ask, "Boy, do you see the light?" I would say, "Yes," because I knew that if I didn't, he would keep pushing down hard.

When the preacher wanted people to come forward to the altar to be saved, it didn't seem to matter to my mother that I had just been saved the week before, or the week before that. No sooner would the preacher say, "Get saved," than my mother would jerk me by the arm and say, "Get up there, boy. You need saving." But I saw the same thing happening to other kids in church. Their parents would shove them up to the altar to be saved over and over again too.

My father and brother didn't get along well working together. They would come home late and drunk on pay days, and they would be arguing. One night, when I wasn't at home, my father and brother came home and they had been drinking. An argument broke out between them. My father hit my brother, Bob, in the face with his fist knocking him out. My brother hit the floor like a rock. My mother came running out to put cold towels on his face to get him to come to. We had no telephone to call for medical help. There was no ambulance service. In those days of hard times, when somebody got hurt, people had to help each other as well as they could.

Not long after that my brother left home and struck out on his own to find his place in the world. He was about eighteen years old. I missed him. My mother and father argued more than ever after Bob left home. And my father drank more because of the incident with Bob. No one in the neighborhood of Curry Hollow liked my father or the way he treated his family.

2

THE ARMY SENT MY BROTHER HOME IN A CASKET

In 1938 a baby girl, Marguerite, was born. Now there were four girls left at home and one boy. Donna was no longer the youngest in the family.

In 1939 my father was out of work because the job he and my brother had worked on was finished. I remember my father, on a Saturday, asking me if I wanted to walk to the small town of Dravosburg. He wanted to get a haircut. We walked the three miles down the railroad tracks to get to Dravosburg. He took me into the barbershop with him.

It was about noon as my father waited his turn in the barber chair. I sat looking at books. When the barber was done cutting my father's hair, my father said to me, "Son, you stay here in the barbershop." He said he had something to do and that he would be right back.

After four hours had passed, and my father hadn't returned, the owner said to me, "Well, boy, I don't think your father's coming back. Maybe you better go home." The shop was about to close.

I left and walked to where there was a tavern. I was too young to go in by myself. I waited outside, and as each man came out I would ask him whether my father was inside. None of them knew him, but at last one man did come out who knew my father. He had worked with him on a job. He told me that my father had been in the tavern most of the afternoon, but that he had left about thirty minutes ago.

I walked home along the railroad tracks thinking that maybe my father had drunk too much and just forgot that I was waiting for him in the barbershop. When I arrived home I found out that my father had not returned. I told my mother that he left me in the barbershop. I told her all about it. My mother said, "Well, he must be out getting drunk on what little money we have left."

Months went by and nobody knew anything about where my father might have gone. My mother took a bus to town to apply for welfare. There was nobody working to bring home any money now. We were dirt poor. In those times there was nothing anybody could do about a father who wouldn't support his family.

I didn't miss my father. I was glad he was gone. I felt at ease knowing that he wasn't around to kick me or slap me for no reason. I wanted to help my mother, but the best I could do was to get a paper route. It was a walking route. I didn't own a bike. I was nine years old at the time.

Another way I found to make small change money was to sell scrap iron. Every week there was an old man with a horse-drawn wagon who would come down our dirt road wanting to buy scrap iron. A friend of mine and I would walk up and down the railroad tracks looking for scrap iron. Sometimes trains would be pulling rail cars full of scrap iron, and some of the scrap would fall off. If we were lucky, and the train stopped for some reason, one of us would get on top of the rail car and throw scrap iron down while the other one would keep on the lookout for a railroad man.

During those years America was selling a lot of scrap metal to Japan. This was before World War II. I gave most of the money I made to my mother from selling scrap metal and from my paper route. I wanted to help out. It didn't help much. We depended on welfare.

All the kids would go barefoot in the summer so we could save our shoes for school. This helped, but there were still times when we all had to put cardboard down on the insides of our shoes because of the holes in our shoes. My mother would send me down the road with my homemade, little pull-wagon made of wooden boards and small iron wheels. Once a month the welfare office would give out food supplies to families on welfare.

I had to go down the road about three miles with my wagon. The welfare worker would load the wagon with our family's supply of food for the month. That usually consisted of flour, sugar, cooking oil, a big sack of navy beans, some fat-back, and a big jar of applebutter. In place of butter they gave us oleo with a package of yellow liquid to mix in the oleo to make it look like butter. It was terrible. But we didn't really know how terrible it was because we had never tasted real butter.

We used the jar of applebutter instead of oleo. My mother tried to make Christmas for all of us as happy as she could. We kids were only allowed one gift each. One year I asked for a Red Rider BB gun. My mom made sure that I got my BB gun. Some of the other boys in the neighborhood got BB guns too. Sometimes we would get together and compete to see who the best shot was. We would shoot at empty cans coming down the creek. I wasn't into shooting birds. I loved all animals and I was growing up at this time. I had a German Shepherd Police dog that I had had from a puppy. He was my best companion, and he was an outside dog.

I had a friend who lived up the road from us. He also had a German Shepherd Police dog and a BB gun. Sometimes we would walk down to the tavern and at just about dark, my friend would hide in the bushes on one side of the tavern door. I would hide in the bushes on the other side. As the drunks came out we would shoot at them in the butt.

We had a good time watching them jumping and letting out a howl. Nobody ever caught us because we had a good hiding place. And we had it planned that if someone did see us and came running after us, we would just run through the swamp. It was close by the tavern and covered by tall swamp grass. The swamp extended for about half a mile. My friend and I knew every inch of the swamp. We would often wade in the swamp looking for frogs, snakes and tadpoles. Of course my mother never knew that I was doing this. She would have taken my BB gun away from me.

I didn't get to see my brother, Bob, much after our father abandoned us. My brother, Bob, was interested in girls. He would drop by the house maybe about once a month. My mother did not say so, but I think my brother was living with a girl at the time. I think the girl was in the little town of Dravosburg. When he was ready to leave he would ask me if I wanted to walk with him down the dirt road to the main road, and then to the bus stop. I would wait with him until the bus came. Just before the bus came he would put two dimes in my pocket. Then he would wave to me from the window of the bus.

I would be so happy that I'd run and hop-skip back home. I didn't tell my sisters because they would have been jealous. And besides, I didn't think Bob would want me to tell them that he was giving money to me and not to them.

There was a candy store close to the school in Dravosburg. After school I would make a beeline for the store to buy some candy. I would share the candy with my sisters sometimes. My brother, Bob, was the male figure in my life. He was the one I looked up to. I missed him after he moved out of our house. There was no one bringing home money, and my mother had a new baby.

My mother knew that if our family kept living in a tar-paper shack in Curry Hollow that we would never be anything but poor. So with what money she had hidden from our father, she went to the outskirts of McKeesport, a place called the Tenth Ward. She found and rented an old two-story house. It was a big house. Railroad tracks ran behind the house and our backyard was small. In front of the house there was a small yard, then a public sidewalk. There were trolley cars and automobiles running down the main street. It was

1940 when we moved into this house.

In this house we had hot and cold running water, a big white bathtub and for heat we had a coal furnace. My sisters and I thought it was incredible to have hot and cold running water and a bathtub to take a bath in. I was so happy that I didn't have to carry water anymore. And I didn't have to look for coal on the side of the railroad tracks. But I couldn't use my BB gun anymore. I would have been in big trouble in the city. My dog was unhappy. I had to keep him tied up all the time. Living in town was better in some ways, but worse in others. I felt that I had lost my freedom, and my dog had too. We couldn't run in the woods or look for frogs in the swamp. But I knew that it was better for the rest of the family.

The school was only about eight blocks from our house. The elementary school was on Atlantic Avenue in the Tenth Ward of McKeesport. I will never forget the school principal. He was a big man. I was always getting into trouble. I was bigger than all the other kids in my class, and I felt funny being in the same class with them. I was defiant. I didn't do my assignments and I didn't do anything the teacher wanted me to do. I didn't listen. I didn't like any of the other kids in the class. They had all been brought up in a big town, and they thought they were smarter than I was because I had come out of the woods.

Many a school day the woman teacher would escort me to the principal's office. Then she would tell him things that I was doing in her classroom. She wasn't going to put up with me. When she was talking to him, she would even add a few things that I hadn't done because she didn't like me. One day she said that she didn't want me in her class. She said that I upset the other children.

That made the principal mad. He had a big, flat wooden paddle behind his desk. He took it out and told me to turn around. Then he hit me with the paddle hard a number of times.

After having been taken to the principal's office almost every week, I learned something about him. I was told that he had been in the Army and had been nerve-gassed in World War I. Because of this he would sit behind his big desk and close his eyes for long periods of time as he would talk.

The next time I was taken to his office I waited for his lecture. I was standing in front of his desk and he was telling me why I was about to be punished. When he closed his eyes, I quietly, but very quickly, got out of his office and out of the school building before his eyes opened.

That was the beginning of my playing hooky from school. I didn't care if I never went back to school. I started hanging around Newt Harrington's candy store and Sam Larson's drugstore. That's where all the kids would go to sit at the soda fountain and drink milkshakes for ten cents.

Sometimes during school hours I would walk over the big bridge from the Tenth Ward to uptown McKeesport and hang around outside a movie theatre waiting for it to open. I could see a cowboy movie for ten cents. If I didn't have the ten cents to get in, I would sneak in the theatre when the doorman wasn't looking, or when he left his post for some reason. I would stay in the movie theatre all day and watch the same movie over and over. I'd watch the movie clock, and when it was time for school to be let out, I would go home. It didn't take long before the school sent word home to my mother that I was missing school. My mother convinced me that I should go back to school.

I went back to school and told my teacher that I wasn't going to let anybody hit me with a board again, and that I would be ready to fight if I had to. I knew when I told her this that she would tell the principal what I'd said. She must have, because I was never taken to the principal's office again.

I hadn't seen my brother, Bob, for quite a while. And my mother was keeping his whereabouts a secret. I did overhear my mother tell my older sister, Jane, that Bob had made a girl from the town of Dravosburg pregnant, and that Bob was now on the run. Only my mother knew where he was. In that same year, 1940, my mother applied for a divorce on the grounds of non-support.

Not long after the divorce my mother received word that my father had just returned from a trip to China. He was in the Merchant Marines, and he was, at that time, in a hotel in McKeesport and wanted to see his children. We were to go over to the hotel and meet with him. I didn't want to go but my mother talked me into it. My mother said that if my father was mean toward me that I should just leave and walk back home.

Not all of the kids went to see him. My sister, Maxine, nick-named Mickey, and Donna and I went to meet with him. My father looked good. He had a fresh haircut and a shave. He smelled like he had been drinking, but no one could tell by looking at him. We all met outside the hotel. My father gave the two girls a kiss on the forehead and he patted me on the top of my head and said, "Hi."

He took us to a bar and grill to get us something to eat. We sat in a booth and ordered food. My father didn't order food, but he did order a small glass of whisky and a small glass of beer. He would drink half the whisky, then wash it down with half a glass of beer. He had about three servings of whisky and beer while we were eating our food.

We left the bar and grill and my father took us to a clothing store and bought us some clothes, shoes and socks. Then we went back to the bar and grill. He bought us all soft drinks while he drank another whisky and beer. My father could hold his whisky. He wouldn't get to the point that he would stagger or slur his words. After a lot of drinking he would get mean and sleepy. He would go and lie down and sleep for three or four hours, then get back up as sober as a judge. Then he would start drinking again. At the bar and grill we said goodbye. He said he was going to sail out to sea in a day or two. That was the last we saw of our father for another year or two.

I was at the age that I was now interested in girls. There was a girl in the neighborhood who was about four years older than I was. She went to high school with my sister, Mickey. I will never forget her because she was my first love. Her name was Doris. I was eleven years old. She and I had a love affair. We would meet in dark places because her parents were strict with her and because they didn't like me. I was just starting to adjust to city life a little.

My dog didn't like city life. He didn't have any freedom. He had to be tied up. I started hanging out at the pool hall with boys older than I was. I liked standing outside the pool hall with the other guys in the evening watching the girls go by. If we saw a good-looking girl we would give out a whistle catcall.

In those years of the forties it was a coming thing what boys and grown men would do when they saw a good-looking girl or woman. Most of the ones we whistled at seemed to like it. They would smile and blush. Some would even make it a point to make more than one trip past the whistling cat caller just to get the guys to whistle at them again. Those were the good old days. Today whistling at girls would be considered sexual harassment. Our society has changed.

My next to the oldest sister, Jane, went to work at Grant's Five and Dime store in McKeesport. My mother took in a male boarder. His name was Bill. We all knew him from Curry Hollow. He was the father of three children, and he and his wife were divorced. The ex-wife had the three children. Bill was my mother's age and he was good to us kids.

Bill was a foreman on the Union Railroad who never missed a day of work. He was a father who paid his child support every month. He drank one quart of beer on Friday nights. He treated my mother with respect. That made all of us kids happy.

My older sister, Jean, married Ralph Wyke, the son of a family that my family had known for many years. Jean and Ralph had grown up together. They married in 1941. Jean married a good man. Ralph was the kind of person that everybody liked and could get along with. Ralph liked working on overseas construction jobs. Right after they married the two of them went to

Puerto Rico on a big construction job.

That year we got another big surprise. Our brother, Bob, came to our house in McKeesport to see us and he was in uniform. He had joined the Army in 1940. My mother was the only one who had known where Bob was, and she hadn't told any of us. My brother looked good in his uniform. All the family was proud of him.

Bob stayed at home with us for about two or three days, and during that time there was no mention of the girl in Dravosburg or that she was having a baby. The next time we heard from Bob was in 1941.

He had been upgraded to sergeant. We were all happy. I wanted to go out and brag to all the other kids in the neighborhood about my brother. I wanted to tell them that my brother was a sergeant in the U.S. Army, but my mother told us kids never to tell anyone that Bob was in the Army. She said that if anybody should ever ask about Bob, we should say, "I don't know anything." It sure was hard for me to keep that secret. I wanted to brag about my brother, but I made a promise that I wouldn't tell and I didn't.

Another big event of 1941 came over the radio. The Japanese surprise attack on Pearl Harbor sank the bulk of the U.S. Pacific Fleet. This sent a shock through everyone in America, young and old. People sat by the radio listening for news. On December 8,1941, President Roosevelt declared war against Japan. Three days later Germany and Italy declared war on the United States. I was young at the time, but I had been told a lot about World War I, so I knew what was happening. It was remarkable the way the neighbors all came together.

We all knew that we were all in this together. Our American pride and patriotism to our country came through in all its glory. We all felt it. Everyone was thinking and asking, "What can I do to help my country and to help the servicemen fight and win this war with Japan and Germany."

The Draft Board went into high gear. All men eighteen years old and up to forty years old had to report to the Draft Board. The branches of the services were taking married men with children. It didn't matter. One of our neighbors who had four children was drafted into the Army. Everyone was touched by the war years. Every household had to live by rationing of a lot of food and gas. Ration card books were issued to families.

There was a shortage of everything. Even women's nylon stockings were a rationed item. If the women could even find a store that might have gotten a small supply in, there would be a hundred women standing outside the store waiting for the door to open to buy nylons. Coffee was a big rationed item. Those who could began growing vegetables to try to supplement food for the family. These were called "Victory Gardens." Cigarettes were also rationed to the public. Most people started rolling their own. Most Americans didn't complain, and when someone did complain about the shortages, there would always be someone to set them straight by saying, "Hey, don't you know there's a war going on."

With all able-bodied men being drafted into the service, there was a shortage of manpower for jobs. Women who could work did so in steel mills, factories and on assembly lines. There was such a shortage that if you didn't like the work you were doing, you could quit and go to some other place and be hired for a job the same day. You didn't have to have any job experience. They would train you for the job. Things were booming. Everybody was making money. My family even got off welfare.

We had paychecks coming in. There was a popular song at this time about women who took over industry jobs, "Rosie the Riveter." She worked at a fighter plane factory pounding rivets into the new plane structures with a rivet gun.

In the war years of the 40s mothers who had husbands, sons, or daughters serving in the Armed Forces were exceptionally proud even though they might fear that something might happen to them when they were sent overseas. Just about every house in America had a small blue flag hanging in their window symbolizing that they had someone in the family in the service. A blue star on the flag meant that they were serving. If the serving person became wounded, the blue star would be changed to silver. If the serving person was killed the star would be changed to gold. In some family homes there were as many as four or five or more stars showing on the little flags in the windows.

I will never forget the first one killed in action from our neighborhood. He was a young man who was serving his country in the Marine Corps. He was the son of the Flegel family who lived on the same street as our family. Everyone in the neighborhood felt the loss as one of our own. We were all saddened. The next one on our block was John Vargo. He was a gunner on a B17 Bomber. His plane went down at sea. I remember John because he was a good neighborhood friend of mine. He was about five years older than I was.

I remember that he and I would go down to the cellar of his house and eat caramel popcorn. His dad made caramel popcorn to sell at ball games. Another thing I remember about John Vargo was that he would sometimes let me watch him play the accordion. Both of these brave men made us all proud to be Americans and proud to have known them. They will always be in my memories as the ones who inspired my young life in the war years.

The year 1942 will stay in my memories. This was the year my mother received a telegram from the Army telling her that our brother, Bob, was admitted to the Walter Reed Army Hospital in Washington D.C. This news put us all in shock. That's all that we were told, that Bob was in the hospital.

My mother packed her bag and took a train to Washington D.C. to be with Bob. Mother stayed at Walter Reed Hospital for about two weeks before she came home. She tried to explain to us kids why our brother was in the hospital. When Bob was home on leave we all noticed a very large scar on the side and in the palm of his left hand. He never told us how he got the scar and we didn't ask. But we did notice that he couldn't hold anything in his left hand without dropping it. Mother told the family that he had leukemia and that he wasn't doing well.

Mother stayed at home a couple of weeks and then went back to be with her son, Bob. At that time we didn't have much knowledge about the treatment of leukemia. We didn't know how serious this was for our brother. Our mother did tell us that a bayonet wound caused the scar on my brother's hand. The Army had treated the wound with sulfur powder. They didn't know during the war that using sulfur powder on wounds could cause complications.

We all wanted to go and visit Bob at the hospital, but there was not enough money for all of us to go. My mother made several trips to and from the hospital.

One day my mother was cleaning house and she had the feeling that something was wrong. She called the hospital and was told by a nurse that the doctor wanted to talk to her. He said, "We did all that we could. Sergeant Robert Clark has just passed away." The news was devastating to our family.

That was in April of 1943. I had just turned thirteen years old. The Army sent my brother's body home in a wooden casket draped with an American flag. The color of the casket was Army olive drab. Not long after Bob's funeral our sister, Jane, joined the Navy Waves. Then we had a gold star and a blue star on our little flag in the front window of our home.

3

I WAS ARMY DRAFTED AT THE AGE OF THIRTEEN

The war overseas was raging and everyone wanted to get into the service. My sister, Jean, and her husband, Ralph Wyke, returned from the construction job in Puerto Rico in 1943. They didn't come home empty handed. They brought a new baby girl, Betty Jane, and that made me an uncle. I was proud to be an uncle at the age of thirteen.

Ralph didn't waste any time after getting back home. He went down to the Navy recruiting office and joined the Seabees. Before long he had to go to Pittsburgh to take his physical. I remember that day. He let me go with him. When he got to the testing and the physical place, there were hundreds of others doing the same thing Ralph was doing. They wanted to serve their country. I could see that everyone was happy. You could just feel the enthusiasm.

After Ralph took his written test, the Seabees wanted some proof of his past construction work. He asked me if I would go back home to pick up the papers. I did. It was a long way back to McKeesport and then back to Pittsburgh, but I made it in time before they stopped giving physicals that day. So Ralph went into the Seabees and we had another blue star on our flag in the window.

In 1943, and not long after Ralph left to serve his country, I went over to the tenth ward of McKeesport to visit a friend. When I arrived I found everyone happy and celebrating because my friend was leaving the next day for the Marine Corps. I couldn't understand that because my friend was only fifteen years old.

I asked him how he did it. He said, "It's easy. All you have to do is go down to the draft board and tell them that you just turned eighteen." All men at this time had an obligation to report to the draft board as soon as they turned eighteen. He told me to have it all figured out, the year I was born. I said, "What if they ask me for my birth certificate?" "Don't worry," he said, they don't ask for anything. Besides, you're big for your age. You can pass for eighteen." I knew he was right because I was as big as he was, and he was two years older than I was.

The next day, without telling my mother or anybody else, I walked over to the town of McKeesport to the draft board. I thought, "Well, the worst thing they can do is laugh at me and tell me to come back when I'm old enough." Well, things turned out great. They handed me a form to fill out that asked me a lot of questions. I filled out the form to the best of my ability by lying about my age. They didn't ask me for any proof of age, so that day I became eighteen years of age.

I didn't feel bad about lying about my age because when we moved to the big city of McKeesport I always told everyone that I was older than I actually was because I wanted to hang around with older kids. Kids my age acted like babies who were still hanging onto their mothers' apron strings.

A week went by and I received a draft notice from the draft board telling me that I was being drafted and I was to go take my physical in Pittsburgh. That was the same place that I had gone to with Ralph Wyke, my brother-in-law. So I knew right where to go. I went there and they gave me a battery of tests which I passed. These were written tests. Then came the physical. I knew that this was going to take all day. We walked from one military doctor to another in our underwear. They checked out every part of our physical being.

I remember that they sent about twenty of us to the men's room at the same time with a glass jar wanting us to urinate in the jar. Well, I just didn't have to go, so I got up enough nerve to work my way up to this long urinal that guys were urinating in. I looked over at the guy next to me. I could see that he was really filling his glass jar up fast. I said to him in a whisper, "I can't urinate right now. Could you put some in my jar?" He smiled and said, "No problem." He took my jar and filled it up half way.

So we went out of the men's room to get into a single line and wait our turn at a table where they take your urine and test it right there. They put the results on a chart which we carried with us from one station to another. I made sure that I didn't get in front of or behind the guy who urinated into my jar. I got my turn at the urine test table. He put the count number of the sample on my chart. At the next station, the guy who gave his urine asked, "How did I do?" I said, "You passed again."

We looked at my chart, and his chart showed the urine count number was three points higher than the count on my chart. We both laughed. After a long day of going through the physical, I went home to tell my mother what I had done. She couldn't believe that I had enlisted in the draft. She didn't want me to go through with it, but I talked her into it. She knew how much I hated school and having no father. Finally she agreed that maybe the service would do me some good. I said, "Thanks, Mom."

About a week later I received a draft notice of a classification that put me in 1-A which meant that I had passed everything. Boy, was I happy. I was going to take my brother, Bob's place in the Army. My orders read that I was to report to Army personnel at the train station at downtown McKeesport, and a group of us draftees would be escorted to Pittsburgh and taken to the same building where we took our physical.

There we took our swearing in. After all of us took the oath, the Army officer who swore us in said, "Congratulations. All of you are now in the U.S. Army. All of you will be on a train tonight for Fort Dix, New Jersey Induction Center." When we arrived at Fort Dix we were marched to a clinic to receive our shots. We were all still in civilian clothes, and all the other soldiers who had been there a week before us were shouting, "You'll be sorry."

After the shots we were marched to a warehouse for fitting us up to our uniforms. I came out of the warehouse with two big bags of clothing and shoes. Receiving so many new things overwhelmed me. I felt like I had just hit the jackpot. I just couldn't believe it. We all had a hard time carrying all this baggage back to the barracks.

They were wooden, two-story barracks. They told us to get rid of our civilian clothes, and that from now on we wouldn't be allowed to wear civilian clothing while the war was on. For me that was great. Army clothes and shoes were the best I had ever had.

During the two weeks we stayed at Fort Dix we were put on clean-up details around the fort and put on K.P. in the consolidated mess hall. And I can tell you, we worked hard. Those on K.P. got a wake-up call at three o'clock in the morning, and then they had about fifteen minutes to report to the mess hall.

Usually the mess sergeant was a mean old bulldog type. One very important thing I learned fast was, "Never volunteer for anything." One day a sergeant came in the barracks wanting two volunteers who had truck driver's licenses. It didn't take long before two men showed their licenses. Well, later that day I saw the same two men pushing wheelbarrows hauling rocks.

After two weeks the Army gave a large group of us orders to take our basic training at Camp Walters, Texas. They put us on a troop train to take us to Camp Walters. This was the longest train ride that I ever took. On the train there were only soldiers. The Army served nothing but field rations. Every soldier took his mess kit and had to go to the dining rail car to get warm field rations. We did have sleeping berths on the train.

The most exciting thing that happened was when the train would stop at a train station. The soldiers would hang out the windows of the train and give whistle catcalls to the girls who would be on the station platform. I think the people knew that there was a troop train scheduled to stop at a certain time because there was always a bunch of girls at the train stations. The soldiers and the girls would exchange addresses. It was great. I got about five girls' addresses. Now I had someone other than my mother to write to, although, before I left home my girlfriend, Doris, promised that she would write to me.

It took about six days to get to Camp Walters, Texas. We didn't know it, but this would be a very hard thirteen weeks of basic training. It was hot. The first thing they taught us when we got off the train was, "Keep your mouth shut and salute anything that moves." The mean-looking sergeant told us to take our hats off as he went up and down the ranks.

"Well," he said, "I see our well trained barber is going to be very disappointed because they sheared you 'bag-a-bounds' at Fort Dix. Here at Camp Walters you'll get a haircut once a week. And from now on the Army will do your thinking for you. Do you understand what I just said?" All at the same time, everyone said, "Yes, sergeant." Then he said, "There will be no talking until I tell you you can talk or when I call your names." Then he said, "The names I call out will be assigned to my barracks." After he had called out the names, and we were moved over to one group, he told us that we were to follow him. And he said, "There had better not be any stragglers or they will pay the price."

We all knew what he meant. There we were with two big heavy bags of clothing and field gear. We all looked at each other without saying a word. We knew we were in for it. The sergeant said, "Follow me."

Well, he took off walking like a racehorse and we remembered what he said about not straggling behind. I wasn't up front, but I wasn't going to be at the tail end either. We were all huffing and puffing and straining. I'll bet we passed fifty barracks and none was his. We were all thinking and hoping that the next one would be his.

The sergeant kept turning around as he was walking, shouting, "Close it up." My hand and arm felt numb, but I didn't dare drop my bags. At last we reached the barracks. The sergeant's assistant was a corporal. As soon as we arrived, the corporal jumped down from the porch of the barracks where he was standing, and with notebook in hand, he bellowed out, "I want the names of you two stragglers there at the end." Needless to say, the two stragglers were on the black list into the first week of basic training.

I got assigned a bunk upstairs in the barracks. I was glad because downstairs was the main entrance and there was a lot of traffic. The upstairs did have its disadvantages. When the sergeant blew his whistle for us to get outside and stand at attention in four ranks, it took the guys upstairs longer to get out of the barracks.

At that time the Army didn't issue boots. We were issued two pairs of canvas leggings that laced up on hoops, and you had to lace them up on the outside of your legs. The first week of basic training some soldiers would forget and lace them up on the inside of their legs. Then, when the whistle was blown, we would see some of them falling on their faces because the hoops on the leggings would come together and lock your ankles together. Then down on their faces they would go. It didn't take long after that for them to learn to put them on the right way.

Our sergeant and the corporal were very strict. The sergeant said, "When you men hear the whistle I will close my eyes, and when I open my eyes I want to see four ranks standing at attention in front of me." At that we all bellowed out, "Yes, sergeant." We were all issued rifles and bayonets along with a rifle belt for ammo, a canteen, and a first aid packet which contained a bandage and a pack of sulfur for wounds.

It wasn't long before we were out on the rifle range after hiking eight miles to get to it. We all had to qualify with our weapons or they would keep us on the "hot" range until we did. The next day was the pistol range, and then the machine-gun range, and then the 60mm mortar range. After firing all these weapons, we had to take them apart and clean them, and then the sergeants and corporals would inspect them.

It was really hot at this time of the year in Texas. It was nothing to see soldiers pass out all around you from heat stroke. If a soldier passed out next to you while standing at attention at any time, you were not allowed to help him in any way. You were to remain at attention as if you hadn't seen anything. If the soldier passed out while we were marching we were to walk around him. There were trained medical soldiers with us who would take care of them.

Before we left the barracks to go out to training, and while we were in ranks, we had to take the tops off our water canteens. Then the sergeant and his assistant would come around and put in three or four salt pills in our canteen of water. This was to stop us from drinking too much water. We marched everywhere. I never did get to ride in any Army vehicle all the time that I was in basic training. When we got back to the barracks in the evening we would be really tired.

The food in the Army during the war was always beef liver, beef hash, and S.O.S., sheep and goat meat and fish. That's all the Army seemed to know. We never did get chicken, pork chops, or steak.

The mess hall sergeant was meaner than a rattlesnake. The tables in the mess hall were picnic style tables with wooden benches to sit on. There were about twenty tables. You would stand in the chow line to get in. Once in, you would pick up a tray and a knife, fork and spoon, then go through the serving line. After receiving your food you would go to a table that was pointed out to you either by the mess sergeant or by his assistant. They would point out a table where everyone at that table was standing at attention with their tray of food on the table in front of them. No one at the table was to sit until the last man arrived. There were eight men to a table.

The mess sergeant or his assistant was the only one allowed to give your table the order to be seated, and there was no talking allowed except to say, "Please pass . . ." this or that. If the mess sergeant caught you talking he would tell you to get out of his mess hall. Smoking was not allowed.

Pulling K.P. in his mess hall was hell. But he sure kept a clean mess hall. We would go on fifteen- or twenty-mile marches with our sixty-five pound field packs strapped to our backs, and carrying a rifle and steel helmet, and if you happened to be in the machine gun squad, you would be carrying that too.

The mess sergeant and his cooks would set up a field mess tent when we arrived and it was eating time. There was a place at Camp Walters they called, "Hell's Bottom," and it was just that. The company I was in stayed at Hell's Bottom for two weeks.

We dug foxholes and slept in them or in trenches. This is the place where they wanted a soldier to get the feel of the real thing in war. They had simulated artillery going off all around you day and night. They would use explosions for artillery. This was also the place they would teach you to throw hand grenades.

There were houses that covered about a block long with empty houses on both sides of the street. This was to simulate a German village, and this was to train us in the principles of how to clear out house-to-house fighting. They would send each twelve-man squad in at a time. They had simulated German soldiers in and around each house.

The squad would plan who would go where, and each man had to know what to do. It was important to work as a team. We would go in with bayonets on our rifles. We would be firing blanks and throwing smoke and fragmentation hand grenades. Each squad was scored on their ability to work together as a squad, and each man was scored on his ability to perform as a fighting soldier.

At Hell's Bottom we received a lot of training in running through the bayonet course. There were dummies that would pop out at you. You had to be quick to thrust your bayonet into the dummy or shoot it. Every soldier was scored on his performance. If they didn't like the way you performed, you were sent through it again until you got it right.

Another obstacle course they put us through was the infiltration course. We crawled on our bellies and sometimes on our backs in mud and on wet ground. We crawled under barbed wire and through other obstacles while they fired live bullets from machine guns over our heads. You had to keep your rifle with you at all times, and you could not let it get dirty. As they were shooting over our heads they kept yelling, "Keep your heads down."

Two weeks at Hell's Bottom was hard, but good training. It was to get us ready for combat conditions. What I dreaded most about Hell's Bottom was the snakes. There were rattlesnakes under every rock you turned over. There was also the long wooden shed they called the "latrine," the Army's term for toilet. There were two long boards on each side of the shed with holes cut in them to accommodate ten men on each side. This was not a favorite place. I think the smell had something to do with it, but I think the main reason why people dreaded going in and staying for any length of time was the warning sign in big bold letters above the door, "Beware of rattlesnakes in the rafters." When we got back to the barracks we all felt and smelled like worn-out pack mules.

When we weren't out in the field we did get Sundays off to go to church, or to sleep in on Saturday nights. If a soldier was up to it we would go to the service club on the campsite. They would bus in some local girls for us to dance with, and the service club gave out free refreshments. If you weren't dancing you could just sit and talk to the girls.

The girls were older than I was. They ranged in age from eighteen to older. I never told anyone my real age. If they asked me, I would say, "Eighteen years old." I was thirteen. I had always tried to act older than my real age. I loved to dance, and it was at the service clubs that I learned to dance, and at U.S.O. clubs.

We didn't get passes to go to the small town of Menial Wells until after our six weeks of basic training. The soldiers called the town, "Venereal Wells." All I saw in this small town were bars and grills, and the town was full of soldiers and military police just waiting for somebody to mess up.

The first three weeks, other than drill and weapons instruction, we were shown a lot of films on venereal diseases and frostbite of the feet. They usually showed these films just before we were supposed to eat so that we would lose our appetites. In the barracks' latrines there were posters on the walls of gorgeous looking women usually wearing a short and tight dress leaning against a lamp post on the corner of a street. At the bottom of the poster it said, "She may look clean, but she has venereal disease."

A person would think after a while that maybe the Army wanted us to turn against women. But, if they did, it didn't work. For one thing most of the soldiers in my barracks, and in all the other barracks, were married and had children at home. In all the barracks' latrines the toilets had no partitions between the toilets. There were about six or seven toilets in a line. If you were the shy type, you were in trouble. Also the Army set up two toilets mostly on the end. On would have a sign above it that read, "Soldiers with V.D. only." Another toilet would have a sign that read, "Soldiers with crabs only." Sometimes you would go in the latrine and all the toilets were taken except those two. They would always be empty. But if you dared sit on either one of them, no matter how bad you had to go, you would be a marked person in the barracks, or even in the whole company. No one would get near you. There were times when I had to go so bad, and if the toilets were full, rather than use the marked toilets, I'd run to the next barracks to use an unmarked toilet.

Pay days in the Army in 1943 and 1944 were once a month. The pay for a private was fifty dollars a month. That was the most money I had ever made. Since I was a thirteen year old, I felt rich. Although I had an allotment, thirty-five dollars a month was going home to my mother, I kept fifteen dollars for myself. And even that was a lot of money for me. The movies in the evenings at the camp were twenty-five cents.

Our PX, which was a barracks-type building, had wooden tables and chairs. The PX sold bottles of beer for ten cents a bottle, and you could sit right there and drink beer. Candy bars and chewing gum were two for a nickel. I was in my glory. I could buy all the candy and gum I wanted. Cigarettes were ten cents a pack, one dollar a carton. I put a false bottom in my footlocker that was at the end of my bunk. I had layers of gum and candy in the false bottom.

At inspection time, when we had to leave our lockers open, they never did find my candy and gum. I had to be careful not to have gum in my mouth during training. That was frowned upon. So after we got back to the barracks in the evening, and after a show, I would put a whole pack of gum in my mouth at one time. I couldn't do that when I was growing up. Neither my family nor I had the money to do things like that. So now I just went crazy.

One of the best things soldiers looked forward to each day when we got back to the barracks in the evening, and after chow, was mail call. They would hold mail call at one time for three or four barracks. The mail clerk would have a bag full of mail. He would position himself high above everyone, and the crowd of soldiers would gather round, each one hoping to hear his name called to receive a letter. The mail clerk would call out a last name, and if it was your name, you were to sound off with your first name and middle initial. If the letter was for you, the clerk would throw it at you over the heads of all the men, or it would be passed to you by everybody standing around.

Mail call was a time that everybody looked forward to. Every mail call left some soldiers disappointed. When you did receive a letter, you wanted to be alone. Solitude was hard to find in a barracks full of soldiers. Well, it wasn't long before I received my first "Dear John" letter. It was from my sweetheart, Doris, my first love. The letter said, "Dear Jim, I'm sorry, but I got married to a guy named, Chester." She said that she just couldn't wait. What surprised me was that I had just received a letter the week before telling me that she missed me and loved me. "Oh well," I thought, "I still have my Mom and my sisters to write to me, and I've got a foot locker full of candy and gum to help me chase the blues away."

One thing was for sure, I wasn't alone when it came to receiving "Dear John" letters. Some of the guys in the barracks got "Dear John" letters too. They took it hard. Some, like me, said, "What the Hell. There's a lot more out there waiting."

We were getting close to the end of our thirteen weeks of basic training, and we were all dreading the last big road march that was coming up. It was a thirty-mile hike. But then, too, we all wanted to get it over with.

We were all hyped up the day the sergeant ordered us to fall out in four ranks with full field packs, our weapons, and steel helmets on our heads, and our ammo belts with water canteens on our belts. Some carried machine guns too. And they were the old water-cooled machine guns which were heavier than the thirty cal air-cooled machine guns the Army has today.

We all had salt tablets put into our canteens. They told us that we would be going at a fast pace and that we would be given a ten-minute break every hour. They also stressed that they didn't want any stragglers.

I learned very quickly why stragglers aren't liked. If you should get behind someone who is not keeping up the pace, all those behind the straggler will have to work that much harder to catch up once you pass the stragglers. You almost had to run to catch up. I learned who the stragglers were in the platoon, and if they started out in front of me, I made it a point to get ahead of them just as soon as we got started.

We began our thirty-mile hike in the evening after the hot Texas sun went down, and we were warned not to eat a big meal that night. It was just beginning to get dark when we started out. We walked and walked, and we sweated, and the only time we were allowed to bring the canteen of water to our mouths was during our ten-minute breaks.

You didn't dare take the backpack off during breaks no matter how hot you got. I had made up my mind that I was not going to fall out or be a straggler. I never did fall out of the march during basic training, and I wasn't going to start now.

After about the first fifteen miles I could feel blisters forming on the heels of my feet because none of us had been in the Army long enough to really break in our shoes. I knew that I wasn't the only one getting blisters. We would just put it out of our minds and pretend that it was all in our heads, that we just thought that blisters were forming on our feet.

We walked all the rest of that evening, all night and into morning. We had Army medical men riding in an Army ambulance taking care of the men who would fall over in a ditch from heat stroke or when their blisters got to them. Then there were the ones who felt sorry for themselves and they would just fall out no matter what they were doing. Medical men would check out the ones who fell out or passed out, and if they thought the person's situation was serious enough, they would put them on a big truck and let them ride.

I always said about the ones who might be just acting, "Take a ride without any pride." When we arrived at the barracks we were shown ten soldiers who either fell out into the ditches along the dirt road or who just couldn't make it.

We sure were glad it was over, and we felt good about ourselves. We did complete the march without any help. When I took off my high-top shoes and socks I could see that my blisters were bleeding. I knew that we must have stopped just in time. My shoes wore holes in my socks. The medical soldiers came to our barracks to check us out and to treat the blisters. They would swab our feet with brown looking stuff that would almost make you climb the walls. The Army let us recover the next morning. We didn't have to wear our shoes to the afternoon class. We all lived through it.

I was one of 25,000 soldiers that Camp Walters trained, and I'm proud I did it. The other reason I was proud to have been trained as an infantryman at Camp Walters was that it was this camp that one of my heroes was trained at. A Texas boy named Audie Murphy, also brought up in poverty, and who also joined the Army at a young age trained at Camp Walters. Audie Murphy saw two years of continuous combat on the battlefield. He received more medals than any other American soldier in World War II, including the Congressional Medal of Honor. He also received a battlefield commission. After being discharged from the Army, Audie Murphy became a Hollywood star. He will be remembered as one of America's best warriors. He was the kind of infantryman that any soldier would want by his side in combat.

Audie Murphy was in the movie, "To Hell and Back." I personally feel that if Audie Murphy had stayed in the Army, he would have made the rank of General. Even today a big portrait of Audie Murphy hangs in the Capitol Building in Austin, Texas. May America never forget this great hero.

I'm glad the Army sent me to Camp Walters for my training. A week before we finished training at Camp Walters, the Army recruiting officer wanted volunteers to go to Parachute Training School at Fort Benning, Georgia. Those who volunteered would not receive their fifteen days of leave to go home after completion of training at Camp Walters. Those who volunteered would receive their leave after parachute training. I volunteered, along with about ten other men in our barracks. The last day at Camp Walters we all shook hands and said our goodbyes. Little did I know that almost all the men I had trained with at Camp Walters would be killed or wounded at Normandy under the command of General Eisenhower.

I was back on the train again headed for Fort Benning, Georgia. The training was mostly physical, like running five miles before breakfast. After breakfast there was more physical training in a place they called, "The Fry Pan." I always had to give some airborne instructor sergeant thirty or forty push-ups because I blinked my eyes. Once while on a break I walked out to a water drinking fountain that was located in the middle of an open field. That cost me fifty push-ups. An instructor said, "Soldier, you never walk anywhere in this training at Fort Benning, not even when you're on a break."

Well, now I understood why everyone was running to get a drink of water at the fountain, then running back to the break area. Another way the instructors would give you push-ups to do was they would come up to you, and in the middle of what they were telling you, they would say, very fast, "Jab," or "Jab, Jab, Double Jab."

They wanted you to jab yourself with your fist and drive your fist right into your left shoulder. That would be one Jab. Two Jabs would be your left fist into your right shoulder. The thing that you really had to pay attention to was the last count of jabbing the instructor had said. If he left off with a double Jab, then you would pound your right fist to the left shoulder, and then the left fist to the right shoulder, and in this case, you would leave your fists where they landed until the instructor told you to recover. Then you would take your arms down. If you did any of the Jabs wrong, the instructor would have you doing push-ups until you were blue in the face.

You might think all this was harassment, but it wasn't. It was to keep us alert. The school was good. I liked it. We would jump out of a mock-up airplane that was a small distance off the ground. We were learning how to fall. Then, jumping off a wooden tower, and harnessed up, we were sent down a steel cable into sawdust to break the fall.

We were taken to a big hangar where we learned to pack parachutes and go to classes. Then we were trained on the big steel towers. The parachutes were already open, mechanically operated. It would take us up high, and when the rig holding the open parachute released the parachute, we got a big thrilling ride back down to the ground. It wasn't long before we were loading up on a real plane and thinking, "What the Hell am I doing up here?" But you always let your fellow soldiers think that you thought, "This is great fun." After going through parachute school, I was going home.

4

HONORABLE DISCHARGE

I was on my way home for my first fifteen-day furlough to be on my own. I was back on the train, but this train was mostly all civilians. There would be some servicemen going back to their bases, or they, too, would be going on furlough. The train, at that time, was how everybody traveled. People didn't fly on planes as they do now.

Military police would come on the train while it was stopped and check all the servicemen's furlough papers. During the war all service personnel in uniform would ride the train at half the price.

I liked riding the train because you could get up and walk around, and more times than not you would meet a good looking girl sitting by herself. You could tell whether they were on the make or not by walking up and down the train. Just smile at them or wink, and if they smiled or winked back you would more than likely make a home run. Another good place to make out with a girl was in the club car. If you saw a good looking girl in the club car alone, buy her a drink and start talking.

My line was usually, "Pardon me, pretty lady, isn't your name . . . ." I would think up some fictitious name. Then, "I'm sure I know you from some place." And of course she would say, "No, that's not my name." And then I would say, "A pretty girl like you surely must have a pretty name." If she gave me her name, then I'd know I could start an exchange of conversation. Then maybe I could talk my way right into where I could sit with her.

On the other hand, if she told you to get lost right from the very beginning, then I would mark her off the list of possibilities. I would check the next train car, but I would change my approach. I would say, "Pretty lady, I seem to have lost my phone number. Can I have yours?" In those good old days a serviceman riding on a train all day and all night was sure to find a woman to sit with before midnight. On a long train ride it would be more enjoyable for both of them. I could almost bet that a lot of couples met like this during the war years, and their casual meeting on a train blossomed into a love affair and then marriage.

I was really excited to be going home to visit my mother and sisters and all my friends. My sister, Jane, who went into the Navy Waves wrote me a letter and told me that since the train I was going home on went through Washington D.C., I should get off and visit with her for a day. She said that she would show me around the city. She sent me directions to get to her place of work at the Department of the Navy.

Well, I did just that. I got off the train in Washington and took a taxi to her place of work. There was nothing but people in Navy uniforms. I was the only soldier in the building, and it sure was a big building my sister worked in. I told them at the information desk who I was looking for, and they escorted me through a hallway and up elevators to the office where she worked. The place was big and full of good looking ladies in Navy uniforms. The supervisor of my sister's department took me to Jane's desk. My sister, Jane, didn't see me coming into the office. She had her back turned and she was typing. The supervisor announced my presence. Jane saw me and she jumped up, threw her arms around me and said how happy she was to see me. Jane said that she didn't really think that I would stop and come to see her.

Jane's supervisor told her, "I'm sure that you want some time with your kid brother, so take the rest of the day off." Jane introduced me as her kid brother, and I was holding my breath hoping she wouldn't tell them that I was only thirteen years old.

A lot of the girls in the office came over to Jane's desk, and boy, there sure were some good looking ones. Jane introduced me to them and said, "Sorry, my brother and I have a lot of places to see." Jane hurriedly got me out of the building. We got a taxi and went to a nice place to eat.

I asked Jane why she was in such a hurry to get me out of her office. She said, "Little brother, if you think I'm going to introduce you to the girls in my office, and then you date one of them when they are in their twenties, well I just don't know what I would do." She said she just didn't know how she could explain a situation like that. I told her, "I've been out with ladies older than I am." And she said, "I'm sure you have, but not any from my office." We both laughed.

After eating we stayed and talked about the hard times of our childhood and about the death of our brother, Bob. She told me how much she missed him. After we had a long talk she asked me what I would like to see in Washington, D.C. I told her that my time was short because I had to catch a train at a certain time. She suggested that we visit the Washington Monument.

She told me that there were no elevators and that we would have to walk up a lot of stairs. I said, "Let's go." After we got there and started walking up those narrow, spiral steps, I thought they would never come to an end. But we made it to the top and looked down from the little window at the top.

We had a good time that day. Jane went with me to the train station. I had a little time before my train was to leave so we stopped at a cocktail lounge and had a mixed drink together. When the drinks came I saw a smile on her face. I asked, "What's so funny?" And she said, "I was just thinking. Here I am sitting and drinking with a minor, a thirteen year old, in a bar having a mixed cocktail." I said, "Jane, I'm a soldier and this isn't my first time to have a drink." We both laughed. Jane went with me to the train and we said our goodbyes. She told me to be sure to tell everyone at home that she was thinking of them, that she loved them, and to give Mom a kiss for her. I remember telling Jane just before I left the gate to board the train, "You are a gorgeous looking lady in your Navy Wave uniform." She blushed and smiled and said, "Thank you, little brother." We parted and I got on my train.

I arrived at home and it was so good to be back home. It seemed that everyone loved a serviceman during World War II. The older people really showed their appreciation toward service people. They would invite you to their homes for a home cooked meal. They went out of their way just to talk to a service person. I never took them up on their invitations to dinner. They usually had a son or grandson in the service. They would want to know whether I knew him, or they would show me their son or grandson's picture in uniform and ask if I had seen him. They just didn't realize how big the service branches were, and how many Army, Marine, and Navy camps there were.

I loved going to town. I didn't have to walk now because in almost all towns they would let service people ride free. When a service person would step aboard a city bus, the driver would cover the coin box with his hand, meaning, "It's a free ride." Movies were free, but taxis you paid for like everyone else.

I was thirteen years old at this time. I had learned in the Army how to act and how to control myself. When drinking alcohol, I could walk into any bar or tavern, sit at the bar and order a beer or a shot of liquor. I was thirteen years old, and I was never asked for proof of my age. It was against the law to serve anyone under the age of twenty-one then. But since I was in uniform that was good enough for the bartender. They felt that if a person was old enough to wear the uniform that was good enough for the bartender. They felt that if a person was old enough to wear the uniform, and maybe have to die for his country, then that serviceman was old enough to drink at a bar.

I wasn't the sort of teenager who would smell the fumes from a bottle of beer and then want the world to know that I had been drinking. I knew my limit, and the more I would drink, the more I would try to act sober. I never let myself get to the point at which I would stagger or slur my words. These were the good old times. Most of the time when I went into a bar during the war years, I would no sooner be seated at the bar when the bartender would give me a glass of beer and then refuse my money. Someone at the other end of the bar would have said, "Give that soldier a drink. It's on me." There were times when it seemed that everyone in the bar was paying for my drinks.

This would not have happened if the bar was full of uniformed men. I didn't spend much time in bars. My interest was in girls, and the women I was interested in didn't hang around in bars.

The best places I found for drinking, and places where the ladies looked good, were the hotel lounges and the cocktail lounges. McKeesport had a nice roller skating rink. That was a good place to meet girls. As I walked around town, I would meet some of my old buddies that I used to hang out with. When they saw me in uniform they couldn't believe it. They had thought I was sixteen or seventeen years old when I was hanging out with them. They would say, "We didn't know you were of draft age." And I would say, "Well, I didn't want you to know that I was older than you." None of them ever knew that I was only thirteen years old when I joined the military. Most of them could hardly wait to reach eighteen so they could get in the service.

All their talk was about which part of the service they were planning to go into. What really bugged them was seeing me going into a bar for a beer when they couldn't even get inside the door. They would be run off by the bartender who was usually the owner of the bar.

I saw my old girlfriend, Doris, downtown shopping. We talked about her new married life. She seemed to be happy. She said the guy she married installed and repaired neon signs for businesses. I casually asked her, "How come your husband isn't in the service?" He was six or seven years older than I was. She said that he was classified 4-F and the service wouldn't take him. I told her that I was happy for her, and congratulations on her marriage. We parted, going our own ways.

I was having a good time home on leave. I went to a lot of house parties where there were other service people and girls. We all got along well because the one thing in the serviceman's thoughts was that with the war going strong, this might be his last time to be at home with friends.

While I was at home my mother pointed out to me, and I could see for myself, that the little flag she had in the window now had one gold star for my brother, Bob, and three blue stars, one for my sister, Jane, one for my sister

Jean's husband, Ralph, and now, one for me.

Almost everyone living on both sides of the street now had these little flags in their windows. But as the months passed by, one could see the blue stars changing to silver, which meant wounded, and then to gold, which meant died or killed in action.

The war was taking a toll on American fighting men in service. It was now getting to the point that mothers and wives were afraid to answer the door when someone knocked for fear that it would be a telegram from the War Department saying, "We are sorry to inform you . . ." that a husband or a son had been killed or wounded. In the war years just about every household had someone serving in the military, and they were all hoping and praying not to receive a telegram from the War Department.

My mother told me while I was at home that my father had left the Merchant Marines and joined the Army. That was hard to believe. First, I wondered how he had managed to stay sober long enough to take a physical and then do basic training. I just couldn't believe it. I was sure that when they drew his blood during his physical they would be able to see that all they were getting was alcohol from his veins. My mother said that he was in the Combat Engineers, a branch of the Army, and that it was Engineer's Basic Training that he was put through, not infantry training as I had done.

She also told me that my father was too old to be in the Army, and that he had lied about his age to get into the service, but not like I had, making myself older. My father lied to make himself younger to get into the Army. My father had served in World War I in the Army. That made him too old for the Army in World War II. But he got in the Army anyway.

My mother and I thought that maybe the Army would do him some good and maybe keep him sober. My mother never did put a star on the little flag for my father. He was never a good husband or father, and he didn't want to be a part of our family.

While I was home on leave my mother told me that I should go down to my old grade school in the Tenth Ward neighborhood. There were a lot of names on a marble monument that was put up on the street corner where the school was. It was in dedication to all those serving in the military from the Tenth Ward. I found my brother, Bob's name, and there was a gold star after his name.

I also found my sister, Jane's name, and my name. As I looked at my name on the bronze plate I thought to myself, "Well, they finally gave me a good grade on bronze. That's better than the grades I was getting when I was in this school." But I also realized now that I had been at fault. I didn't apply myself.

It was too hard on me being raised out in the woods of Curry Hollow.

I just couldn't adjust to living and going to school with city kids. We just didn't understand each other's ways. But that was all in the past. Now I looked to see what the future would hold for me down the road.

While home on leave there was another war tragedy that touched and saddened the whole United States. The newspapers reported that all five sons of the Sullivan family had been killed in the war. The five Sullivan brothers were serving aboard the same Navy ship when it was torpedoed and sunk by the Japanese. Everyone felt the loss of these brave brothers. I remember reading about them in the newspaper when all five of them enlisted in the U.S. Navy. I hope this country never forgets the brave men like the Sullivan brothers.

When my leave at home was just about over I was invited to a private dance party at the home of a couple of other service people who were also home on leave. They said there would be a lot of single girls there. That evening I went with them to the party, and I sure was glad I did.

I met a really nice girl. She was about seven years older than I was, but age was never a part of our conversation. We danced until about three o'clock in the morning. We got along really well. She promised to write to me and gave me her address. My leave time was over and I had to report to my new duty station, an Army camp at New Comberland, Maryland.

I was at New Comberland for about six months of training. I was there long enough to be eligible for another five-day furlough to go home. I got to see my mother and sisters and the nice girl I had met at the house dance while on my last leave home. She had her own car. She and I had a ball together, but then my leave was over, and again we had to say goodbye. Back at camp, and while sitting around the barracks, some of the soldiers were bragging about lying about their age to get into the Army.

Some of them said, "I was sixteen when I first came into the Army." Now they were all eighteen. More than one was bragging about coming into the Army under-age. Without thinking I opened my big mouth and said, "I came into the Army at thirteen, and I'm still underage." Little did I know that I had just made a big blunder.

I tried to cover up by saying, "I'm only kidding. I just wanted to beat you guys." But I could see some uncertainty on the faces of my fellow soldiers. Not much more was said about it until a week later. Some of the soldiers and I received orders for Fort Dix, New Jersey. After arriving at Fort Dix, I was ordered to report to the commanding officer. When I went into the office there were about five officers sitting around a table. One of the men said, "It has been reported that you, soldier, are not old enough to be in the Army. Is this true, and if so, how old are you?"

I knew that I couldn't lie or I would be in trouble. I admitted that I was fourteen. I could see some of the officers' mouths drop open. Without asking me anything more, they told me that I would be confined to my company area until further notice. About two weeks went by before an officer who said he had been appointed to act as my attorney, told me that the Army was going to court-martial me for fraudulent enlistment. He also said that I would receive a dishonorable discharge. He told me that the Army was getting tougher on soldiers who lied about their age to get into the service. He said that I had one thing going for me, a good record, except for falsifying my birth certificate. I told him that I had not falsified my birth certificate or anything else. I told him that the draft board hadn't asked me for any proof of my age. The attorney said, "Well, you do look old enough."

The attorney told me that he would delay the court-martial for a time until I could come up with evidence that I had not falsified my birth certificate or any other papers to get into the service. He said that they were going to check with the draft board.

In the meantime the attorney wanted me to come up with a copy of my birth certificate and a sworn affidavit from my mother showing proof of my age. He said that if I could come up with those two things that he could get me out of this mess.

Two or three days went by. I had a lot of time to think and to look back to how I had gotten into this predicament. My first mistake was telling the other soldiers in New Comberland. I had opened my big mouth and bragged about being younger than any of them were when first getting into the Army. I hadn't thought about it before I ran off my mouth. But then, I would never have thought that any of my fellow soldiers would turn me in. I was disappointed in myself. I couldn't eat. I thought about all the good things that I could have done if only I had made the Army my career. I could have retired from the Army at the age of thirty-two or thirty-three with twenty years of service. I don't think that I could have retired that early out in civilian life.

My mother sent me all the documents related to my age. I gave all this to my attorney and a week later the court-martial convened. My attorney went with me to the court-martial. Charges were read, and "Fraudulent enlistment." My attorney did all the talking. He began by telling the court that I had a good service record and that I did not falsify my birth certificate or anything else to get in the service.

He told the court that I had lied about my age to the draft board, but that the draft board hadn't asked for any proof of my age. He told them that I took my physical, passed all the tests, and was given a Class A classification, and then drafted and inducted into the Army.

The attorney's closing statement to the court was, "This soldier is a minor. He doesn't know his own mind." I didn't like that remark, but I thought as long as the court was accepting what my attorney was telling them, I should keep my mouth shut.

After my attorney showed the court my birth certificate and the sworn affidavit from my mother, the officers on the court martial board looked at me, then at each other, shook their heads, and the one in charge said, "This case is closed." My attorney told me that I would be given a good discharge. He shook my hand and said, "Good luck. Come back in the service when you're the right age."

5

A CIVILIAN AGAIN

I was overjoyed that the Army hadn't given me a dishonorable discharge. I was given the freedom to move around the camp, but I was getting what I didn't want, a discharge from the Army. I felt that I had let my country and myself down. The Army had taken me in and given me structure in my life. The Army taught me how to work as a team member and they had instilled discipline in me. Now I had to take responsibility for my actions. I should not have told anybody that I was only thirteen years old.

I had to move to the other part of the camp, to the separation center. There were a lot of soldiers being discharged for all kinds of reasons, but none like my reason. In the barracks I met one of the soldiers that I had taken basic training with. He was surprised to see me, and even more surprised to learn the reason why I was being discharged. It took about a week to be discharged. I was honorably discharged by reason of being a minority under the Army's Sec. IV AR615-360, paragraph 56. I was given mustering out pay of $200 and a lapel pin that discharged soldiers called, "The Ruptured Duck." The pin signified that I had been honorably discharged from the service of World War II.

An Army friend who was also being discharged told me that if I ever needed a job to give him a call. He gave me his home phone number and address in Orange, New Jersey. I thanked him for the offer.

I had a year of service in the Army when I was discharged. I received the full G.I. Bill for schooling and the unemployment checks that an ex-serviceman could sign up for. They called it the 52-20 Club, which meant that you could sign up at the unemployment office for fifty-two weeks and receive a $20 check each week. I signed up for these benefits.

When I arrived home, the newspaper had received word that I was the youngest veteran ever to be discharged from McKeesport, or any other place in the United States. A news reporter came to my home. They put my picture in the newspaper, and my picture was also in some popular magazines. With that, the fan mail began.

The mailman would come into our house and practically dump his mailbag with fan mail from all over the United States. The letters were mostly from young boys who wanted to know how I had fooled the U.S. Army. They wanted to know so that they could try to get into the service too. There was so much fan mail from young kids that there was no way I could ever have answered all the mail I received. The American Legion in McKeesport's Burt Foster Post No. 361 recruited me. I became the nation's youngest Legionnaire after taking the Legion's oath. This too made the newspaper. I expressed to the members of the Legion that I missed being in the service, and I told them how much I loved the military life.

Members of the Legion tried to help me as much as they could. They went out of their way. They took me to Pittsburgh to get me enrolled in a military school. At the military school I saw little boys who were my age, and I saw how childish they acted in their little toy soldier uniforms. I knew I wouldn't fit in after having been with real soldiers, and after having done things real soldiers do. I thought to myself, "I will never get a free drink in a bar wearing that uniform." No, that was not for me. I knew the American Legion meant well, and they were trying to get me back into what I wanted most, the military.

After being at home a month, I went to work on the Union Railroad repairing railroad boxcars between Pittsburgh and McKeesport. To get the job, I had to show my discharge from the military. They thought that since I had a discharge that I must be old enough to work. During the war, in the forties, there was a push on to hire veterans for jobs. That was a great thing for our society to think of those who had served first. That's more than they do today.

During the war years I carried a copy of my discharge. It got me a lot of jobs. I worked on the railroad for about three months and then quit because I was given a job on a riverboat called, "The Old Stern Wheeler," and steam boilers. This is what made the boat move in the water. The boat traveled up and down the Allegheny River and the Monongahela River.

The boat was more of a flat-bottom boat that pushed coal barges from the coal mines to the steel mills around McKeesport and the other cities with steel mills. It was a good job. I worked in the engine room as an oiler. It was interesting going through all the boat locks on the rivers, and this was the time when I had to be on the alert in the engine room. The pilot would be working the boat's indicator. This would send the same signal from the pilot house to the engine room, and give the pilot what he wants, like "full ahead," or "half ahead," or "full astern," or "half astern."

I had my own cabin on the boat, and there was one old lady on the boat. She was the maid and she made all the beds and cleaned up the cabins. The food was very good. The pay was also good at that time, ten dollars a day. I didn't have to pay for my cabin or my food. I had to stay aboard the boat for ten days, and then I would have five days off. I worked for about six months sailing up and down the Allegheny River. One day I quit because the ten days on the boat made me feel trapped, and it kept me away from girls.

As I look back on the civilian jobs that I have had, I think this one was the best. What I didn't see at the time were the chances for advancement on this job. I could have worked as an oiler, then from oiler up to chief engineer over the years. But that's all hindsight now.

It wasn't long after I left the riverboat job when my mother told me that she had received word that Congressman Samie Wiese from Pittsburgh wanted to see me. So Mother and I went to his office. The congressman said he had read about me in the newspaper and he asked if there was anything he could do to help me. I told him there was nothing he could do, but that I missed being in the military. He came up with the idea that maybe I could join the Army in Canada by lying about my age again. My mother told him that our family didn't have the money to send her son to Canada. At this Congressman Samie Wiese said, "I'll tell you what I'm going to do. I'm going to give your son, Jimmie Clark, a hundred dollars out of my own pocket for him to go up to the border of Buffalo, New York and Ontario, Canada."

We thought that might work, and if it did, I would be back in the military. The congressman gave me the money right out of his wallet. My mother and I went home and I packed a bag and got on the Greyhound bus for Buffalo, New York. I arrived in Buffalo late that evening, so I got a hotel room. I could see out the hotel window that Buffalo was a big city. The next morning I caught a taxicab and told the driver to take me to Canada. We got to the border and the border police at the gate asked me why I was going to Canada. I told them that I was going to join the Canadian Army. He told me to join my own Army, and he wouldn't let me into Canada.

This was very disappointing. I felt that I had let everybody down who was trying to help me. I walked around the big city of Buffalo. I came to a big theatre, a burlesque theatre. I paid five dollars to get in. I had nothing better to do. The burlesque was a great play, lots of pretty girls. I went back and stayed another night at the hotel. I didn't want to go home as a failure again.

As I was going through my wallet I found the address and phone number of the Army friend in Orange, New Jersey who had offered me a job. I called and asked him if his offer was still on. He said to come on down to New Jersey. So I got on the Greyhound bus again.

My friend picked me up and I stayed at his house. He had a wife and three children. I went to work with him the next day and was hired that same day. It was hard and hot work, but the pay was good. I worked at the American Smelting and Refining Company from 1944 until 1945. They made copper pipes. My job was to feed the blast furnace. I worked for about four months and then all the workers went on strike. I wasn't in good standing with the Union because I wouldn't walk the picket line. I thanked my friend and left.

I went to another town in New Jersey called Perth Amboy and rented an apartment. I looked for work and saw a sign at the Strand Theatre for ushers to show people to their seats when the movies were playing. I talked to the manager and was hired at twenty dollars a week, seven days a week, from 11:00 am until 9:30 pm.

I had to wear a monkey suit with a bow tie. The only equipment I needed was a flashlight to escort people to their seats. The ushers' dressing room was a large room up on the stage behind the picture screen. The dressing room had metal wall lockers for the ushers to use when changing their clothes. The door to get into the dressing room could be locked from the inside. In the dressing room was a small Army bed to be used in case an usher should get sick. I never did see anybody get sick.

The usher job didn't pay much, so I lost my apartment. There was no place for me to stay, so, without anybody's knowing about it, I slept in the ushers' dressing room. I convinced the manager that I was a dedicated usher. All the other ushers would leave at about 9:30 in the evening when the last show would come on. At about 9:15 pm the girl selling tickets would close down her booth and take the money up to the manager's office.

I would stick around until the last movie was over, then help turn on all the lights and greet everyone leaving the theatre with a "good night." When the manager and the ticket girl were up in the office counting money, I would go to the back of the theatre to one of the exits and remove the 2 x 4 board from the inside. That board kept people from sneaking into the theatre from the outside.

When the manager would come down from the office to leave and lock the front doors, I made it a point to be right there in my street clothes. Sometimes he would ask why I hadn't left with the others. I would say, "Well, I don't have anything else to do, and I'm not in a hurry." The manager would walk out to the parking lot and drive off. Then I would walk down the alley alongside the theatre to the exit that I had removed the board from. I would open the door, replace the board, then go up and down the rows of seats to see whether anybody had dropped something. I was never lucky enough to find anything other than quarters and small change.

After that I would wash up and brush my teeth in the men's room before the janitor arrived. I knew when he would arrive. It took him about two hours to clean the theatre. He never did come backstage. I locked the door from the inside of the dressing room, so I was safe. No one could walk in on me. I knew that the manager arrived every day at 10:00 am. I made sure that I was out of the theatre by 8:00 am.

I would go to the YMCA, take a shower, and then eat breakfast at a greasy-spoon restaurant. Then I would be the first usher to arrive at the theatre. The Head Usher, who didn't have to wear the usher's uniform, dressed in a suit. He would always stay out front and collect tickets from people.

One day he told me he had another job that he might be going to, and the theatre manager had told him that he was thinking about offering the job as Head Usher to me. The manager never did say anything to me.

One night, after closing the theatre, I was going up and down the rows of empty seats looking for anything people might have dropped, and I found a men's gold wristwatch. I knew it was an expensive watch, and I had no intention of keeping it. That next morning when I arrived at the theatre, a man came in and wanted to see the manager. I called the manager on the theatre phone. He said that he would be right down.

When the manager came down I moved off to get ready to carry the new film up to the projector room when I heard the man tell the manager that he thought he had lost his watch at the theatre the night before. He wanted to know whether someone had found it. I spoke up and asked the man if he could identify the watch. I told him that I had found a men's gold watch the night before and that I was going to turn it in to the manager this morning.

The man did identify the watch. I took it out of my pocket and gave it to him. He was so happy to get the watch back that he offered me five dollars as a reward. I wouldn't take it. Then the theatre manager spoke up and said how proud he was to have honest people working for him like Mr. Clark, and he said that Mr. Clark was going to be the next Head Usher.

I told the manager thanks, and the man with the watch left happy. About a month later the Head Usher left and I was given his job. I went to a second-hand store and bought a suit and a tie. Now I could stand out front and collect tickets. I received a ten dollar pay raise. Now my salary was thirty dollars a week.

It wasn't long before I noticed that the girl selling tickets was not only a nice person but also a pretty girl. Her name was Judy. I don't remember her last name. She was about four years older than I was, but she didn't know it. I asked her if she had a boyfriend. She said that she didn't. I asked her if she would have breakfast with me some morning before work. She said she would love to. This was the beginning of our going together. After making Head Usher and getting a pay raise, I rented myself a cheap apartment. I had one day a week off, and Judy had the same day off.

I took her out one day row-boating on a lake and then to dinner. Judy lived with her mother and father. I think she was an only child. Judy and I were just kissing friends. I wanted more but Judy didn't want to go all the way.

One day she invited me to dinner at her parents' house. She had told me that her father owned a family business. I think she said it was a furniture store. I did go to her home for dinner because I knew that Judy's parents wanted to meet me. We had a good dinner, and then her father asked me a lot of questions. After dinner Judy and her mother went out to the kitchen.

When we were alone Judy's father asked me if I knew that they were Jewish. Then he said that he didn't want Judy to marry outside the faith, and that they had worked hard for their family business and he wanted to keep it in the Jewish faith. Then he came right out and asked me if I had been circumcised. I thought, "This guy is being damn right bold," and I said, "Hell yes." Then I got up out of the chair and made my way out of the house. I could see that he did not want me in the family.

Judy and I still met and enjoyed each other's company. I had been working at the theatre for about four months when Judy accepted a good job in Newark, New Jersey. Judy went to work on the train and came back on the train. She wanted me to meet her at the train station when I could. I did meet her five or six times. Judy was a good and sincere person. I was falling in love with her, but I knew that I had nothing to offer her. I felt that I wasn't good enough for her, and I knew that her family didn't approve of me and never would. I never did tell Judy about the conversation with her father. Ours was a relationship that would have put a wedge between Judy and her parents. So I thought it would be better if I just removed myself from her life.

I quit the theatre and left town without saying goodbye. I didn't know where I was going. I just started hitch-hiking. I ended up in Plainfield, New Jersey. As I was standing on the roadside hitch-hiking, there was a Borden's Dairy Farm that had a big sign. The dairy needed workers. I went to their office and they hired me. They even furnished living quarters, barracks style, with fifteen people upstairs and fifteen people downstairs. When I got to the barracks they wanted me to come in.

I learned that most of the men were drifters like me, and when I entered the barracks, I was asked by one of the men if I was a Yankee from the North, or a Rebel from the South. I said, "Rebel." They said, "Downstairs. Yankees are upstairs." So I found an empty bed downstairs.

I was told that they worked three shifts a day at the dairy and that I would never have the same job from one day to the next. Each week I would be working a different shift. They had a small snack bar on the farm where a person could buy something to eat.

My first week was working in a big building where loose, fresh-cut grass, clover and alfalfa were dried and dumped into a big pit by trucks. There were two of us who used a pitchfork to throw the forage out of the pit and onto a wide, moving leather belt. At the end of the belt a crew of two men would bail and weigh the square bales.

My next job was working around the cows. Because I was new, they gave me the dirty job of steering the cows that were ready for milking down a long trench path that had cement walls on both sides. It was a narrow passage. I had to keep them moving in a single line. I was given a water hose to spray on them to keep them moving. This was one of the worst jobs. I had rubber boots on and I was covered with mud and cow s_ _t from my head to my boots.

The next day I was given the job of wiping the cows' milk bags off with warm rags. One cow after another, they would just keep coming. The next job was steering the cows onto a very large and slow-moving merry-go-round. As soon as the cow was fully on, I would lock his head and neck into an iron gate so that the cow couldn't move his head or get out.

Then the next day I was shown and given the job of sitting on a wooden stool, with a handful of tags with strings on the tags. My job was to test each tit on the cow's bag to see if there was a bad tit out of the bunch of tits. If the cow kicked and squirmed, that usually meant that the tit was bad. I had to put a tag on that tit, so the workers who were putting on the milking machine would pass by the tagged tit.

I worked at the dairy for about three months. One Sunday evening we were throwing a small birthday party for one of the guys downstairs. Some of the guys had musical instruments. They started playing and singing country songs. We had beer, but nobody was drunk. Things were going good for about an hour when the guys upstairs started yelling down to us, "Stop playing that damn dumb Rebel music." At first we just didn't pay any attention to them. But they kept yelling that if we didn't quit playing and singing, they were going to come down and kick some Rebel butts. Well, that did it. Everyone at the downstairs party stopped singing and playing. The instruments were put away, and all of us who were partying went upstairs and the rumble was on. The fighting started, things were thrown, windows were broken, and some guys were thrown down the stairs. This went on for a long time until the police arrived and booked just about all of us. The next morning we were all taken before a judge with all our injuries, some with black eyes and bruises. I had a cut above my eye. The judge had a list of all the damages to the property.

I don't think the judge liked anyone from outside the state of New Jersey. First, he made the remark that, "Drifters come to Plainfield and make trouble." We tried to explain how it all got out of hand and who started the trouble. The judge wouldn't listen. He told us he wanted all the people not from New Jersey to be out of the state by that evening, and that we were going to be escorted back to the dairy farm by the police. We should pick up our belongings and the wages we had coming, that we would be given our wages in cash, and that we would all have to split the cost of the damages to the barracks. The dairy people had the bill ready when they gave us our money. There were about ten of us Rebels.

We received our pay minus what we had to pitch in to pay for the damages. None of the Yankees who started the trouble in the first place were disciplined. They all stayed working at the dairy farm. The police took us to the train station and they looked over our shoulders to see to it that we bought train tickets out of the state of New Jersey on a train that was to leave that day. Then the police stayed right there to make sure that we all got on the train. I was the only one who bought a ticket to New York City. The other guys went South. Some went back to where they came from. I didn't know anybody in New York, but I had heard so much about Broadway and all the famous places in New York. I didn't have much money left after paying for my part of the damages, and after buying my ticket. The police said to each of us as we started to board a train, "Don't come back or we will lock you up."

6

NEW YORK CITY

I arrived in New York at Grand Central Station. I was astonished to see how big it was and that there were so many people coming and going or waiting for a train or waiting for someone. There were shops, men's rooms, waiting rooms, and lockers for checked bags.

After looking the station over, I found that I could buy a hot dog on a hot steamed bun and a soft drink for only twenty-five cents. I thought that maybe I could live at the station until I landed a job. I knew that I would have to sleep sitting up because I was sure they wouldn't allow a person to take up all the space by lying down. That would take up an entire bench. I bought a newspaper and checked the want ads. There were lots of jobs but a person would have to know his way around the city or get lost.

That was one of the reasons why I didn't want to leave the station. The first day I was there I took a seat next to a guy who was about my age. He was three years older than I was. I was then fifteen years old. He was also reading the want ads.

We struck up a conversation and I found out that he was also on the road from another state. He said that he had been at the train station for three days. He also said it was rough trying to get any sleep in the train station because of all the people moving around, talking, babies crying, and small kids kicking you and bumping into you.

He told me the station police started keeping an eye on you if they saw you at the station day after day, and if you were sitting with your head hanging down and your eyes closed, they would wake you up and ask you, "What are you waiting for?" If you said, "A train," they would ask to see your ticket.

This stranger I was talking to told me he told the station police that he was waiting for his pregnant wife who was coming from Florida, but that he had forgotten which day and time she was to arrive. He also told them that he had no place to stay or live until she did arrive. He had to meet her at the station.

The guy told me that the station police must have bought his story because they quit bothering him when he closed his eyes and tried to get some sleep.

He also told me that I would be safe that first night, and that if they should ask me if I were waiting for a train, to tell them that I was waiting for a relative to arrive. He said that I should pick out a gate number and know where the train was coming from and the time it was supposed to arrive.

Well, the first night the station police left me alone. The second night they tapped me on the shoulder every time I closed my eyes. The third night I thought I might fool them by going into the men's room and getting some sleep sitting on the toilet. I had to put a dime in the coin box on the floor for it to open. Once the coin is put in, nobody else can get in. The door is locked.

One night of that was enough for me. I met the guy again who was pretending to wait for his pregnant wife. I would see that he felt like hell. There was just no way a person could get any rest trying to live at Grand Central Station.

We met and talked to another homeless soul who was trying to live this way. He told us that sometimes, during the week, a city police van called a Paddy Wagon would pull up in front of the train station. Then the city police would round up all the people they had seen hanging around the station day and night.

Those people would be put in the Paddy Wagon, taken to the City Jail, booked, and sentenced to thirty days on a vagrancy charge. A vagrant is a person who has no home, no place to live, no income, and no money. That person is not allowed to be free in society even if he is not bothering anybody.

I told my station friend, after I learned about the round-up, that I was not going to hang around the station any longer. I had just about enough money out of my last job to get a cheap room for a week or two until I could find a job doing anything. He said that he was in the same situation, and that if I didn't mind, he would like for us to share a room or an apartment.

I could see the guy was a straight guy by the way he looked at girls, and the conversation we had was all about the girl friend problems he had in his home state. In a way he was doing the same thing I was doing. We were both trying to find a place in society. I agreed that we should pitch in on getting a place to stay and try to help each other with getting jobs. So we walked and rode the subway reading the want ads in the newspaper.

We found a two-room apartment. No cooking was allowed. We had to eat out. We paid fourteen dollars a week. We split that amount. It sure did feel good to sleep on a bed again. And it was good to sleep without the fear of someone tapping you on the shoulder, and without the fear of being locked up. Now I had a mailing address. I wrote home and told my mother that I was doing great. I told her that I had an apartment and a job. I didn't have a job, but I didn't want her to worry.

After walking around and seeing all the shops and restaurants, I noticed that there were a lot of Italian restaurants. Many had a sign in the window showing a big plate of spaghetti with meat balls for just sixty-five cents. Just about all of the restaurants had a help wanted sign in the window. So I got a job as a dishwasher in an Italian restaurant. I got all the spaghetti I wanted and was paid twenty-five dollars a week.

The owner made sure that you earned every penny of that money. I had to work ten hours a day, and at closing I had to sweep and mop the eating area and the kitchen, scrub pots and pans, scrub garbage cans, and take out the garbage. It was a job. The other guy also landed a job. He worked as a bus-boy in a bigger restaurant than the one where I worked.

One day I received a big shock. A letter arrived from my first childhood love, Doris. I don't know how she got my address. Maybe one of my sisters gave it to her. She told me that she had a baby girl now. She wasn't happy in her new marriage and was thinking about coming to New York to see me. She gave me a phone number and the time and date to call her. She said that she would explain more on the phone.

I told this other guy who had the other room next to mine about the letter and that she wanted to come to see me. The guy said, "See if she will bring a girl friend." Well, I called on the date, and at the time she requested. She told me that she wanted to get away from McKeesport for a while and she asked if she could stay with me. My first thought was, "This is great." I asked if she would bring a girl friend with her. I told her that I had a great friend for her girl friend and what he looked like, and his age. She said that she did have someone who would come to New York with her. I thought, "Great. This is going to work out good." Doris told me when she would arrive.

So this guy and I went to the train station to meet them. Well, the girl Doris brought with her was a lot on the heavy side. I had seen her before in McKeesport with Doris. We all went out to eat at a greasy-spoon restaurant. Then we took them to our rooms and we had a great time. I found out that Doris had a lot more sexual experience than I had had. It was because she had been married and had received more training in the subject of sex. She assured me that she would show me what it was all about, and she did. Now I was hooked on having sex with her.

The two girls went out looking for jobs. They didn't seem to have any trouble finding jobs. Doris got a job as a waitress and she did well on receiving tips. I can't remember where the other girl got a job. Doris told me one night as we were lying in bed together that her marriage wasn't working out. She said that she and her husband constantly had arguments about me. Her husband thought that she was in love with me.

I was in shock when she told me this. She said that she was still in love with me. I loved having Doris in my bed, but one thing I could see was that her girl friend had all the control when it came to making decisions that involved both of them. After staying with me for about six weeks I could see that Doris was starting to worry about her baby and about what her husband might do. Doris had left him and her baby to live with another man. I got the impression that the heavy girl Doris came with was getting homesick. I thought she wanted to go home, and that she would try to get Doris to go home with her. Doris was a follower.

The girl friend succeeded because after staying with me in New York for six weeks, Doris told me that she wanted to go home to see her baby. I tried to talk her into staying, but I also knew that since she was separated from her baby, there was really nothing I could do or say that would make her stay with me. I had the feeling that the other guy didn't give a damn whether they stayed or left.

So we all went to the train station. They bought their tickets for McKeesport, Doris gave me a hug and a long kiss, and that was the end of a good romance. After the girls left the other guy said he didn't really care for the fat girl and that he was glad to see her go. I felt more alone than ever after Doris left. But I also felt that I had to look forward. About a week after the girls left, the other guy in the other room told me that he had had his fill of New York and he was going back to his home state.

After he left I had to find a cheaper place to stay in the big city. Now I found myself all alone again. I kept my eye on the newspaper want ads. I didn't know my way around New York. I made it a point not to wander off too many blocks going north or south.

One day I remember being on 42nd Street and the Avenue of the Americas. I wanted something cold to drink. I saw this nice place on the corner. It was a cocktail bar. When I opened the door and stepped inside, the place was so dimly lit that I couldn't get my eyes adjusted right away from coming in from the sunny outside. It was like going into a dark theatre.

As soon as I was inside I could smell lots of different perfumes. I thought to myself, "I'm in luck. There must be lots of ladies in this place." I just stood there by the door for a few minutes trying to get my eyes to adjust to the dim lighting. About that time someone put a hand around my arm and in a soft, high-pitched man's voice said, "Let me direct you to the bar." When I got to the bar my eyes had adjusted. I sat on a bar stool and the man who had led me to the bar said to the bartender, "I'm buying this gentleman a drink." Then he sat on the bar stool next to mine.

At first I didn't think much about it until the bartender said, "What are you going to have, you sweet thing." Right then I became a little suspicious that there was something different about this place. Then the guy who bought me the drink started asking me questions like, "What's your name?" I gave him a false name. I looked at the booths behind me to see how many women were in this place.

Well, what I saw was two men sitting in each booth holding hands and necking. There wasn't a woman in the place. I thought to myself, "I'm getting the hell out of here, and now." I didn't even touch the drink the bartender had put in front of me, nor did I thank the person who bought me the drink. I couldn't get out the door fast enough.

Once I was outside I felt safe. I just wanted to tell everyone on the street what had happened. And I wanted to ask why the city would let a place like that cocktail lounge do business. I didn't say anything, but I just couldn't get over seeing two men in a love embrace. I wanted to throw up just thinking about it. So I put it out of my mind and stayed with getting my cold drinks from sidewalk vendors. That way I could see what was going on around me.

I got a cheaper room and continued to work as a dishwasher in the Italian restaurant. But I knew that I had to get out of that city. It was no place for a person from the woods like me. One day I overheard two guys in the restaurant talking about a big resort in Bear Mountain, New York. One said he had just quit a good job there. I asked him, "Where the hell is Bear Mountain?" He told me and even showed me on the map. He said they had good jobs there for anyone who wanted to work. The next day I found them in the telephone book. I talked to a supervisor at the main desk at the resort. He said, yes, he did have openings, but he wanted to hire ex-servicemen. I told him that I was coming up for an interview. So I told my boss that I was quitting and thanks for the job. I was to the point by then that it didn't even matter whether I got the job on the mountain or not. I had had my fill of New York too. I received what money I had coming and a plate of spaghetti and meat balls. I gave up my cheap, bed-bug ridden room, and with my carry bag and a map, I took off for the Bear Mountain Resort.

I was surprised when I arrived at the resort. It was a big place sitting at the bottom of a big, snow covered mountain. There were lots of cars in a big parking lot. I was told that West Point Military School was not far from the resort.

I went to the main desk and asked for the man I'd talked to about a job. The person I had talked to came out and we went into his office. We talked and he gave me an application form to fill out. I showed him my discharge from the Army. He just looked at the front. He didn't see my real age.

He told me that they had a big dining hall and sometimes held big banquets, and that what he as looking for were sharp bus-boys who don't trip over their own feet. He said they had to be clean shaven, keep their hair cut, wear shiny black shoes, black slacks, and black bow ties. They also had to wear clean white shirts and black vest-type jackets. He said the most important things was the ability to work with a woman waitress sometimes, and at other times, two or three at a time.

I told him that I was sure that I wouldn't have any problem with what he required, and I told him that I would like to work there. Then he told me that they would furnish the required clothing, but that I would have to buy my own black shoes and socks. He also said that if I wanted, they would provide living quarters. They had individual log cabins for the employees who wanted them. The resort would take twelve dollars out of my pay every week for the living quarters. To me this was great.

They took me to a row of log cabins where most of the male employees stayed. It was just a short walking distance from the resort. I was given my own log cabin. There was one large bedroom, a small kitchen, and a bathroom with a shower. I had hit it lucky again. I was fifteen and a half now, and World War II was over. There were a lot of ex-servicemen looking for jobs, so I was lucky that I had landed this one.

All the employees at the resort worked shift work. So it seemed that the other occupants of the other log cabins were coming or going to work at the resort. Some were cooks, bell-hops, and doormen who also parked people's cars as they were checking into the resort or checking out. My shift changed every week. I was given time to go buy black shoes and socks. Then I was ready.

They assigned me to the big dining room, but first they gave me some training on how to stand off to the side and close to the five big round tables that I was responsible for. I had to stand with a white dishtowel hanging from my arm. They showed me how to carry a big round metal tray full and stacked high with dirty dishes. It was carried by one hand, the fingers and thumb of that hand at shoulder height, and of course, without dropping the tray of dishes.

The waitress carried the food out of the kitchen and served the plates of food. If things got too busy, then I was supposed to help her bring out the food orders. I had to keep the water glasses and coffee cups full. When the customers left, it was my job to clean off the table and then set it up again for the next customers.

A waitress that I was going to be working with told me that if we worked as a team, and if we were polite to the customers and kept them happy, they would leave a big tip and come back again as customers. All waitresses, by rules of the resort, were to give a certain percentage of their tips to the bus-boy they worked with. I never had any problem with this rule because I usually worked with the same waitress. But some of the other bus-boys complained that their waitress cheated them.

After working at the resort for four months another bus-boy told me how they ripped off the waitresses. I was told that a waitress has five big tables to take care of. When the customers at one table have eaten and are ready to leave, they leave more than one dollar. Maybe they leave two five-dollar bills, or two tens. The waitress is concentrating on the other four tables, and she doesn't know how much the customers left for a tip.

The bus-boy is the first one to reach that table to clear away the dirty dishes. He uses a white cloth napkin to cover up one of the bills left as a tip. He will leave the other bill and clean off the table. The last thing the bus-boy will do is pick up the napkin with the bill under it. Then he carries his tray back to the kitchen. Once in the kitchen, he pockets the money.

I knew the waitresses were aware that this was going on. I told the waitress I was working with that she had nothing to worry about, that I had no reason to rip her off because I found her to be more than genuine with me. A lot of times, if the tips had been good, at the end of the shift she would give me extra money, more than the percentage she had to give me. I had no reason to rip her off.

I became friends with the bellhops. They couldn't go into or out of the kitchen, and I could. They wanted me to bring them food sometimes down to the basement. Sometimes there would be a woman or two who had spent all her money on a room and at the cocktail lounge. The women wouldn't have money for food. So the bell hops would have me take food to the women, and then they would take it out in trade. I got on the good side of the bellhops. They trusted me. And they let me in on what they were doing.

It had to do with the bridal suite at the resort. They showed me what they had done. We went into the unoccupied room next to the bridal suite. They took down a small framed picture on the wall. They had drilled a hole in the wall, right through and into the wall of the bridal suite. They let me stand on a stool and look through the drilled hole. It was a straight view of the bed in the bridal suite. We then went into the unoccupied bridal suite, and there was a large, framed picture on the wall of a fall season with leaves falling off trees along a waterfall. The hole in the wall went right through one of the falling leaves in the painting, and the hole blended so well that no one would ever detect it.

The bellhops promised me that they would let me peek through the hole the next time the bridal suite was occupied. But, they said that I would have to stand in line and wait my turn.

At the peep hole, as time went by at the resort, I can truthfully say, "Yes, I did take my turn standing on a chair and looking through the hole in the wall." But I didn't see anything more taking place than what I had been doing with a woman when I was twelve years old. It was like watching a skin-flick movie.

The resort attracted a lot of famous people from all over the United States and from other countries. Ski champions and the people who liked skiing, football players, and honeymooners all came to the resort. I liked working there, but after a while I thought it was time to move on. I was still looking for my place in life and I knew that staying there was not what I wanted to do for a career. I let the resort know that I would be leaving.

The bellhops and waitresses told me they would miss me. I told the bellhops that the next bus-boy would probably get food for them. All they would have to do was give him a turn at looking through the peep hole.

The day came for me to leave. I wanted to stay, but I wanted to leave also. I flipped a coin in the air. It came up the way I called to leave. I went up to the resort's main office to tell them the log cabin I had been staying in was ready for inspection. They sent one of the supervisors to look at it. The cabin passed inspection. I turned in the key, picked up my small bag and my sleeping bag, and then went to the bus station for a bus to take me back to the big city of New York.

7

THE HOBO LIFE

I stayed at the YMCA. The next day I went to the Greyhound bus station and bought a ticket to Morgantown, West Virginia. This is where my sister, Jean, and her husband, Ralph moved to after Ralph got out of the Navy Seabees. My sister, Jean had another baby, a boy they named, Buzz. When I got to Jean and Ralph's they said I could stay with them until I decided what I wanted to do.

Ralph was working for a big chemical company, and he told me that he could get me a job there. I went to work with the chemical plant which was right on the outskirts of Morgantown. I was almost sixteen. The chemical plant hired me after I showed them my Army discharge. They didn't look at the back of my discharge which showed my real age.

It was winter when I was at my sister's place. I remember the cold mornings when Ralph and I would go out to the old Model T Ford. He had to take us to work, and when the battery would be down on the car, and the car wouldn't start, I had to get in front of the car and with a metal crank try to crank the engine, while Ralph pushed the starter and pushed and pulled on the choke. More often than not, the car was hard to get started on those cold mornings, but with a lot of cranking and swearing, we would get the car started and go to work.

While I was staying and working in Morgantown, I decided to call Judy in New Jersey because I missed her. She was happy to hear from me, so we started calling each other by phone. On my birthday Judy sent me a real nice gold wristwatch. I never did tell her about getting run out of the state of New Jersey. I stayed with Ralph and Jean for about three months, and then I wanted to travel. I thanked them for letting me stay at their home in Morgantown.

I started hitchhiking south. I wanted to see Florida. I had been told by one of the bellhops I was working with at Bear Mountain that in Florida bellhops and busboys were making fifty dollars a day working at some of the big hotels in Miami. I believed what he told me, so I wanted to see for myself.

I started hitchhiking in the forties. People didn't have any fear about picking up a hitchhiker in those days. In the forties there was no talk about drugs and marijuana, or newspaper reports of hitchhikers killing the person who picked them up, or of the driver killing the hitchhiker.

In the forties people seemed to have more morals and respect for each other. Hitchhiking was easy then. I found the only time it was hard getting a ride was when it started to get dark. Then drivers didn't seem to want to pick up hitchhikers. I didn't blame them. It didn't take me long to learn the ropes.

One of the most important things is to have a map and not get stuck in small towns, because they don't have any missions or a Salvation Army that will give drifters a place to stay for the night. Also, small towns are leery of drifters in their towns. When I did get stuck in a small town after dark I would go out to the outskirts of that town and try to find some kind of shelter near the road I was traveling on.

The shelter would usually be a big tree to get under, or under a bridge on the road, or under a railroad bridge. In a large city a person on the road can find a mission or a Salvation Army to take them in. I have never been refused a bed in either one of them. The Salvation Army would give a drifter something to eat, a place to take a shower, clean sheets, and a bed for the night.

The missions I found would do the same thing for a drifter, but they would usually hold religious services at all times of the day, and they wanted you to attend those services. They also expected you to sing and go forward to the altar and be saved. I had been saved so many times growing up that I thought I had enough salvation to last a lifetime.

Missions I stayed at all required that I attend services before they would give me something to eat and a bed. Usually both the missions and the Salvation Army would fill out a form wanting my Social Security number and letting me and the other drifters know that this was for one night's lodging and not a place to homestead. They meant, "Stay one night and then move on."

During my travels I learned a lot and met many interesting poor people traveling as I was, on the road hitchhiking, and some who would rather hop on a slow-moving freight train and then just go where the train takes you. But I met some hobos who could tell you where a freight train was headed, and then it was up to you to decide whether you wanted to go and jump off when the train slowed down. The railroad has people working for them who keep on the lookout for hobos.

They are like railroad cops. They look out for the interest and safety of the railroad, but some of them let the authority go to their heads, and sometimes they just take matters into their own hands when they catch a hobo or a drifter riding in an empty boxcar of the freight train. I heard stories from hobos about being beaten up with clubs and then thrown off a moving freight train.

I considered myself a drifter, a person who wanders from place to place and from job to job. I would never lower myself to beg people for money. I would work my way. I learned that most bums I met would not work, and most of them have no pride. When they're not bumming for money they're drinking cheap wine. Now a hobo I got along with. They wander aimlessly but they will usually work their way, and the ones I met weren't into asking people for money.

There were times during my travels down to Florida when I slept under railroad bridges and would come upon a hobo jungle. I would always ask the group if I could join them. They could see that I was on the road, and I never got turned down. They would welcome me, but they would usually ask me what I could contribute to the pot of Mulligan Stew. They had a cardboard box and they wanted me to put any kind of food I had in it. They preferred vegetables so that a stew could be made. The first time I stayed with hobos they were a friendly group.

I told them that this was the first time for me to be on the road and there was a lot that I had to learn about their ways. They welcomed me and wanted to know what I was doing on the road. I told them about my Army background and they were amazed that I had been in the Army at thirteen years of age. I showed them my discharge and it seemed that they started to show me more courtesy. The hobos seemed to know each other, and I noticed that there was always one hobo in the group who was more respected by the others and seemed to be the leader. And that hobo seemed to be older than the others.

At my first camping with a hobo group, one of them, in a nice way, told me to start carrying something in my bag to contribute to the Mulligan Stew. I was also told to get myself some eating utensils the next time I should visit a restaurant. He told me to also get a coffee cup. I assured him that I would.

When the stew was done cooking and the leader of the group filled his large can full of stew, all the other hobos helped themselves. After they had all served themselves, I was invited to help myself. One of the hobos gave me a spoon and an empty bean can. I filled the bean can with soup and joined them for dinner sitting on a wooden box. The stew was real good. After we all had all the stew we wanted, the hobos sat around a small fire and they would swap stories of their past lives in society and stories of their travels as hobos.

They gave me a lot of good tips that would help me on my travels. They showed me on paper how to read the hobo code. The older man, and leader of the group, took me off to the side so the others wouldn't hear what he had to say. He told me that as long as I was on the road I shouldn't wear rings or a watch. He was referring to the new wristwatch I was wearing that Judy had sent me for my birthday. I took his advice.

That same night I put my watch inside my boot. This older hobo gave me more advice. He said, "Settle down. Be somebody. Don't be a hobo or bum." I assured the old fellow that I would take his advice. The old fellow gave me a big piece of cardboard to put under my sleeping bag. It seemed like everyone went and sacked out about the same time that evening.

Early the next morning they seemed to split up in pairs of two's and all went in different directions. I didn't want to be the last one to leave from under the railroad bridge, so I made it a point to hurry and roll up my sleeping bag and get out on the main road. I heard some of them talking about what time a freight train would be coming and slowing down near this spot. They intended to hop on the freight train. When I thanked them for letting me camp with them they wished me all the luck in the world. I left them thinking to myself, "What a nice bunch of human beings. They're not just hobos."

Later that day as I waited for someone to pick me up, I looked over the code that the hobos wrote down on paper that would help me in my travels. Most of the code they gave me had to do with going to people's houses to ask for food and work. That I was not going to do, but there were other things on the list that were nice to know. They told me that the code should be left in a viewable place of a residence last visited by a hobo so the next hobo could read the code and know what treatment he would receive. The code mark could be left on a tree, on a fence, or on the side of the residence mailbox. I had no intention of going to someone's house to ask for food or money. I would rather eat grass first.

Hitchhiking is definitely not a fast way to travel. A lot of the local people around the small towns, and farmers especially, wanted to be helpful. But they would only take me a short way down the road and then say to me, "Well, this is as far as I'm going." They would take me two or three miles down the road and then drop me off in a place that would be hard to get a ride from. Four-way stops are good spots, and a Y in the road is another good place.

I also found that placing myself under a street light helps a person to get a ride. If another hitchhiker is already at the place you wanted to be, and you are both going in the same direction, it was always common courtesy to walk up ahead of that hitchhiker and let him get his ride first. I have been in situations where the driver of the vehicle would pick up the first hitchhiker then come down the road and pick me up.

There are three main points that I think help any hitchhiker. First, keep a clean appearance, and that includes being clean-shaven and keeping your hair cut. You should not smell like a polecat. Use cologne. In my time on the road the only cologne a man could get was Velvet or Old Spice. The second point is, stand and face the driver, smile, and hold your arm out in front of you with your thumb pointed in the direction you're going. Finally, don't have a lot of baggage. I carried one small handbag and my sleeping bag strapped on top of my handbag.

When I was hitchhiking there were no freeways. I traveled on routes that took you right through the middle of big cities and towns. Countrysides and filling stations were few and far between. There were no fast-food chains as there are today. Sometimes I would come upon a Mom-and-Pop hamburger place, and hamburgers were fifteen cents. A soft drink was five cents. I would keep my shaving up by carrying a mirror and razor in my bag. A lot of times I would shave and wash up as much as I could at gas stations. When I was stranded out in the country I would look for a creek where I could wash up and shave.

During my travels I would drop my mother a postcard telling her not to worry, that I was doing just great, and that I was getting plenty to eat. One time an old chicken farmer outside of Charlotte, North Carolina picked me up in an old truck, and he, like so many others, told me he was going down the road a short way.

I thought, "What the heck. The old guy just wants to be nice." After I got in his truck he asked me if I wanted some work. He said he had a week of work for someone who wanted it, and he would pay me seventy-five cents an hour and give me meals and a place to sleep. He told me that his wife was the best cook in that county. Without asking what kind of work I would be doing I agreed to take the job. I wasn't in a hurry to get to where I wanted to go.

The old farmer took me to his chicken farm. The chicken houses were as long as Army barracks. He took me in his house and told his wife that I was the new hired hand and to put on another plate for dinner. He told me to follow him and he would show me where I was to bunk. He took me to the barn and pointed up to the hayloft. There was a wooden ladder up to the loft and lots of hay. Then he showed me an old outhouse he wanted me to use. Then he showed me a long wooden horse and cattle drinking box. It was empty and it looked clean. There was a water hose nearby to fill it up. He said, "This is where you can take a bath."

I was starting to wonder, "What the hell did I get myself into," but it was close to dinner time, and his wife's cooking smelled good. I also thought to myself, "His wife's cooking had better be good or I'm getting the hell out of here and back on the road." The old farmer gave me a pair of rubber boots to wear and two pairs of coveralls to wear for the work he wanted me to do. When he gave me these things I knew right then and there that I wasn't going to gather chicken eggs.

I was invited into the house for dinner, and it was a very good, home-cooked meal. His wife was a great cook. They wanted to know all about me, where I was going and where I had come from. After we got all the small talk done, the old man told me what he wanted me to do. He said he had a batch of new chickens coming and he wanted me to clean out the chicken house.

I thought that shouldn't be too hard to do. He told me that we would start work right after breakfast and that he would wake me up at five-thirty. The old man showed me the light switch in the barn. I fixed a nice place for my sleeping bag in the hay. After about two hours into the night I felt something run over my face. I could hear something moving in the hay. Before I got into my sleeping bag, I had put my flashlight in my sleeping bag with me. I quickly turned on the flashlight and I could see that the place was crawling with field mice. I turned on the barn light and let it stay on all night. It seemed that the mice stayed in their hiding places when the light was on.

The next morning the old man woke me, and at breakfast he asked me how well I had slept. I told him that his barn was full of mice and that I'd rather sleep in the bed of his truck outside. He told me that would be fine. So after the first night I put loose hay in the bed of his truck and that's where I slept. The old man showed me what he wanted me to do. He gave me a pick and a shovel and he wanted me to pick and shovel chicken s_ _t that was at least twelve inches thick and as hard as a rock. He said that when I had a wagon full that I was to shovel it off the floor and put it into the big field wagon. He had a mule hitched to pull the wagon. After the wagon was full, we were to take the load of chicken s_ _t and scatter it on the field. After working like a jackass in that chicken house I started to get chicken lice all over my body. So I told the man that I needed to take a hot shower every day because the lice were getting to me. So the old man agreed to let me use the shower in the house after shoveling chicken s_ _t.

I sure was glad when that job was finished. It took a full seven days to clean out that mess in the chicken house. The old man and his wife thanked me and he paid me my hard earned money. His wife packed me a lunch to take with me on the road. We said our goodbyes. They told me that if I was ever out that way again I should stop by and see them. When I went down their road, and after they couldn't see me, I put the hobo's code on their fence where it could be seen. The code meant, "You can sleep in the barn."

8

HITCHHIKING MY WAY TO FLORIDA

What money I had with me I wanted to save for when I arrived in Florida. I could get a room and also have enough money to tide me over until I landed a job. For the rest of the time on the road hitchhiking, I came up with a plan. The next time I was given a ride I was going to trick the driver into buying me food without asking. This way I wouldn't have to spend any of my money for food.

The next guy picked me up. He was a talkative guy, so I held back from putting my plan into action. I waited until things got a little quiet. All of a sudden I bent forward in the car seat, and at the same time grabbed my stomach, and with grunts and groans made face movements that made it seem that I was in agony.

I would even let out strong outbursts of grunts and groans as if I were in complete physical pain. But I didn't have to carry on my act for very long. The driver was shocked and hurriedly pulled over to the side of the road and kept asking, "What's wrong? What's wrong?" When I felt that the driver didn't want me to die in his car, and when he thought he had a person in his car who needed emergency medical treatment, and when I could see that I had him believing that I was almost dying, I said, waving my hand at the same time, "I'm O.K., I'm O.K. It's just my stomach. My little gut is trying to eat my big gut because I haven't eaten in three days."

"You haven't eaten in three days?" he asked. "That's right," I said, "Three days, because I haven't had any money to buy food." Then I would pretend that I was just coming out of an emergency situation. I would throw my head back on the headrest and groan slightly. The driver said to me, "If you can just hold on a little longer I'm going to buy you something to eat." He pulled back onto the road and began to look for a restaurant to get me something to eat.

I sat back in the seat with a sad and bewildered look on my face. Well, my plan had worked. The driver found a restaurant. When he parked the car, he got out and hurriedly opened my door and wanted to help me out of the car. But I said, "No thanks. I can make it."

When we were seated in the restaurant the guy told me to order what I wanted. I started with soup and salad. Then I ordered something good from the menu. I'm not a hard guy to please. I went light on the guy's wallet. I wouldn't order the most high-priced thing on the menu. I would eat fast and clean the plate to the last crumb, and I wouldn't say anything while I was eating. I wanted the guy paying for the food to feel that he was helping to feed a starving person.

After we got back in the car I thanked him for the food and told him that I was grateful and would never forget the good deed he had done. I could tell that when the driver let me out, that was as far as he was going in my direction. I could also tell that he was glad to get me out of his car before I should die in his car of hunger pains.

This was my plan and it worked. So I used it time and time again. I only had one guy tell me that he was broke or he would buy me something. I used this method quite a few times. Whenever I found myself in a good-sized town and they had a Salvation Army, I would stay there and they would give me food.

If there was no Salvation Army, I would look for a nice restaurant. I would go in and ask for the manager. I made it a point not to talk to anyone except the manager. If for any reason the manager wasn't there, I would just leave.

If the manager was there and I was able to talk to him, I would ask to talk to him in private. Then I would tell the manager, "I'm going to put it to you straight, Sir. I'm on the road and I'm headed for Florida. I've been on the road now for many days, and I haven't had anything to eat now going on three days. Now, I'll tell you what I'll do for you. I'll wash your dishes and your pots and pans. I'll scrub your floors, scrub your garbage cans, and wash your windows. I will do all this for a bowl of soup. And I'll give you a good day's work for a bowl of soup."

I would say all of this in a fast-talking fashion so the manager couldn't interrupt me. What I was trying to do was to work on the manager's sympathy. This method always worked for me. More times than not, the manager would be more than generous. I had one manager tell the waitress, "Give this man the menu and let him order what he wants." They would feed me, and usually the manager would tell me if he had work for me to do. Usually they did have work for me to do, and I was always ready to accept work. One manager put me to work and asked me if I would stay. He said that he had a steady job in the kitchen for me. But I wanted to keep moving and get to Florida.

I found that being on the road as I was wasn't all that advantageous. At times I found myself very much alone, and I never knew where I was going to sleep when dark closed in. I had no one to talk to, no one to help me figure out what my next move should be. Sometimes I found myself out on a country road, no traffic coming in either direction, and it was getting dark. Sometimes it would start raining. I learned very quickly to think for myself and to look for shelter. There was always one thing I was positive about, and that was that God had sent an angel to watch over me. Many a time during the day and at night I prayed to God for guidance and asked God for help. I always found shelter and food, so I know that my prayers were answered.

Another thing that's hard to do when hitchhiking is staying on the numbered route you want to travel. Sometimes the drivers would think they knew the best route, and before I knew it, the driver would take me out of my way and miles off my route. Sometimes I would fall asleep, then open my eyes and find myself on another route and going in a different direction. I found that hitchhiking a long distance isn't that easy.

There is one ride I will never forget. I was dropped off out in the countryside. I was way out of my way and there was no traffic on the road. The blacktopped road ended and a dirt road began. A situation like that gives a person a strange feeling, and a feeling of being alone in the world. I thought, "I'll be stuck on this road for the rest of the evening." So I started looking around to find shelter for when it became dark. I sat on the side of the road waiting for more than an hour and no cars passed by either way. There was white cotton lying on the ground on both sides of the road that had blown off trucks carrying cotton from cotton fields.

I was sitting there and I could hear something like iron wheels on a wagon. As I looked down a side dirt road near where I was sitting, I saw a horse-drawn wooden buckboard with an old black man and a small boy sitting beside him.

I didn't think anything about it. They waved at me, and then when they got to where I was, they stopped. The old man told me that he was only going about three miles down the road, but that there was an intersection there where there would be traffic. He told me to climb aboard on the same seat with him and the boy. So I did. The horse was old and slow, but I really appreciated that this old fellow gave me a ride off a road I would never have gotten a ride off of. The old man told me that the boy was his grandchild, and they wanted to know where I had come from and where I was headed.

The old man said he and his family lived on a cotton plantation and that he had never traveled anywhere. The old man let me off not far from an intersection where cars were traveling. I thanked the old man and the boy for giving me a ride. I took a dollar out of my pocket and offered it to the old man, but he wouldn't take it. So I put it in the little boy's pocket and told the boy, "Make sure your grandpa buys you some ice cream." I got a big smile out of the boy. The old man said, "Good luck, and God bless you on your travels." That was the first time anybody had ever said to me, "God bless you," other than my mother. That was a ride I'll always remember.

After a lot of hitchhiking I finally reached Florida. It was a long trip. I checked into the YMCA in Jacksonville, Florida before hitchhiking down to Miami, which I had been told, was the place to make big money. I was sixteen and a half when I arrived in Florida. After resting for three days I worked my way down to Miami. The place was pretty with all the big hotels along the ocean beaches and all the palm trees.

As soon as I arrived I went to the state unemployment office. I stood in line and when I reached the service desk and turned in the application form they had me fill out, the man at the counter said, "I see you're from out of state." Then he told me that he was sorry, but Florida didn't have enough jobs for their returning veterans, and it would be hard for me to get a job through them. But he said he would put my name at the bottom of the job list and that I should report to their office once every two weeks.

As I walked around the town of Miami I saw a lot of private employment offices. In their windows they had lots of jobs, bellhops, busboys, and a lot of other jobs. So I went into one of their offices and filled out an application. When I was interviewed I found out that the agency wanted me to buy the job as a busboy or bellhop. They wanted seventy-five dollars up-front, and then a certain amount of my first five paychecks. If I should quit or get fired before the agency got all the money that was due to them, then they had arrangements with the employer that the agency would get the money I had coming to me. I told the guy at the agency that if I had seventy-five dollars I wouldn't be looking for a job. So that was the end of that.

I started to feel disappointment about coming to Florida. As I walked down a main street and heard people talking, all I could hear was Cuban. It made me feel that I was in a foreign country. I rented a cheap room. I had a feeling that things were not going to be good for me here in Miami. I visited a lot of restaurants but they didn't need dishwashers or busboys. I started hanging out at a park along the docks where tour boats docked that took tourists out on the water to look at the fish. Some of the boats had glass bottoms.

The park had a lot of benches and coconut palm trees. Now and then a coconut would fall out of the tree, and the park had a coconut opener mounted for the public to use. I would buy myself a newspaper to look for work.

One day I walked down toward where all the fancy and expensive hotels along the beach were. I saw a flat-bed truck parked alongside one of the hotels and a bunch of painters in white coveralls. I asked to see their boss. He was in the hotel at the time, so I waited until he came out and then I asked him for a job. He asked me if I were a painter. I told him I'd done a lot of painting. I told him this because I needed a job, and I thought to myself, "What's so hard about putting paint on a wall with a paint brush?"

The boss said he was short a painter and that he would like me to come to his hotel the next morning at seven am. Now, I was starting to feel good. I had landed a job. Well, the next morning I was at the hotel at six-thirty am. I was the first one to arrive. The flat-bed truck and the painters arrived on time and men got into their white coveralls. The boss gave me a pair of coveralls to put on. Then he told me that he was going to turn me over to his lead painter for the day because he, the boss, would be gone most of the day.

Well, the lead painter took me up to a room on the second floor of the hotel. He told me that all the rooms on the second floor were empty and they had to paint them all. There was another painter who went up to the second floor with us. The lead man told him to start painting a room, and then he assigned me the next room. He showed me what had to be painted, the one big room, the bathroom, a large closet, all the walls and ceilings, and I was to use different colors of paint. All the work was to be done with brushes.

In the forties painters weren't using long-handle rollers, and we were using sticky lead paint. As soon as the lead man gave me my instructions regarding how he wanted the room painted, he left me alone. I had a ladder to stand on and rags for cleanup.

Well, I really wanted to do my best. I was careful not to get paint all over the place. I started in the bathroom. I thought I was doing pretty well, but now and then I would look at myself in the bathroom mirror and I could see that I had paint on my face and in my hair. When I was painting the ceiling, paint started to run down my arm.

I didn't see the lead man all morning. Another painter came down the hallway yelling, "Lunch time," so all the painters stopped painting and went down to the truck to take their lunch break. I was a little late joining them because I was trying to clean the paint off my face and hands.

When I did join the other painters the lead man asked me how I was coming along with the painting. I told him, "Just fine, no problem." I finished the bathroom and moved the ladder and paint into the closet of the large room. I got all set to paint the closet when I thought I would go over to see how the painter was coming along in the room next to mine. When I walked in and looked in the bathroom, the closet, and the big room, I found the guy cleaning his brushes. I complimented him on a good job of painting. I just couldn't believe that this guy was finished. I asked him if he had done all that painting by himself. His reply was, "Of course." He acted like I was asking that question to offend him. I went back to the room where I had been painting. I knew right then I was in trouble. It was around three o'clock in the afternoon when the boss and the lead man came into my room. After they looked in the bathroom and then came back out to where I was, I could see that they were shaking their heads in disbelief. I knew what was coming. The boss said to me, "Mister, you told me that you were a painter."

I said, "Yes, I did, because I needed a job and I thought I could do the job of painting." He said that he would have to let me go but that he would pay me for the hours I did work. He told me that he was on a time contract and he just didn't have the time to train someone to be a painter. So that ended my experience as a painter in Miami.

I went back to the park during the day and to my cheap room in the evening. About a week later I saw a job in the newspaper that said, "No experience needed." It was working on a dredge boat in the Everglades, and they would furnish room and board on the dredge.

I went to the office in town to apply for the job. I told them I had worked on a riverboat. Out of five people, two of us were hired to work on the dredge in the Everglades. We were told the wages would be seventy cents an hour and room and board. I gave up my room the next morning. The people who hired us took us out of the city, and way out into the country and into the swamps. When the truck stopped along the banks of the swamp, there was a worker waiting for us in a motorboat to take us out to the dredge.

We went a long way down the swamp, and then the boat operator said to us, "Welcome to the Everglades where the alligators, all kinds of snakes, and lizards live." I got the feeling this guy was trying to put the fear into us two new workers.

After about a five-minute ride we came to the dredge boat. We climbed up on a ladder and the foreman of the crew gave us a handshake then took us to where we would be bunking. It was a large cabin with five beds. The foreman said, "This is the cabin you two guys will bunk in." I noticed that all the bunks had mosquito netting over the beds.

The foreman showed us the place where we would be eating, and he told us the times when food would be served. Then he explained how a dredge operates. It sucks all the mud and muck from the bottom of the Everglades waterways. Then all the stuff that is sucked up from the bottom is sent through very large pipes at a rapid rate. The pipes go out the back end of the dredge and down the middle of the Everglades. Each pipe is about fifteen or twenty feet long and are bolted together by very large nuts and bolts. The nuts in size were about four inches. The pipes would extend for about a half-mile down the middle of the Everglades. The pipes take a turn onto a high spot in the Everglades, and all that mud and muck would stack up and make land. The pipes on this end had to be moved every so often to another spot.

The foreman told the new man and me that we would have the job of moving the pipes at the end when they had to be moved, and that we would stop all leaks in the pipes where they are joined with nuts and bolts.

We would have to go all around the pipes and tighten the nuts so they didn't leak. The foreman told us that we were to wear life jackets when working from a motor boat. He said that we should expect to be wet all the time and that we would be working twelve hours a day. He also told us to be alert because there were poisonous snakes in the water, and they liked to sun themselves on the pontoon. And he said there were alligators in the water. I was wishing then that somebody else had been chosen for this job. But, I was there, so I'd have to give it a try. At night the mosquitoes came at you like a swarm of bees.

They gave me and the other man a four-inch wrench that had about a three-foot handle, and the weight of the wrench was about five pounds. We were to follow the pipeline from the dredge and step up on the floating pontoon and stop any leaks. We didn't have to look for leaks because all the pipes were always leaking. We looked like drowned rats by the time we would finally get a leak stopped.

One day we had to move the end of the pipe to another location. I got out of the boat and stood on the new ground that the mud had made. The guy in the boat yelled for me to look out behind me. I did, and I saw one of the biggest hard shell crabs I had ever seen. I just stood there. The crab looked me over and then started coming at me with his pincers held high.

I grabbed my big wrench. I could see the crab wasn't going to stop. I had to hit that crab with that iron wrench at least two good blows before I stopped it. I told the guy I was working with, "It's your turn to be the first one out of the boat the next time."

Every now and then we would see snakes swimming really fast, just skimming on the top of the water like they were in a hurry to get to where they were going.

Sleeping aboard the dredge was very hard because all the digging would go on all night, and all the machinery would always be running aboard the dredge. And the dredge would suddenly lift up a little out of the water when the big clawed bucket was lowered, and the big bucket would take a big scoop from the bottom. The dredge would also heave to the left and to the right. It was very hard to get to sleep.

The guy I came there with told me that he was quitting after we had worked on the dredge one month. I said, "When you quit, so am I." So we quit after working one month. We went up to the main office in Miami for our last paycheck.

I went back to the unemployment office. This time at the unemployment office there was a man waiting on people that I hadn't seen before. He seemed to be a very friendly fellow. When it came my turn at the counter, and he asked my name and address, I told him I didn't have an address, that the city park would be my address until I found a job. He said, "You poor soul. I'm sorry, but we don't have any jobs for you at the present, but check back here each morning. And make sure that when you come in you talk to me."

I went back to the city park and staked out my park bench. This was where I was going to spend my days and nights until I could find work. I found some cardboard to put down on the bench for a mattress and I had my sleeping bag. I had a little money from the dredge boat job. I wanted to save that money for food and not spend it on getting a cheap room. I knew if I did, what little money I did have wouldn't last long.

It wasn't too bad sleeping on the park bench. The nights were warm. The mosquitoes were a bother, and I would cover up my whole body with my sleeping bag. There were other drifters sleeping on other benches and no one ever bothered me at night.

During the day I would sit up and read the paper looking for work, or I would walk over to where the fishing boats were coming in and unloading their big fish catch, and weighing the fish right there on the dock.

Boats were coming in and going out with people all day long. I made friends with two other young drifters in the park. They were buddies and they were in the same situation I was in. They were from out of state and looking for work. They, too, had gone to the unemployment office and been told there were no jobs, and what jobs there were would be given to returning veterans of Florida.

These two drifters were occupying park benches near the one where I was sleeping. Since we were in the same situation we made an agreement that whoever found work first would come back to the park and tell the others, and then try and get them hired on the same job.

Two mornings went by before I went back to stand in the long line at the unemployment office. I made sure that I was in the line of this counter guy I had seen before. When I did get to talk to him he acted surprised to see that I was still around. He said he still had nothing in the way of work for me and for me to keep checking back.

I was starting to get to the point of giving up on trying to get work in Miami, and I was ready to start hitchhiking to California before I ran completely out of money. One day the weather in Miami started to get wind-stormy. I thought it would pass over. There had been talk of a hurricane that might be on the way to Florida.

I didn't take it seriously. The wind was starting to bend the palm trees in the park. I saw a policeman talking to people and asking them to leave. When he came over to the park bench that I was occupying and told me that I couldn't stay in the park, that a hurricane was on the way, I told him that I didn't have any place to go. He told me that the Red Cross was taking some people in and giving them shelter. He gave me directions to the building the Red Cross had set up to shelter homeless drifters like me. The Red Cross assigned me a cot and a blanket and served sandwiches.

I was in luck being out of the storm. The two other guys that I had made friends with in the park were also in the Red Cross shelter. I stayed in the shelter two days, and after the hurricane was over, I went to the park. The place was a mess. Trees and trash were everywhere. All the benches were turned over and a lot of them were broken.

I knew that I couldn't stay in the park any longer, and I remembered being told that there was a mission at the end of town that took in homeless men. When I got to the mission I had to sign in and attend religious services before they would give me a bed and food. The mission was full of drifters and bums.

The beds were double-deck bunk beds. I had a bottom bunk. That night I took off my shoes and put them under the bed. I was going to sleep with my clothes on. I noticed that the guy in the bed next to mine kept looking at me. I asked the guy, "Is there something wrong?" He said, "This must be your first time to stay at this mission. I noticed that you put your shoes under the bed. If you want them you'd better sleep with your shoes on or tie them around your neck." He said, "This is just friendly advice." I thanked him and tied the shoelaces around my neck and put a shoe on each side of my face.

I went to sleep and at about four o'clock in the morning the city police came into the room where we were sleeping. They had turned on the lights and they started pointing at some of the bums and drifters and saying, "You, and you, get your clothes on and go outside." One of the police officers looked at me, but didn't say anything. And he didn't say anything to the fellow who had given me advice about my shoes.

I didn't know what was going on. The police took about half the people out of that big room. After the police left, taking all the people they wanted, they left the room and turned off the lights. After all that I couldn't get back to sleep. I got up and went out to the main office and asked why the police were taking the men away.

I was told that this was one way the City of Miami used to get cheap labor to clean up the city after the hurricane. The guy at the desk said, "They will charge the men they took last night with vagrancy and give them thirty days in jail." He told me that I was lucky that I was as young as I was, otherwise the police would more than likely have taken me too. I noticed when I first arrived in the state of Florida that they still had a chain gang. The prisoners wore black and white striped pants and shirt with a round hat to match, and the ones I saw working along the roadside had an armed guard standing watch over them.

I counted my blessings that the police hadn't taken me that night. I surely didn't want to get a police record being this young. I didn't want to break the law in any way. I knew the Army wouldn't want me with a police record.

I had my seventeenth birthday in Florida and I was still a drifter. I stayed at the mission, and every day I would go uptown to see if any of the stores or restaurants had signs in their windows saying, "Help Wanted." I found none.

There was one really nice restaurant that I remember quite well. Each time that I would walk down the main street of Miami I would make it a point to stop and stare in their big front window. They always had a big round roast cooking and turning on the grill. It always looked so brown, and standing outside the window, I could smell the aroma of that delicious looking roast. I could tell that this was an expensive restaurant and out of my class. I would just have to settle for the bread and lunchmeat I had in my carrying bag.

Then one day as I was watching the roast being cooked, to my surprise, out of the door of the restaurant, and picking their teeth like they had just eaten a Thanksgiving dinner, came the two guys I had met in the park and made an agreement with about helping each other find work. As they came out of the restaurant they saw me looking in the window. I said to them, "Looks like you guys hit it big being able to eat in a place like this." "We sure did," said one of them with a big smile on his face. "And," he said, "We have reservations to stay at one of the best hotels in the city. And that's not all. We get to eat breakfast in the morning at this same restaurant."

I stood there dumbfounded. Then they told me how they had come by all this good luck, and they told me that I could do the same thing. They had signed up to join the Army. They had taken their physicals and tests, and passed, and they were to ship out tomorrow evening. Since they had no residence in Florida, the Army recruiter gave them meal tickets for the restaurant and a place to stay overnight.

I told them they sure were lucky. They told me that I should go and see the Army recruiter, and that maybe I could get in the Army again. The two guys told me to go to the Post Office, that the Army recruiter had an office there.

I thanked the two guys and high-tailed it down to the recruiter's office right then. I showed the recruiter my discharge from the Army, and told him the reason why I was discharged. The recruiter could see that I was discharged under the Army's code of Section Four, which means that I was under-aged at the time. The recruiter told me that since I had lied to get in the Army the first time, and since I had just turned seventeen years old, that I would have to get written permission from my mother to go into the Army again and that it would have to be signed by a notary public. Also, I would have to show a copy of my birth certificate and provide a sworn affidavit from three persons who had known me all my life and could verify my age.

I could see the Army wasn't going to take any more chances with me. The recruiter told me that the war was over and there was no longer a draft. The Army was now an all voluntary force, and in recruiting for the Army, they could be more particular. He told me to come back when I got the papers from my parents. I really started to feel good. My mother had a phone now and I had the number. The first thing I did was to get a personal post office box. Then I called my mother and told her what the Army recruiter wanted.

My mother told me that if that was what I wanted, then she would have all the papers I needed on the way as quickly as she could and she would send them to my post office box. I thanked my mother and told her not to worry about me, that I had a job and was doing just fine.

I had to lie because I didn't want her to worry about me. When I went back to the mission I told the management that I wanted to get back into the Army and that my mother was sending me all the papers I needed. I asked the management if it would be all right for me to stay at the mission until I received the papers from home. They told me that they would be more than happy for me to stay until the Army accepted me.

It only took about five days before I received all the papers from my mother. I couldn't get to the recruiting office fast enough. He looked over the papers and he was pleased. He asked me if I would be ready to take a physical with a group of volunteers the next day and a battery of tests. I assured him that I would be at the place the physical was being given, and that I would be at the door long before they opened.

Well, I was the first to arrive. I passed the physical and tests which took all day. Out of all the volunteers I was the only one who had been in the service before. As the Army clerk was typing my new records he asked me what my occupation was. I said, "Drifter." The clerk said, "No, we won't put that on your new records. I will type in that your occupation is laborer." The Army recruiter told me that I was the only one of all the other new recruits who didn't have to take Basic Training because I had already taken Basic Training when I was in the Army at the age of thirteen. The recruiter told me that all those who passed all the tests would be sworn into the Army that evening, and that we would be on a train by noon the next day for Fort Dix, New Jersey for assignment.

The recruiter told me that I would be in charge and responsible for getting myself and the other thirty new recruits to Fort Dix. I would have to carry on my person all the sealed records of all of us new recruits. We were to be standing outside the recruiting office the next day at 10 am. After being sworn in, we were all given meal tickets to eat at a nice restaurant. It was the one I had spent a lot of days looking in their big window watching that roast cooking. Now I had been given a ticket to go and sink my teeth into that delicious roast instead of just looking and smelling its aroma.

We were given tickets to eat breakfast at the same restaurant, and some of us were given tickets to stay at a really nice hotel. I was feeling good and happy that I was going to be back in the Army again. We all went to eat at the nice restaurant and I don't think I have to tell anyone what I ordered to eat.

The roast was even more delicious than I had imagined. I felt like a king as I was eating. I never did tell the other guys at the table with me that I had come to this restaurant many times just to look at the roast cooking in the window, and now I was finally getting to sink my teeth into that roast at the Army's expense.

It was just great staying at a nice clean hotel and getting to take a bath in a tub and sleeping between two white sheets. After a good night's sleep we all checked out of the hotel and went back to the restaurant to use our last meal ticket for breakfast. I was beginning to wish they would never end, but I had made a three-year commitment to the Army. To me it was like getting to go back home.

The recruiter got us all to the train station. He made roll call and gave me a box of records for all us new recruits. The recruiter gave me a train travel voucher for all of us. I was to give that to the conductor. And he gave me vouchers so that we could eat in the dining car. The recruiter also gave us all strict orders that there would be no drinking of alcohol and that there would be military personnel to meet us at our destination, Fort Dix.

Knowing that I was back in the Army again I felt that I was going back to where I had security. I know that during all the traveling I did at a young age God was watching over me. My mother once told me that I was born under a wandering star.

9

ABOARD A TROOP SHIP BOUND FOR GERMANY

When the train arrived at our destination the Army representatives were right there to meet us. They came aboard the train, counted all of the recruits, then took the records from me and told everybody to get off the train and get aboard the waiting buses.

When we arrived at the camp they started processing all of us. After all the paperwork, all the recruits were told that in about two or three days they would be sent out to another camp for basic training, "except one of you." That meant me. I would be going overseas for re-assignment.

We were taken to the warehouse to fit us for uniforms and to issue all our Army clothing. Then they assigned us to the barracks they wanted us to be in. I was separated from all the ones I arrived with and assigned to a barracks that had soldiers who had a lot of time in the Army. They had been sent to this camp for shipment overseas.

I kept my mouth shut. I was in uniform like the rest of them. I had thrown away all my civilian clothing. I stayed at Fort Dix, New Jersey for two weeks. They kept us all doing something. I found myself on K.P. duty just about every other day in a consolidated mess hall, which means one big mess hall that fed damn near everyone in this large camp. There was no liberty, so in the evenings just about every other bed in the barracks had a poker game being played on it.

I didn't gamble so I would go to a movie on the camp. The movie price was twenty-five cents. I was glad to be back in the Army again. This time I had the determination that I wanted to be a soldier, and this time I made a pledge to myself that I was going to stay in the Army and fulfill what I had started out to do at thirteen years of age.

The Army had given me a second opportunity, so now I was in my glory.

What a good feeling it was that I didn't have to make any transforming changes this time as I had when I left civilian life to enter military life the first time. I knew what the Army expected of me. I knew to keep my mouth shut and not to volunteer for anything. It was good to be back in a military camp again and to hear the bugle being blown, playing taps in the evening right at 2100 hours (9 pm).

The bugle sound floated across the entire camp signifying the end of a military day and that all barracks lights were to be turned out. The sound of the bugle would be heard again in the morning for reveille for all soldiers to get out of bed. These sounds were music to my ears. It made me feel that I was somebody again, and that my time as a wandering drifter had been nothing but a dream. I called my mother and thanked her for sending all the papers I needed to get back into the Army at seventeen years of age, and I thanked her for giving her consent for me to go back into the Army.

I was at Fort Dix for about two weeks before the Army told us that everybody in my barracks would be shipping out for Germany. It wasn't long before we were carrying our duffel bags on our shoulders and walking up the gangway boarding the biggest troop ship I had ever seen. To me this was all a new adventure.

As we came aboard the ship I was in the group leading the way down to the bottom of the ship into a big room they called compartments. This big compartment had canvas cots hanging three high and no mattresses. I ended up with the one in the middle. To get to my canvas bunk I had to step on the railing of the bottom bunk and the guy on the top had to climb and step on the first and middle bunks to get into his canvas bunk.

We were like sardines in a can. There were about seventy-five of us crammed into this compartment. The first two days out to sea were nice and calm. Each morning, after we got up for reveille, and roll call to make sure no one had jumped over the side of the ship, we went up on the main deck to line up for chow. The line roped around the ship three or four times. The chow line was so long that when the last man in the chow line reached the serving line, in the mess galley they were getting ready to serve dinner, and the troops on the ship were starting to line up for that dinner. To stand in line, to get to the galley, the troops were exposed to the outside.

After eating we were to report back to the compartment for cleanup. After cleanup of the compartment, everyone, except those picked for more cleanup detail, were to go topside on the upper deck, which was out in the open. We were not allowed to go back to our compartments until later in the day.

Everything was going good at sea, but then after the third day the sea started to get rough, and being up on deck we would get sprays of salt water. There were no chairs to sit on. If you wanted to sit you just had to sit on the cold deck, if you were lucky enough to find a place to sit. There were that many soldiers on this ship. All the officers were on the deck above us. They had deck chairs. We lower rank soldiers were not allowed to go up to the officers' deck. Also, the officers had nice staterooms aboard the ship, and a nice dining room with tables that had white tablecloths. The tables would seat four to a table, and to top that off, they had waiters to wait on them.

The trip to Germany would take about eleven days. It wasn't long before the ocean started getting rough, and we were starting to get some big gales and salt water spray in our faces. A lot of the soldiers would crowd for cover in stairways that led down to the different compartments, or they would get under anything for cover to get out of the sea water spray blowing across the ship's deck.

I walked around the ship's deck. I could see a lot of soldiers getting seasick and a lot of them hanging their heads over the railings to vomit their guts out. I was one of those who had their heads hanging over the railing. When the sea got so rough that you had to fight to hang on, then, and only then, would they announce over a loud speaker that we could go down to our compartments. After about four days out to sea they opened a big room on the ship where we could sit in chairs and on benches to get out of the bad weather.

I noticed that the chow line aboard the ship got shorter because of those of us who were seasick. Even the smell of food made us sick. In the evening there was a compartment where they would show a movie. There were no chairs to sit on. We sat on the hard deck. Some soldiers would go and get their pillows off their bunks to sit on and watch the movie. I was one of them.

This was the only entertainment we had aboard ship. After eleven days the ship docked at Bremerhaven Port in Germany. It sure was good to get off the troop ship. I was seasick all the way except for the first three days out to sea.

The Army disembarked all of us soldiers, put us on buses and took us to a replacement center for re-assignment. Everyone was broke. Those who smoked had no money to buy cigarettes or anything. It was in the middle of the month, and the Army only paid their soldiers once a month. I guess the Army felt sorry for us because they set it up so that we could sign the upcoming payroll and receive a partial pay of ten dollars. All the soldiers called this the "Flying Ten," which meant that after you received the ten dollars, it would leave your hand fast for things at the Post Exchange, like soap, shaving stuff, cigarettes and beer.

We stayed at the replacement center for about five days before the Army assigned all of us to different units throughout Germany. There was a small group of us who went to Berlin. It was at this time that the cold war was going on about Berlin. This is a place that all the soldiers were hoping they wouldn't get assigned to. Lucky me. All of us soldiers whose orders read, "Berlin," started getting jokingly harassed by the other soldiers about going to Berlin. The Russians had their Army surrounding Berlin and they had set up a blockade around the city trapping the Americans, French, and the British. The blockade kept all land traffic from entering the city.

The Russians could do this because to get into Berlin everything had to go through the Russian Sector of Germany. The Russians also controlled the trains going through their sector into Berlin. They only allowed so many trains a week going into or out of West Berlin.

The Army took us down to the train station, destination Berlin. When we boarded the train we were assigned four men to a private compartment that had sleeping berths overhead for each of us and nice seating, two men on each side facing one another. There was a sliding window for us to look out of.

There was no dining car. We were given cans of field rations. We did get to see the ravages of war that Germans had brought down on themselves. The train stopped at a lot of stations on our way to Berlin. At every station there would be poor and ragged looking children and adults who crowded up to every window of the train begging for food or cigarettes. They tried to sell us bottles of German liquor. All the guys in the compartment were leery about buying anything liquid that they were trying to sell us for fear there might be urine in the bottle.

The train was coming into the Russian Sector of Germany. It was starting to get dark and we were all given orders to pull down the window shades, and nobody was to look or peek out the windows. After a long ride through the Russian Sector our train was stopped and Russian soldiers came aboard. Our In-Charge American officer gave the Russian officer a manifest which showed the number of troops and the names of every American soldier aboard the train. Russians only allowed a small number of American soldiers to be stationed in Berlin.

Also they didn't permit any tanks or artillery going into the American Sector of Berlin. The Russian soldiers made a head count of all of us aboard the train by coming into each compartment and looking to see that the manifest of the number of American soldiers on the train was correct. When they were satisfied our train was permitted to proceed toward the American part of Berlin.

When we arrived at our destination we were all loaded up on an Army truck with our duffel bags and taken to a very small camp consisting of nice, red brick, three story buildings. There were about five buildings that housed soldiers, one building for the Post Exchange, one for the service club, and another for the commanding officer. The buildings were laid out so that they formed a square with a big parade ground in the middle and a flagpole almost in the middle of the parade ground.

At the base of the flagpole flowers were planted. The new name of the camp was The Roosevelt Barracks, and it was located right in town. After we were assigned to the building they wanted us to be in, the group I arrived with was all split up to various buildings. Each building housed a company of infantry soldiers.

I was assigned to "I" Company whose commanding officer was an old, gray-haired captain named Winters. He had a stone look on his face all the time, and he had a mean military disposition. I had the misfortune of experiencing his mean disposition time and time again while under his command.

The next morning, after our arrival at Roosevelt Barracks, the battalion commander wanted to give us a welcoming speech which began, "Welcome to the outpost of Berlin." He continued. "As all of you know, we are surrounded by the Russian Army, and we are here to serve as the American Military Occupation Force, not as conquerors of Germany. You are to conduct yourselves as an occupation force." Then he went on to explain how Berlin had been broken up among the four powers, that there were four sectors, American, British, French and Russian. He said that the Russian Sector was off limits to every American soldier. He explained that if we went into the Russian Sector there was a chance that we would never be heard from again.

The next thing the battalion commander was firm and explicit about was V.D. He told us that if any soldier under his command went into town and contracted a venereal disease, he would be taken out of his assigned company and placed in a V.D. platoon for thirty days under a sergeant in command with orders to rule that platoon with an iron fist. The V.D. platoon had to sleep outside in pup tents. He went on to explain that soldiers with V.D. would not be allowed to eat with the other soldiers in the mess hall and that they would be the last to be fed. They had to bring their field mess kits, go through the mess hall serving line, and then eat outside sitting on the ground. He said, "Each V.D. soldier will wear a sign around his neck saying, 'I have V.D.'" Then he told us that he would personally write a letter to the wife or parents of that soldier and let them know that their son or husband had contracted a venereal disease while serving in Berlin, Germany.

He told us that if a soldier should go to a German doctor for treatment of

V.D., that soldier would be court-martialed by military court. "There is no excuse for getting V.D.," he said. "Each company will have free condoms made available for when a soldier signs out to go on pass." After the battalion commander's remarks to us we were left with a safety first when it came to having sex with German frauleins. Before the battalion commander's warning about V.D., other soldiers who had been in Berlin a while had told us that the ratio of females to males in Berlin was seven to one.

When I heard that I thought I had just arrived in Paradise. But after hearing about what happens to a soldier who gets V.D., I thought maybe this paradise could turn out to be Hitler's revenge on American troops. One thing for sure, the commander's welcome speech left us all thinking that we had better let our heads do the thinking for us rather than letting the lower parts of our bodies do the thinking. We did not want the humiliation that would go with getting V.D.

I was assigned to the weapons platoon of the "I" company as a 50 caliber machine gunner. This is how an infantry battalion is made up: the manpower is about 850 to 950 which has three rifle companies, a heavy weapons company, a headquarters, and a headquarters company. In an infantry rifle company there are approximately 203 in manpower strength and these are broken down into three rifle platoons and one weapons platoon. This platoon is armed with 50 caliber and 30 caliber machine guns, 57 mm recoilless rifles, and 60 mm mortars and Browning automatic rifles, plus, each soldier carries his own personal weapon.

In another American camp near this one was a constabulary unit. In all, the headcount of American soldiers in Berlin at that time, 1947, was approximately 3,000 troops. The Russians had the American, British, and French sectors of Berlin surrounded by their large army and artillery batteries and armored tank regiments. This gave us American soldiers the feeling that we were to be sacrificed for the beginning of a war with Russia.

Berlin would have been a battlefield of Armageddon. We would have been wiped out because we had a military weakness compared with what the Russians had and there was no place for us to retreat to. The company I was in kept us on a rigid training schedule all the time and always made us aware of being trapped in Berlin by the Russians.

All the companies were very strict about liberty passes. A pass to go out of camp and to the city was a privilege that had to be earned, and a privilege that the company could take away from a soldier at their discretion. Each company only allowed a small percentage of their soldiers to go on pass at any one time. A week day pass was from six in the evening until 11:30 pm. That evening a soldier had to sign in at the orderly room under the supervision of the sergeant on duty. Overnight passes were only given out on weekends, and these passes were restricted to about three overnight passes per company.

A soldier on an overnight pass had to be back for reveille the next working day morning. This battalion and the companies were very strict about all soldiers being in their beds at bed check time, which was twelve o'clock midnight. Each company's duty sergeant made the bed check. He would carry a flashlight with him and check each room for soldiers in their beds.

There were four soldiers to a room. If a soldier missed his bed check, the next day he would have to report to the company commander who would give the soldier the old Article (104) under the Uniform Code of Military Justice. Under Article (104) a soldier could be reduced in rank, and if the soldier had no rank, punishment included ten days of company hard labor from after supper to up to bed check time, twelve o'clock midnight. The hard labor would be carried out under the supervision of a non-commissioned officer.

The Army, at this time, would not tolerate a soldier who was disobedient to orders or military regulations. This was a voluntary Army, and the soldier had asked for it. The Army was quick to give a soldier a bad conduct discharge just for missing bed check three times or punishment under Article (104) more than three times.

I've seen a lot of good soldiers receive a bad conduct discharge. The Army, at that time, felt that anyone could be replaced, so the Army would lay it on a soldier, "Do as we say and the Army will do your thinking for you." Another motto was, "If the Army had wanted you to have a wife, the Army would have issued you one."

The rigid schedule was every soldier out in front of the barracks in formation for roll call and reveille. The duty officer would stand out in the middle of the parade field and take the report from each company of those present or absent. It was always "all present and accounted for" in the report.

No one would dare miss roll call and be counted as A.W.O.L. One of the rifle companies in this square of barracks around the parade field was an all black company. At this time in the Army we were segregated. The black company was the 555th, and every morning at reveille, this company's report to the duty officer would be in a loud voice that could be heard all over the parade field, "Triple nickel all present, Sir." We would all get a big chuckle out of that report.

Every evening, Monday through Friday, at five in the evening, retreat was held, which is the lowering of the American flag ceremony. All the companies would stand outside in front of their barracks. This formation was always held in full class A uniform, and each soldier had his individual weapon. An inspection was held by each platoon leader and platoon sergeant. They would check each soldier for close haircuts, clean shaves, clean and neat uniforms, shoes shined and a clean weapon.

Roll call was also made at this formation. If a soldier didn't pass inspection he was not allowed to go on pass to town. These inspections at reveille and retreat and for being checked for clean shaved were strict. Even if a soldier only had fuzz on his face they wanted it off. It got to the point that I had to shave twice a day. Because I had to shave off my face fuzz when I was in the Army at age thirteen, and from that time on until I was seventeen, my facial hair was dark and thick. I had started shaving at an early age.

The soldiering in Berlin was a spit and shine outfit. We all had to get our uniforms cut to fit. They didn't want any baggy-fitting uniforms. Each company had its own German tailor. There was a tailor's shop down in the basement of each barracks. Each soldier had to pay for his own uniform tailoring, and at the end of each month, on payday, each soldier had to give so much out of his pay to keep the tailor employed.

The Army still paid one time a month. A private received fifty dollars a month. The Army would get each soldier to sign the supplemental payroll one week before the actual pay day. In signing the supplemental payroll, there was a small block the soldier was to sign his name in, and the Army was adamant that a soldier should not go outside this small block with any part of his signature. If a soldier did go out of the block in any way, he would be red-lined, which meant that he would not get paid that month. There was an old Army saying at that time, and that was T.S., which meant tough s_ _t.

When anything went wrong with a soldier the leaders and other soldiers would tell you to take your T.S. card to the Army chaplain and he would punch it for you. The T.S. card was just an imaginary thing the soldiers would say, and that was about all the sympathy one soldier would get from another soldier.

Within each battalion when you had a problem each company had their own beer hall also down in the basement of each building. It would open at 6:30 in the evening and stay open until ten o'clock. Privates and non-commissioned officers could drink together, which was not really a good mix. After so many beers anger would flare up between privates and N.C.O.'s and then fights would break out.

I remember that this is where I got in trouble. There was a private first class I just did not like. A private first class held a lot of authority in the Army at that time. Rank was hard to come by. All the squad leaders were private first class, and they wore one stripe on their sleeves. As a squad leader they had twelve privates under their command.

I was not under the command of this private first class, but for some reason he didn't like me, nor did I like him. This night I had a few beers and he happened to be in the beer hall at the same time. A fist fight broke out between us. Usually when a fist fight broke out between soldiers it wasn't stopped by the bystanders in the beer hall. They wanted to see the action until, of course, things started getting smashed or wrecked.

Most of the time the others would try to direct the two fighting men out of the beer hall and into the long hallway and then let them go at it. Then, when it was all over, all was forgotten, unless one or the other of them got hurt or was bleeding and had to go to the medics to get patched up. Then a report was made out by the medics and given to the commanding officer of the company the next morning.

As the old saying goes, "Someone has to be the fall guy," and since everyone knew that I was the one who provoked the fight, the blame was on my shoulders. We both had to report to old man Winters, the company commander. We each had a patch on our faces, and I had a cut above my eye. The private first class got a verbal reprimand and was restricted from the beer hall for two weeks.

I received an Article (104) and was restricted to company barracks for ten days with hard labor every night after supper for five hours each night, and was restricted from going on pass. I was also restricted from the beer hall for a month. This was my first awakening to the fact that I was in an all volunteer Army, and they knew you asked for it, and they were more than ready to lay their military regulations on a soldier.

My first night of labor punishment was under the supervision of a corporal. I was to scrub the long hallways on my hands and knees with a foot-long hand brush and a toothbrush with a bucket of hot water and bars of G.I. brown soap and rags to wipe up the water.

I was not allowed to use a mop. The hallways were the full length of the building. I had to do all three floors' hallways. I didn't have to do the basement floor, but the last hour of each evening I had to clean each large latrine, one at each end of the building by myself.

Scrubbing the hallways on my hands and knees was hard, but what really made me feel bad was watching all the other soldiers getting dressed in Class A dress uniforms ready to go to town on pass to go dancing and then shacking up with German frauleins. And there I was with a two-striped corporal standing over my shoulder pointing to a spot I might have missed with the toothbrush.

By the end of the ten days I had made up my mind that I would never get into trouble again. I sure didn't want to be discharged from the service with a bad conduct discharge. It seemed that my company never had a shortage of people to scrub the hallways as I had done. Not long after I came off hard labor someone else was just starting his hard labor.

The four-man room I was in faced the parade ground, and out the window I could see the flagpole and all the other barracks. One Saturday evening as I was looking out my room window I saw a buck sergeant from another company walking across the parade field toward his company. He was the only one on the parade field at the time. I could see that he had had one drink too many. He was staggering as he walked. Halfway across the parade field, and to my surprise, I saw him stop at the flagpole, unzip his pants and urinate on the flower bed at the base of the flagpole.

When he was finished he zipped up his pants and continued walking toward his company. Then I saw an officer come out of the headquarters building which also faced toward the parade field. The officer caught up with the sergeant and I saw the exchange of salutes between them. Then the officer escorted the sergeant over to headquarters.

The following week I saw that the sergeant was now a two-striped corporal. Word was all over camp that the battalion commander had also been looking out the window when the sergeant stopped to urinate on the flowers.

The first time I received a pass to go to town I was amazed to see all the young German women and the black-market German men standing just outside the main gate of the camp waiting for any soldier to come through the gate. The black marketeers wanted to know if I had any cigarettes or chocolate that I wanted to sell. The women would be pulling on my arms wanting me to go with them, and they would say, "I will show you a good time." "You come with me." This was great, but that was not the way I wanted to find a woman to be with. I wanted to have time to look around on my own.

The first day I walked around a small part of the city I was shocked at what I saw. I saw a city that looked like an atomic bomb had been dropped on it. Most of the buildings had been apartments. Now only one or two walls were still standing and the insides would be gutted out and in piles of rubble. But people continued to live among the wreckage. The children played around the rubble. Most of the people lived in cellars of bombed-out buildings or in apartments that were only partially still standing from the bombing of Berlin.

I didn't see any grocery stores or food stores, but I did see some cabarets.

I found that the Germans have the best beer I have ever tasted. As I walked down the streets of the city I had little German kids following me asking for chocolate and cigarettes, which I didn't have. This was my first time on pass and I did not know that that was what they wanted.

The children and all the people were poorly dressed. The people were hungry. They got a small ration of food each week from their newly formed government and most of them had no running water. They had to go to a certain place to get drinking water that was brought in to them from the country.

I felt sorry for the German people. Conditions of life were terrible. They had to pay a heavy price. I especially felt sorry for the young children. They were not to blame for what was brought down on Berlin. The adult Germans had no one to blame for what happened to Germany but their leader, Hitler, and those who supported the Nazi Party.

As I looked at the devastation that the bombing had inflicted on the city, I wondered to myself, "What if the Germans and the Japanese had won World War II?" The American people could very well be in this same situation. Would American women have sold themselves to the invading army, or would we all have been sent to concentration camps? In a world war nobody can really predict what the end will be, except that we all know that all the people will suffer, winners and losers.

As I looked around the city I saw the underground subways in Berlin. This was the only mode of transportation that had survived the destruction of war. Some of the German people used the underground subway for shelter from the bombing of the city.

I saw very few running vehicles. There were no gas stations. I did see most of the people, including the German police, riding bicycles. The few automobiles that were running were small, like Volkswagen types. I had the experience of riding in one of these small cars that was a taxi. I had to ride up front in the passenger seat because the back seat was stacked with firewood. The taxi would go ten or fifteen blocks, and then the driver would stop the taxi, get out and go to the back of the taxi, and open up the trunk where he had installed a wooden stove. The driver threw in some wood, which would generate steam to the engine, and we would be on our way.

Most American soldiers would ride on the underground subway to get around Berlin. We didn't have to pay to ride the subway, but we did have to pay to ride taxis. After my first six months in Berlin I pretty well knew my way around the city. A soldier friend of mine would go with me to all the good German beer gardens and we had a good time. We found all the good ones with dancing to the music of an accordion player and plenty of good looking

German girls. They were just sitting at tables waiting for soldiers to ask them to dance, and that would usually lead to going to bed with them. If a soldier had an overnight pass he was in luck. Otherwise, he would have to be back at camp and in bed for the twelve o'clock midnight bed check.

As I got to know the German people I found that many of them still admired Hitler and hailed him as a great leader. I thought the German people seemed to have lost their spirit and were in deep despair. Sometimes we would have a small party at a German cabaret. We would invite some German girls and the German men we knew who worked at our camp. Late in the evening, when everyone was having a good time, some of the German men would let their real feelings be known about the war they lost.

One German man told me, "One of the reasons why the Americans won World War II was because Americans could spend more money faster and waste more military equipment than the Germans could." Another German who had been an artillery man in the German Army told me that the artillery shell casings that the Germans made were of a metal that would rust when stockpiled for a time in bad weather. He said that when his artillery company would be waiting for either the American or the Russian armies to advance, and the winter weather was bad, and their shells were out in the weather, they would rust. Then, when he had to load and fire artillery guns, they had a hard time trying to get their shell casings to go into the breach of the artillery guns because of the rust on the shell casings. He told me that Americans made all of their artillery shell casings out of solid brass, and they never had any trouble loading artillery when the German Army was advancing.

Before the evening was over, and when people were feeling their drinks, I was shocked when all the German men at our tables stood up and started singing a German song, "Deutschland Uber Alles." I think many Germans still had not come to the realization that their dream of greater Germany and the master race had come to an end. I thought to myself, "Here they are. Their country has been reduced to rubble. Their children are hungry, and still, they sing a song of Germany Over All." I was told, and I saw pictures of Berlin before the war. It was a most attractive city.

The American military put all American soldiers on a ration book. We could only buy two cartons of cigarettes a week and one can of coffee from the Post Exchange. These were the things that were in demand on the German black market. They also wanted chocolate bars and chewing gum. A chocolate bar or two would get a soldier an all-night stay with a fraulein. A carton of cigarettes was worth a week of shacking up.

At the time I didn't smoke. And there I was, a young soldier, girl crazy, and in a place where women outnumbered the men. I was in paradise, and I can honestly say that I really got an education in sex at the early age of seventeen.

All the time I stayed in Berlin there was one thing that I always remembered. That was the warning of the battalion commander about contracting a venereal disease and the humiliation that would result. I always had a pocket full of condoms with me. They were free. The company gave them out to anyone going on pass. Most of us soldiers even bloused the bottoms of our trousers over our boots using rubber condoms.

10

BERLIN AT THE END OF WORLD WAR II

As I got to know the German people more every day, I learned that they hated the Russians. Berlin was the last stronghold of the war. The people of Berlin knew that American troops under the command of General Eisenhower were on the outskirts of Berlin. They also knew that British troops were close to Berlin. They decided to stay in the city rather than flee to the countryside. They thought they would be treated humanely. They did not know that Eisenhower had stopped his troops outside Berlin and a deal was made with the Russians that they could take the city.

This was just what the Russians wanted. For the Russians, Berlin was the grand prize of the war. Germans I talked to in Berlin said they were shocked to see Russian tanks and Russian infantrymen shooting their way into Berlin. For the Russians this was pay-back time for what the Germans did when they were fighting in Russia, and especially for what happened in Stalingrad.

I was told that the Russian soldiers who went into Berlin were natives of Mongolia. The Germans said that the Russians came in shooting so fast that they, the Germans, couldn't flee in any direction without seeing Russian soldiers.

They were killing and raping as they moved through the city of Berlin. Germans told me that the Russians acted like savages. If a Russian soldier saw a young girl or an old woman on the street, he would rape her then and there, and if a father or mother or husband tried to object, they would shoot that person then go on with the rape right there in the street.

I heard from one German family that Russians came into their home, raped the women, and because the soldiers were so amazed at the water faucets in the bathroom, they ripped out the faucets and took them with them when they left.

When the four powers divided the city of Berlin into four sectors after the war, the Russians objected to having to give up any part of the city to the other three powers, the Americans, British, and the French. Because the Russians had taken the city by themselves, they felt that the entire city belonged to them. Not only was Berlin highly infected with venereal disease, it was also infested with body crabs and scabies which burrow into the skin and cause a person to scratch so much a sore will develop, and then they spread all over the person.

I know this because I contracted them by jumping into too many beds with good looking frauleins who were more than anxious to engage in casual sex with a soldier for a candy bar or a pack of gum or cigarettes. If I didn't have any of these with me at the time, that seemed to be all right as long as I promised to bring some the next time.

I got a good sex education at the young age of seventeen. This would never have happened in the United States. Most American girls were hung up on, "Not until we're married," or "I'm not that kind of a girl." My not knowing the German language seemed to be no hardship. As for the scabies, the Army medics gave all of us soldiers a medication to get rid of them.

The Berlin Wall, separating the east from the west, hadn't been put up at that time, but the Russians did have barbed wire along the border. There were Russian soldiers patrolling the border and there were checkpoints with road barriers at different points. American soldiers were forbidden to enter East Berlin. It was later, after the wall had been erected, that Russians would shoot anyone who crossed it coming into the East Sector or trying to leave.

The American Army didn't have much of a training area to use for training soldiers in war maneuvers. The nearest woods were about five miles from our camp. The woods, called Grunewald Forest, was not very big. We always marched to Grunewald with full equipment, a horseshoe looking back-pack with everything in the back-pack that a soldier would need in the field for a week. That included half a tent. When strapped to a soldier's back the weight was about sixty pounds. We also carried a 50 cal. machine gun that weighed about fifty-six pounds. The gunner would carry the barrel to the machine gun that weighed twenty-six pounds. Then there was the tripod the machine gun rested on, which was also very heavy.

Grunewald Forest was where the Army's rifle and pistol ranges were. We were not permitted to fire anything bigger than our rifles and pistols in the forest. We were never permitted to fire 50 cal. machine guns or our 60 or 80 millimeter mortars. When we did fire our mortars we used dummy ammunition.

We would stay bivouacked in two-man tents for a week or two out on the ranges or during Army training for war games. When we marched out to this training area we would attract German children who would follow us all the way out to the training area in the Grunewald Forest. The children would stand a short distance away hoping a soldier would throw them a candy bar or some chewing gum. We were given orders not to give them anything because that would just attract more children to our training area.

When we arrived at the training area the children kept their distance and didn't get in our way. The children were waiting for the time when the mess tent was put up and meals were served to the troops. The children wanted what the soldiers didn't eat, and what we had left in our mess kits to throw away in the garbage can. They would stand near the garbage can at the end of the mess tent, and as each soldier went to empty his left- over food into the garbage can, they would put out the small, tin buckets they were carrying between the soldier and the garbage can.

The mess sergeant didn't want us to give them food because he thought it would just bring more children out to the training area. But I noticed something about the old mess sergeant. He always seemed to have his back turned away from the garbage can when we were dumping our mess kits. I also noticed that there was never anything in the garbage can. Some of us soldiers would ask the person serving the food if he would put a little extra food in our mess kits so we would have some left over to dump in the kids' tin buckets.

The forest was the cleanest forest I had ever seen. There wasn't a tree branch or a stick of wood anywhere in the forest. The German people kept anything lying on the ground that looked like wood picked up and then taken to their homes to burn for fuel.

It was not permitted to cut any trees that were standing. We were given orders that if a soldier damaged a tree or carved his name into a tree, that he had just bought a tree that he would never own.

The forest was also where young Germans used to make love in behind the bushes. At times, during our war games, we would come upon them. It was fun to watch them jump up and run. This was good entertainment for us soldiers while on infantry tactics training.

The forest was at one edge of a big lake called, Lake Wannsee. In the summer Germans used this lake to swim in. We soldiers would hurry to get to the edge of the forest that overlooked the beach part of the lake. We would look down from the top of a hill, and with binoculars, we would watch the German girls change from street clothes into bathing suits. They would show no modesty, and we soldiers were glad they were not shy. We spent a lot of our training looking through those binoculars during our war games. During the heavy fighting in Berlin, many of Hitler's top Nazi officers used Lake Wannsee for their escape route from the Russians.

It was while my company was out in the forest for a two-week training, and living in tents, that one of the soldiers who was in the same twelve-man squad I was in, broke out with an infection of body hair crabs. Another soldier advised him to soak a rag in gasoline and use that to get rid of the crabs. When the driver of one of the trucks that belonged to the supply sergeant arrived, the soldier with the crabs talked the driver of the truck into soaking a rag in one of the spare gas cans on the truck. The soldier took the gas soaked rag behind a tree, dropped his pants, and applied the gas soaked rag to his crotch. We all knew what he was up to, and we watched with amusement. It wasn't long before he came out from behind that tree yelling, "It burns. It burns." He was running up and down between the trees. Every one of us who were watching was cracking up. Later, someone said the guy who had the crabs went looking for the field medic to get some medicine to treat the burn he received from the gasoline burn around his crotch.

Duty in Berlin was good, but when it came to making promotions, the Army was tight. Occasionally they would promote a private to private first class, a one stripe. Our entire platoon sergeants were three stripes. They were called, "Buck Sergeants." Squad leaders were mostly one-striped private first class.

The young lieutenants we had in the company were just out of Officer's Candidate School with very little military experience. Some of them were victims of their own mad with absolute power and drunk with authority. They were walled up within themselves and they enjoyed the exercising of their authority.

When an officer was walking in the hallway of the barracks, the enlisted soldier, also in the hallway, was expected to stop, face the on-coming officer in the position of attention, and not speak unless the officer spoke first. Then, when the officer passed, the enlisted man could continue walking down the hallway.

The enlisted soldiers called the O.C.S. second lieutenants "90-day wonders," which meant that that was about as long as it took them to go to O.C.S. and get their rank as second lieutenant. It wouldn't take long for these young lieutenants to learn that the only way they were going to learn was from sergeants who had been in the military for a long time and knew how to display leadership.

Some of our sergeants had seen combat in World War II. Our first sergeant of the company I was in was a big Polack who had a big mouth. When he called the company to attention at formations, he made the buildings shake around the camp. He was always ready and willing to fight any man in the company. Even the young lieutenants addressed him as, "Sir." I've seen many a time this first sergeant would run some of those young lieutenants out of his office.

One evening while our company beer hall was open and the first sergeant was there drinking beer, a private started mouthing off to the first sergeant and was trying to pick a fight with the big Polack. The first sergeant told the private that if he couldn't handle his alcohol he had better leave. The private seemed determined to pick a fight. The first sergeant told the private to leave the beer hall. The private refused. At about this time all of us privates shoved the private who was making trouble out the door and into the hallway, but this didn't do much good.

The private stood in the doorway challenging the first sergeant to come out into the hallway and fight. The first sergeant got off his bar stool, went out into the hallway and started kicking the private's butt. The private started breaking away from the fight and started running up the stairs to his room which was on the third floor. The first sergeant was right behind him all the way up the stairs. The private reached the third floor of the barracks and went into his room. The first sergeant went to the private's room, opened the door, and told the private, "This fight isn't over," and that he, the first sergeant, was going to kick his butt real good. The private opened the room window and told the first sergeant that if he came any closer that he, the private, was going to jump out the third floor window.

The first sergeant said, "Then you'd better jump." The first sergeant made an advance toward the private, and the private jumped out the window. He landed on his head on the rock sidewalk and was killed. The next day the company got a half day off from training to mourn the private's death and to attend church services for the private.

After this incident the battalion commander put out an order that there wouldn't be any beer halls in the companies. We had no privates' or sergeants' club in the camp because it was a small camp. So if a soldier wanted a beer he had to wait his turn to get a pass.

We did have a small service club on the camp where they showed movies and a snack bar that served ice cream. A soldier could sign his German fraulein into the club, but before she could come onto the base, she had to get a venereal disease check from a German doctor and have a picture I.D. card from the German police. Once a fraulein applied for this identification, she was to go back to the doctor for V.D. checkups every so often. Then she would be permitted to be escorted on base to the service club.

The duty in the infantry company had a rigorous schedule calling for a lot of inspections, company and battalion marching parades, and every day's schedule called for platoon or company marching drill, sometimes for two or three hours at a time. The Army's reason for so much marching drill was their belief that it teaches automatic obedience and makes it certain that a soldier will carry out the most difficult orders under fire and work as a team. We had a lot of weapons training even though we couldn't fire some of the larger weapons. We also had a lot of physical and self-defense training.

It was June, 1948 when all eyes and ears were on Berlin because the Russians started to put a choke-hold on Berlin. The Russians figured they would starve the people of Berlin by putting up more blockades, cutting off all traffic coming into the city on the Autobahn. They blocked the waterways, cutting off food supplies from going into the western part of Berlin.

The Russians hoped that the Americans would have no way to feed the 1.5 million people of West Berlin, and then would abandon West Berlin like a sinking ship. But the Russians soon learned that as long as we had an airfield, we were determined to show the Russians that the Americans were staying, and the British and the French as well. The German people would have food, fuel enough to get through the winter and medical supplies.

The airfield, Tempelhof, once belonged to Hitler's Air Force. When the airlift started all military personnel were briefed and given a summary as to how all military personnel were going to take an active part in the airlift. Even the infantry company would have a part. We were also warned to tighten our belts, that the Army mess halls would be getting less food supplies, so they didn't want any complaining. The Air Force started flying supplies into the city.

It got to the point that when one plane was taking off, another was landing to take its place on the airfield. The planes were bringing in food, coal for generating electricity, and medical supplies into West Berlin from Wiesbaden and other parts of Germany. The planes that were carrying the supplies were the C47 aircraft known as the Gooney Bird, which dated back to the mid-1930's and would carry about three tons of cargo. There were other planes that were used to carry cargo like the B-17 aircraft.

My company's first time to work on the airlift was on the night shift, ten in the evening until six in the morning. Each soldier had something to do. Some supervised getting the planes that were coming in unloaded, and some worked in the storage warehouses.

I was assigned a crew of German civilian workers and a large, flat-bed truck with a German driver. It was my responsibility to drive out onto the airstrip and be ready to have the driver back up the truck just as soon as the plane stopped on the runway. When the plane crew opened the plane door I was right there to receive the manifest from the crew that showed me what the cargo was and how much cargo there was. As soon as I got the manifest in my hand, the truck was already backed up to the plane.

I would get the Germans working with me to start unloading, and it was my responsibility to have an accurate count of everything that came off the plane and was loaded onto the truck and then delivered to the warehouse people.

The cargo was counted again. There was no time for breaks. Even the pilots didn't leave their planes because the plane would be unloaded in a very short time, and just as soon as the plane was unloaded, that plane was expected to take off and go for another load of supplies.

When the plane was on the ground a vehicle lunch wagon would accommodate the plane crew with sandwiches and hot coffee. I seemed to have the same German crew working with me every evening. They were ex-soldiers from the German Army. They were good workers and they were very grateful that the Americans were doing all they could to bring food supplies to the German people of West Berlin.

The German crew I worked with knew this was a desperate situation. At the beginning of each of my shifts at the airfield my German crew would line up and shake my hand and say, "Guten Morgen." I wasn't used to this kind of friendly manner the way the people greeted me. At the end of the shift, each worker would shake my hand again and tell me in German, "Auf Wiedersehen."

Each company from the battalion would get its turn working at the airlift. My company would work two weeks in a row, and then another company would relieve the company I was in. When working all night at airlift duty my company would let us sleep until noon. The rest of the day was scheduled for military training. Then, after the evening meal, we would try to get some rest before going out to the airfield to work all night.

It was reported that Russian fighter planes would, at times, harass American planes bringing in supplies to Tempelhof Airfield. The airlift in Berlin started in June of 1948 and continued until May of 1949. The airlift brought in 2,342,257 tons of food and fuel to the enclosed city. There were a total of 279,114 air flights into Tempelhof Airfield.

There were approximately, seventy-eight lives lost during the airlift counting American and British. The Russians found out that they couldn't starve us out of Berlin, and that the airlift was not working to their advantage. The Russians lifted the blockade, and once again food was allowed to come into Berlin by Autobahn and some by railroad.

As I became better able to find my way around Berlin, I found what seemed to be the elite part of town, and that was Ku'Damm Boulevard. There were some nice nightclubs with well dressed women who were friendly. As we entered some of the nightclubs women wanted to check our hats and coats. The drinks were a little more expensive. The nightclub provided a floorshow with some good looking frauleins.

One evening as two buddies and I were looking for a good nightclub in Ku'Damm we walked into a dimly lit cafe. There was a floorshow in progress as we walked in. There were three well dressed, slender German girls in evening gowns and high-heeled shoes. We were escorted to a table in a dark area of the nightclub. Then the three women sat down at the table with us and took our order for drinks. While we were drinking, at about the time I noticed, my friend also noticed that these three women dressed in evening gowns had rough voices under the female voice they were trying to impersonate. One of the guys I was with ran the back of his hand across one of their faces and then said, out loud, "This one has a rougher beard than I do." Then, in almost the same breath he said, "Let's get the hell out of this gay bar."

I think we all three tried to get out the door at the same time. After looking for another nightclub we found one called, "The Horseshoe Bar." There were four Morgan horses going around the outside edge of the dance floor inside the club, and around tables outside the ring where the horses ran around. So a person could either dance or ride horses.

There were wood chips in the trench where the horses ran. We sat close to the horse pit. The horses would kick wood chips into our glasses of beer. We were now in a nightclub where the frauleins were real women. We made sure of that before we left the cafe with them. We did make it back in time for bed check.

There was another German nightclub that was a favorite place of most of the soldiers that was called "Slut's Cafe." It was always full of German frauleins sitting at tables waiting for soldiers to pick them up. American music was always played on the record machine. There was a big dance floor and the place was always crowded.

Slut's Cafe was also a nightclub that was well known for brawling among soldiers. Some of the fights were over some fraulein, or some were the result of a soldier bumping into another soldier while on the dance floor. Fighting would break out, and the wrecking of the cafe would begin. It didn't take much to spark a fight. The owner of the cafe couldn't do a thing when soldiers started fighting. There was no phone service, and American soldiers didn't come under German law at the time. The military police came in sometimes, but it seemed that they were never there when a fight broke out.

I remember one evening at Slut's Cafe. The place was crowded with soldiers and German frauleins. The dance floor was also crowded. I was dancing to some nice, romantic music when suddenly one of the soldiers who was dancing out in the middle of the dance floor, set off and dropped a tear gas canister. He must have gotten it when his company was out on Army training at Grunewald Forest. No sooner had he dropped the canister when the place filled up with tear gas smoke.

The frauleins started screaming and crying at the same time. There was a big scramble for the entrance, which was the only way out. Some people were even crawling on the floor trying to find their way out. Those of us who got out first, gagging and tears streaming down our faces, filled our lungs with air, then went back to help others. Some were afraid and couldn't see to find their way to the front door to get out. A lot of them were falling over tables and chairs trying to get out.

After everybody was out, and everyone had left, my buddy and I went back to the barracks that evening in time for bed check. I went to the room that I shared with three other soldiers. They were already in bed and it was after lights out, so I had to undress in the dark and be quiet so that I wouldn't wake any of them. Not long after I took off my clothes to get into bed, one of them looked up from his bed and said, "What the hell is that smell?" His big mouth woke up the other two roommates. At first I tried to act like I didn't know what smell he was talking about until some of them started gagging. One ran to the two windows in the room and opened them. Then I thought it best to tell them what he smelled and what had happened at Slut's Cafe.

They insisted that I hang all the clothes I had been wearing out the window tied to a tent rope, and for me to sneak into the shower right after bed check was made. This was suggested after one of them in the room started getting watery eyes.

I complied with their request after I realized the tear gas was even in my hair. I made sure that I pulled my dress uniform back into the room from outside the window before daybreak. The room I was in was on the third floor facing the parade ground where my company would be standing for muster call and reveille. My buddy who was with me during the tear gassing told me he went through the same thing with his roommates when he got to his room.

It was two days later when we returned to Slut's Cafe to drink a beer. There was hardly anyone in the place. The owner had the front door blocked open trying to air the place out. My buddy and I didn't get half our beer finished when our eyes started watering, so we didn't stay there long.

There was another nightclub that a lot of frauleins would go to hoping to find a steady boyfriend. One evening my buddy and I didn't have much money. It was close to the end of the month, a time when most soldiers are usually broke, unless a soldier had been heavily into the black market. Those soldiers usually always had money, and they were also into lending another soldier money. They would lend ten dollars now in return for fifteen dollars back to the lender on payday.

One evening my buddy and I were having such a good time dancing with frauleins that we let the time slip away. We had just enough time to make it back to camp for bed check if we took a taxi. We would never make it in time if we walked. After talking with one another, without letting the frauleins know our situation, we found out that neither one of us had any money to get a taxi. So we came up with a plan.

We told the two frauleins that my buddy and I both had a three-day pass and that we wanted to spend the three days with them. But, we told them, we had left our money in our wall locker back at camp. We also told them that we had cigarettes and chocolate candy bars back at camp. They were all excited about that, so all four of us took a taxicab and headed back to camp.

When we got close to the personnel gate there were a lot of soldiers returning from pass to make the twelve o'clock bed check. A lot of the soldiers had their frauleins there outside the gate saying their goodbyes, and as always, the black marketeers were out in front of the gate. My buddy and I told the frauleins we would be right back out after we got our money and cigarettes. The frauleins translated all that was being said and told the taxi to wait. Once my buddy and I were inside the gate, we got to our barracks in time for bed check.

This was a trick that the taxi drivers didn't take long to learn from soldiers wanting to get a free ride back to camp. So the taxi drivers started asking soldiers to pay in advance and then the taxi would take us back to camp.

I was starting to get to the point that I was tired of going to nightclubs and brawling. Some of the soldiers had steady frauleins, so I began to want a steady fraulein too. I didn't really want one from out of the nightclubs, so one day when I was out alone riding the subway around West Berlin and getting off at some places to look at all the destruction of the war, I came upon a place called Schmargendorf.

As I was getting off the subway I noticed a young fraulein also getting off at that station. She was carrying a leather bag with books in it and a paper bag. She had gone to where the German government was giving people their rations. I made it a point to say hello to her in German. She smiled, and then I offered to carry her leather bag of books. At first she acted as if she didn't know whether she should trust me or not. So I reached out and took the leather bag from her. I told her my name and she told me hers was Helga, and we started walking past bombed out apartments.

I tried talking to her, but I soon found out that she didn't know one word of English. My knowledge of German was very little, and what little German I did know was good only to pick up a fraulein from a nightclub. So I just walked along beside her. After walking about five blocks from the subway station, the young fraulein stopped in front of an apartment house that had one side bombed out. She entered the doorway and started walking up some dark looking stairs. I followed her up the stairs wondering to myself, "I wonder who she lives with?"

I soon found out. She knocked on the door at the top of the stairs on the second floor and an old woman who was her mother opened the door. When she saw her daughter with an American soldier she had a look of shock on her face. I was welcomed in and we walked down a small hallway and into a very small sitting room where we all sat and looked each other over.

The young fraulein told me in German that this was her "Mutti," meaning mother. Our communicating was done mostly by arms and hands. I found out the daughter was still in high school and was sixteen years old. Her father had been a German soldier who was killed in the war, and she was an only child. I didn't stay long. I told them I'd be back the next day and I would bring them some coffee. I could tell the mother was pleased to hear the word, coffee. She understood that. The next day I returned to their apartment bringing with me candy bars, gum, coffee and a carton of cigarettes. The mother was really glad to get the cigarettes because she smoked and she could also sell some of the cigarettes. I also took them two bottles of German liquor, which helped us get to know each other. They showed me around their apartment which wasn't much. There was a small sitting room, one bedroom, and a bathroom with a shower. They told me they had just gotten tap water into the apartment and it had to be boiled before drinking it.

There was a small terrace off the small bedroom looking down to the sidewalk from the second floor. On the outside of what was left of the building were small holes where bomb fragments had hit the building. They only had electricity in the apartment for a few hours in the evening.

I started taking the young daughter to the on-post service club after she had her V.D. check and an I.D. card made so I could get her into the camp. Everything turned out good, so she and I went to a dance at the Army service club and she enjoyed eating American ice cream. I never took her to a nightclub. Most of the time we just sat in that small sitting room with her Mutti keeping a watchful eye on her daughter and me.

As time went by we seemed to understand each other more when we talked and each time I was permitted to receive a liberty pass, I would go and visit them. When I couldn't get a pass, I just didn't go visit them. There was no way of letting them know anything because there were no telephones.

I found out that the American Army was going to give up this camp that we called Roosevelt Barracks and give it back to the Germans. We were to move to a larger camp, which was more of a distance from town and more of a distance from the German girl, Helga. The camp was named McNair Barracks. There were already some American soldiers at this new camp which was part of the battalion I was already in. By moving to McNair Barracks we would still be in an infantry regiment, which was about 2,100 soldiers in strength. The Army constabulary unit was already in some of these barracks.

There was more room in the camp and the barracks were nicer than at Roosevelt Barracks. Here we had a nice club where all the companies could go and drink beer. They also had a bigger service club. The disappointing thing was there were no subway stations close to this new camp, which meant that I would have to take a taxi to the subway when coming and going to see Helga.

At McNair Barracks the Army had their Army stockade, which was always full with undisciplined soldiers who were serving six months. This stockade, as well as other stockades that I've seen in the Army, was ruled by a big, rough and mean master sergeant. He usually had a big cigar in his mouth and he ruled with an iron fist. When a soldier got out of that stockade, he definitely didn't want to go back in. They were strict. A soldier could get six months in the stockade for refusing an order or by being insubordinate towards a sergeant or a commissioned officer. Discipline was carried out swiftly.

My company was to go on guard duty at Spandau Prison for a month to guard some of Adolph Hitler's top Nazis. They had been tried in 1946 and were sentenced at the Nuremberg trials. There were twenty-two who were tried. Three were acquitted and eight of them received long prison terms. Many were going to be hanged. One of them cheated the hangman, General Goering. He took a cyanide capsule that he had hidden on himself from the guards. The hangman at the executions was a U.S. Army master sergeant by the name of Woods. All of us soldiers were envious of him.

Since my company was alerted to get ready to move to the prison, all liberty passes were cancelled. We had to load up trucks with all the supplies our company needed to live in the prison. Each soldier had to take his individual bed and bedding. Our mess sergeant had to load up supplies. The Spandau Prison was a long way from McNair Barracks, and we were told that we would be at the prison for thirty days.

I was anxiously wanting to see what these top Nazis looked like. I had read a lot of newspaper reports of what they did and the reason for the Nuremberg trials. Now I was going to be given the duty of guarding them. The infantry company I was in was going to relieve the Russians who had been at the prison for one month guarding the German Nazi prisoners. The prisoners were guarded by the four powers, the Russians, French, British, and the Americans. The British would relieve us when our thirty days were over.

The prison was in the British sector of Berlin. When my company relieved the Russians, it was a formal guard mount where we would be in formation and face the Russians who were also in formal formation. The officer in charge told the Russian officer that the Russians were relieved and we Americans would take the duty and all guard posts at the prison.

As my company was standing the guard mount, some of the Russians who were not in the guard mount formation were still moving their personal things out of the building we were to move into. This building was outside the prison walls. When they had finally moved all their things out, we started unloading our trucks and moving all our personal things into the building the Russians moved out of.

All of us soldiers noticed that the building was not left clean. After we had moved in, and after about three days, all of us started breaking out with an epidemic of body crabs and body lice, and we noticed that we could smell dry urine in the corners of the big room. It didn't take us long to move everything out of the building and give it a good G.I. scrubbing and spray the rooms with D.D.T. We were given powder to get rid of the crabs.

The Russians left one of their officers and two or three of their sergeants to stay and observe that we Americans were following all the regulations on the guarding of the six prisoners.

There were a lot of assigned jobs in and around the prison. The prison was a large building that the Germans had used as a prison during the war. There were a lot of rooms, but with only six prisoners, only one side of the prison was really used.

There was a very large wall around the prison with guard towers at different parts of the wall and large searchlights at each tower. There was one large room inside the prison that was set up for our guards' room. Not all our company was on guard duty at one time. Every forty-eight hours half of us would be inside the prison doing guard duty. After forty-eight hours the other half of the company would come into the prison to relieve us. When not in the prison on guard duty, we were attending training classes.

Me on the right with my dog Vonnie, my sister Donna and her
dog. Neighbor friend and his dog. Our tar-paper shack we lived in.
Picture taken 1939.

James Clark
Finished Army Basic Training
Age 13 years old 1943.

1944 James Clark
Home on leave. Me on the
right I was now 14 years old. My
buddy in the Marine Corps was
15 years old.

Honorable Discharge

This is to certify that

JAMES R CLARK   PRIVATE

1st Parachute   Regt, Ft Benning, Ga

Army of the United States

is hereby Honorably Discharged from the military service of the United States of America.

This certificate is awarded as a testimonial of Honest and Faithful Service to his country.

Given at   SEPARATION CENTER,
FORT DIX, NEW JERSEY

Date   24 OCTOBER 1944

L. F. HAGGLUND
MAJOR, INF.

W. D., A. G. O. Form No. 55
January 22, 1943

My brother Robert Clark
Sgt. US Army.
Died in the service 1943.

My mother Bessie Raygor Clark
Deceased 1971 Houston Texas.

My Father Charles Dayton Clark Served in the US Army
WW I and WW II Now Deceased 1964.

My brother-in-law Jack Healey. Served in the Marine-Corps
Now deceased 1991.

My sister Donna Healey and her children Michael, Jeanne a nurse and
Peggy.

My sister Jean Wyke who has always been there to help her brothers and sisters.

My brother-in-law Ralph Wyke. Served in the Navy Sea Bees WW II Now deceased 1981.

Sister Jane Savage served in the Navy Waves in WW II. Now deceased 1995.

1952 Picture taken in Berlin, Germany. I was going on duty with the Military Police.

My daughter Micki, husband John
Sterbick with daughter Evan.

My daughter Tanya Leach.

My son James Robert Clark.

My grandnieces Danielle Cooper and
Misty Cooper.

My niece Amanda Smith.

Spandau Prison 1949 Formal Guard Mount US Army on the right relieving the Russians, one month duty guarding the Nazi War Criminals. I'm in the back row, Americans on the right.

Regimental review for Gen. Mathewson. Berlin, Germany 1951.

1950 Berlin Honor Guard 6th Infantry Regiment. I'm in the front row 5th
from right.

My sister Marguerite and husband George Smith with
family, Jennifer and Patrick. Houston, Texas.

My sister Maxine McLeroy and son Shawn.
Houstin, Texas.

Niece Betty Jane and husband Bill Cooper on their honeymoon 1965 at Pat O'Bryns place. New Orleans, Louisiana.

Nephew Buzz Wyke, Police Captain Harris County, Texas. Now retired from the County. Served in the US Army in Turkey and Taiwan.

My brother-in-law, Ralph and his construction crew being congratulated
by the late Shah of Iran for building the refinery in the background.

On our way out to sea, from Cam Ranh Bay, Vietnam. On our return trip
we ran into a storm and rough seas. Our front ramp and ramp chains were
broken off. 1968.

Back at Cam Ranh Bay after the big storm. Waiting for a new ramp and chains from the United States that took over a month to arrive. Me standing in front of a boat.

Our boat (L.C.U.) up on the shore of Qui-Nhon Village, Vietnam. Picture shows how big the ramp chain is. One ramp chain on each side of the ramp.

One of the crew members holding the monkey that we traded off to a Navy ship for boxes of steaks.

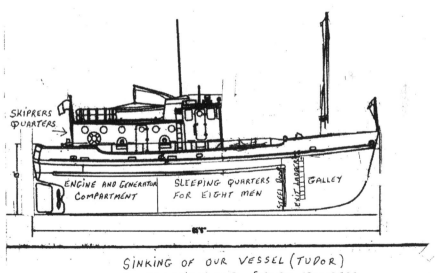

SINKING OF OUR VESSEL (TUDOR) BY THE VIETCONG. SEVEN MEMBERS OF OUR SURVEY CREW WENT DOWN WITH THE BOAT.

DEPARTMENT OF THE NAVY
OFFICER IN CHARGE OF CONSTRUCTION
NAVAL FACILITIES ENGINEERING COMMAND CONTRACTS
REPUBLIC OF VIETNAM
FPO SAN FRANCISCO 96626

NBy-44105

DATE: 26 FEB. 71

TRAVEL ORDER NO. 3208

FROM: Officer-In-Charge of Construction, Naval Facilities Engineering Command
          Contracts, Republic of Vietnam

TO:

        CLARK, JAMES R. B/N 17,148 c/o RMK-BRJ. SAN FRANCISCO, CALIFORNIA APO 96243

SUBJECT: Authorization to Travel | ORIGINAL |

REF: (a) Contract NBy-44105

1. In accordance with reference (a), you are hereby authorized to travel on or about
    ____27 FEB. 71_____ to __Travis AFB, Calif._____.

2. Travel by government air from Saigon, Vietnam is directed. Class __2__ priority
    is certified. In the event space is not available, government air, commercial air
    service Economy class is authorized.

3. A baggage allowance of Sixty Six (66)   pounds is authorized.

4. You are directed to have completed all vaccination, immunization and Vietnamese
    Immigration requirements.

5. These orders are not valid for departure from or entry into Vietnam other than
    through Tan Son Nhut Airport where bearer must officially process with Vietnamese
    Immigration and Customs.

6. This travel order does not constitute authority for payment of per diem, travel
    time, nor travel expense other than provided by the terms of the basic contract.

7. Estimated dollar value of travel is ____$175.00_____.

8. Accounting data:
                                    * Company Business Medical Evacuation
                                    Charge to: Employee Medical Evacuation
                                                7235.01.205

APPROPRIATION	BUCON NO.	AUTH. ACCTG.	OC.	ACCTG. TRANS. TYPE	FUND CODE
17 x 1205.2519	92-246	63185	622	2D	98015 $175.00

C. I. C. T051-3-4-6-1020

for RMK-BRJ, Personnel   JOE BOYD   Director

                                        for A. F. STAUFFER
                                            OICC, RVN
                                            By Direction

DISTRIBUTION·

MORRISON KNUDSEN CORPORATION

MORRISON KNUDSEN PLAZA
P.O. BOX 73/BOISE, IDAHO U.S.A. 83729
PHONE: (208) 386-5000/TELEX: 368439

BRM-0832

February 15, 1999

Dear Mr. Clark:

As a Document Records Specialist of Morrison Knudsen Corporation, I hereby certify that you were employed with Morrison Knudsen from July 20,1970 to June 4, 1971. I have enclosed your employment agreement and various personnel documents which indicate your dates of employment.

Documentation of the sinking of the vessel Tudor, along with the accident and medical reports resulting from the attack, is also enclosed. I hope this will provide you with all that you need

If I can assist you further, please contact me.

Sincerely,

Jill Clemens
Records Management Specialist

Sworn to and subscribed before me
on this __16th__ day of February, 1999

Notary Public

11

GUARDING NAZI PRISONERS AT SPANDAU PRISON

Spandau Prison was built to accommodate 600 prisoners. One big room was set up where the Nazis could hang eight prisoners at a time, and they had a guillotine. There were big furnaces to burn the bodies. The twelve-man squad I was in was one of the first ones inside the prison to relieve the few remaining Russian guards in the wall towers and at the main gates into the prison.

To get up to the wall guard tower, a person had to climb up a ladder. Once in the tower you could see part of the prison yard that wasn't very large. It was a dirt yard with a gravel path for walking. Inside the guard tower was a searchlight that had to be swiveled around by hand by the tower guard.

There was a square metal box with a clock and a key on a chain hanging from the metal box. The Russian soldier couldn't speak English, nor I Russian, so he saluted me, said something in Russian, and climbed down the ladder.

As I looked around I saw the guard tower's instructions on the wall. It was translated into three languages, French, Russian, and English. After reading the instructions, I soon found out what the clock in the metal box and the key were for. Every thirty minutes I was required to put the key in a key slot just below the clock and turn the key. This, in turn, would put a hole in the paper that was inside the clock telling what time the key was turned. This was to make sure the tower guard was alert and not sleeping on duty.

The instructions also told us when to turn on the searchlight and rotate the light throughout the prison yard and along the inside wall of the prison. I was never given any orders to shoot to kill if I spotted an escape attempt, so I guess that was up to me.

Would I have shot to kill? Yes, I would have. That's one thing I was trained to do in the infantry, and knowing the pain and suffering those convicted ex-Nazi hierarchy brought to the world I wouldn't have felt any remorse whatsoever at shooting one of them if they tried to escape.

There was no heat in the guard towers. A soldier had to keep moving around as well as he could in such close quarters. Each one of us tower guards were on duty for two hours. Then we would be relieved and off duty for four hours to rest in the guardhouse inside the prison.

Sometimes we would rotate and be assigned other guard duty inside the prison, which was warmer. Inside this large prison were some of the six top Nazis who were convicted at the Nuremberg trials of September, 1946 and sent to Berlin to serve their time at Spandau prison. The six prisoners were Erich Raeder, Rudolf Hess, Von-Baldu Schirach, Albert Speer, Konstantin Von Neurath, and Grand Admiral Karl Donitz.

Albert Speer was a member of the Nazi party and Hitler's minister for armaments. He directed and participated in war crimes and crimes against humanity. He worked Jews as slave laborers. Speer received twenty years' imprisonment at Spandau prison. He was released in 1966 and died in 1981.

Grand Admiral Karl Donitz was Admiral of the Fleet before Hitler killed himself. He appointed Admiral Donitz his successor to lead the army and Germany. At the Nuremberg trials he was found guilty and sentenced to ten years' imprisonment at Spandau prison. He was released in 1956 and died in 1980.

Rudolph Hess was at one time Hitler's deputy. During the war he commandeered a German plane without Hitler's knowledge and flew over Scotland. Hess parachuted out of the plane and was quickly imprisoned in Great Britain. At the end of the war he was taken back to Nuremberg to stand trial where he was sentenced to life imprisonment at Spandau prison. Hess committed suicide by hanging himself in 1987 at Spandau prison.

Von-Baldu Schirach was the head of the ministry of the Hitler youth. A German youth at the age of ten was to study and learn Nazi doctrine and ideas. At the age of eighteen he was to become a soldier. It was the German Hitler youth who were left to defend Berlin against the Russians at the time Berlin was falling. Schirach was sentenced to four to twenty years at Spandau prison for his authorization, direction, and participation in crimes against humanity, particularly anti-Jewish crimes. Schirach was released from prison in 1966 and died in 1974.

Erich Raeder was Chief of the German Navy, General Admiral of the German Navy, and he participated in war crimes out of sea warfare. Raeder was sentenced to life imprisonment at Spandau prison, but due to illness he was released in 1955 and he died in 1960.

Konstantin Von Neurath was a member of the Nazi party, a general in the

S.S., and President of the Secret Cabinet Council. He was guilty of planning and preparation of the Nazi conspirators for wars of aggression, crimes against persons and property in occupied territories, and crimes against humanity. Neurath was sentenced to Spandau prison for a term of fifteen years. He was released in 1954 due to illness and died in 1956.

Most of these prisoners were convicted of crimes against humanity. Some were convicted of other war crimes. The prisoners who drew the most attention and interest of all us guards were Speer and Hess. Albert Speer was serving a twenty-year sentence. He seemed to be the most intelligent, and he had a better disposition than the others. He also seemed to me friendlier than the others. Speer, on greeting a guard, would give a greeting or a smile. The others acted as if they were mad at the world because they couldn't conquer the world. The others were not friendly at all.

Rudolph Hess acted as if he were in need of some psychological treatment. He acted like a wild animal in a cage. He wouldn't say anything to the guards. He tried to act as if we weren't there. The other prisoners did not like Hess. He talked to himself constantly. Hess was tall and thin with heavy, black eyebrows and black circles around his eyes. When he was out in the prison yard, if he wasn't working in the flowers, he would be walking endlessly back and forth on the gravel path in the garden, or he would walk back and forth in his room. Sometimes at night Hess would let out howling sounds, and sometimes at night I could hear him mumbling. He didn't keep his room very clean.

None of us guards were allowed to have cameras in the prison. We weren't permitted to talk to any of the prisoners, but we did when we could. The Russians, who were supervising when we were guarding, didn't want any of us Americans to become friendly with any of the prisoners.

As the days passed I often saw Speer sitting in the rock garden of the prison, just sitting and thinking. I could see that he was the kind of person who had made up his mind to adjust himself to prison life. In the evening when I would walk past his room I could see that he was always writing. But if he knew that someone saw him writing, he would hide whatever he was writing.

The prisoners were not permitted to be writing any time they wanted to. If they wanted to write a letter to someone outside the prison, they had to get permission, and they were given just a set time to write a letter. They did get visits from their wives once a month for one hour under the supervision of a guard.

In the guardhouse there was always talk among the guards about what they had seen the prisoners do that particular day, and it seemed always to be Hess who was doing strange things that made the guards relay these actions to other guards. Most of the guards didn't have any sympathy for the Nazi prisoners. Many of the guards had lost a relative or a friend in the war, and they had a grudge against the Nazis.

The Army was stricter with the guards than they were with the prisoners. Of all the imprisoned Nazis at Spandau, it was Albert Speer that the Russians wanted most to be sentenced to death at the Nuremberg trials. But Speer lucked out and only received a twenty-year sentence. Hess got a life sentence. The five others received similar sentences. After serving thirty days in the Spandau prison, all of us soldiers were more than glad when it was time for the British to relieve us. We were more than ready to get back to our camp, back into our barracks, back into our training schedule, and to be able to go out on pass.

The day after my company arrived back at camp, and after we unloaded all our equipment, my buddy wanted me to go out on pass and drink beer with him. I did. We wanted to pick up some frauleins. I let him choose the nightclub. While we were at a table drinking beer I saw a German guy I knew walk in. I had shacked up with his sister a time or two when I first arrived in Berlin.

He was a nice guy and he could speak a little English. We invited him to our table for some beer. He told us that he had started a new job working for the Army at Tempelhof Airfield, and he wanted us all to celebrate his getting a job.

We told him that he had come to the right place because my buddy and I are always celebrating. After a few beers, and after looking over the frauleins, the German guy at our table whose name was Hans, said he knew a better place than the cabaret we were in, and the other cabaret had dancing and many frauleins.

My buddy said he was going to stay there because there were a lot of frauleins at that cabaret he wanted to make out with. So Hans and I left my buddy and the nightclub. Hans and I had just walked out the door onto the sidewalk, and I was reaching for my hat that I had folded up and had hanging between my belt and waistline. I was now outside the cabaret and was getting ready to put my cap on my head when a rather large American soldier that I didn't know came walking toward Hans and me. This soldier got up close to me just outside the cabaret and said, "Put your hat on, soldier."

I could tell he had been drinking, and I could see that he was a private first class, the same rank I was. Then he said, "Put your damn hat on soldier. I'm a military policeman." I could tell by the military insignia on his uniform that he was in the military police, but I also knew that he was off duty and he was out drinking just as I was. So I told him, "Buzz off, buddy. I'll put my hat on when I damn well feel like it."

Hans and I continued walking down the street. It was just getting dark. We hadn't walked far when Hans looked back then said to me, "Here comes that soldier." I thought, "Well, I'll bet he wants to start a fight." I didn't look back, but in just seconds the off duty military policeman grabbed me by the shoulder and turned me around. As I turned I kicked him as hard as I could in his family jewels, meaning the groin.

I put all power in that kick. I got a grunt out of him and he doubled up, but then he quickly recovered from doubling up and said to me, "Come and get it." I could see that he had a pocketknife and the blade on the knife was open. I thought, "Well, it's going to be him or me." This was now going to be a serious fight. At about this time Hans couldn't believe that he was seeing an American soldier pulling a knife on another soldier. He was standing off to the side of the soldier with the knife and me. Hans, as soon as he saw the knife, started saying, in German, "Nein, Nein." And then right away Hans stepped between the soldier with the knife and me.

Very quickly, the soldier turned the knife on Hans. The blow of the soldier's arm was moved very quickly, and the knife stabbed Hans in the chest. The soldier said, "Get out of the way, Kraut." This was a slang expression. American soldiers called the Germans Kraut because they liked sauerkraut. When the soldier turned his knife on Hans, this gave me a chance to kick the soldier in his family jewels another hard kick, and I quickly followed up the kick with a hard punch to his face.

He staggered backward and dropped the knife he was holding, trying to use his hands to break the fall. I grabbed the knife, folded the blade, and put it in my pocket. Hans kept saying," He put a hole in my jacket." He said this about three times as he looked at the knife hole in his jacket. Then all of a sudden Hans' temper built up in a furious action. He jumped on top of the soldier who was just picking himself up off the sidewalk. I had to pull Hans off the soldier, and as I was doing this, I told the soldier that now he was in big trouble for stabbing Hans.

I could tell by the soldier's actions that he did realize he had made a hell of a mistake. I asked him what his name was, but he wouldn't tell me. The soldier asked for his knife back. I told him, "Hell no." I told Hans, "Let's get you to a doctor." The soldier started walking toward the cabaret. Hans and I found a German taxi driver to take us to the Army hospital that we had there in Berlin.

It was a small hospital. At first Hans didn't want to go to an American hospital, but I convinced him. I told him I was on his side, and I would tell the American military what had happened. So Hans agreed to go. I looked inside his jacket and I could see there was blood on his shirt. Even at this time the only thing Hans was concerned about was the knife cut in his dress jacket.

When we arrived at the hospital I let them know that an American soldier stabbed Hans. The hospital contacted the military police. When they arrived I reported the incident to them and told them what the soldier looked like, and that he was an off duty military policeman. I gave the pocketknife to the military policeman.

The two military policemen looked at each other as if they knew who I was talking about. I waited while the hospital treated Hans. While they were treating him I filled out the statement about the incident of the stabbing. The MPs told me that I would be hearing from them and they left. I heard one of the MPs get on his Jeep radio and put out a call to pick up this soldier as a suspect.

The hospital took x-rays of Hans' chest and the doctor took care of the knife wound. The doctor said that the knife blade had just missed Hans' lung by a fraction of an inch. The hospital got a lot of information from Hans. They had a German translator and they had Hans fill out a statement. I took Hans home that night and then it was time for me to get back to camp.

A week later I was informed that the soldier who did the stabbing was going to be court-martialed and that Hans and I would be called as witnesses. We would have to give testimony.

Hans and I attended the court martial. We were each called to the stand to give testimony. I was asked why I didn't try to avoid a fight with this other soldier. I told the court that when the soldier put his hand on me spinning me around by my shoulder, I knew that I had to protect myself.

The court martial ended with the soldier receiving a reduction in rank and confinement for six months in the stockade. He also had to forfeit all pay for the six months' confinement. The military police led him away. The soldier was lucky that American soldiers didn't come under German law at that time or he would have received more time.

Hans and I went out that evening to the German beer garden that he wanted to take me to the night he got stabbed. We danced with some good looking frauleins and we drank beer all evening. The last time I saw Hans was when he left the beer garden with the fraulein he had been dancing with. That was the last time I ever saw Hans.

I was now convinced that the only way a soldier was going to stay out of trouble was to get a steady fraulein, so I made up my mind to go back and visit

Helga and her mother on my next pass from camp.

The next day when my company was out on the parade ground, and they had broken us down into our individual platoons to drill in marching, out of the corner of my eye I could see a lieutenant that I had never seen before. He was watching each platoon doing their marching drill when we were given a ten-minute break. Most of us sat down on the ground until our break was over. The lieutenant I didn't know sent word that he wanted to see me.

I thought to myself, "Well, I must be in some kind of trouble." I got up and reported to him. He told me he wanted to see me put my rifle to the right shoulder and march by myself to a distance that he designated, then return to where he was standing. I did as he asked me to do. When I marched back to where he was standing the lieutenant told me to stand at ease. Then he told me who he was and why he had asked me to march by myself. He said that he had been given orders to form an elite honor guard of thirty sharp soldiers to be picked out of the newly formed regiment. He also said that he wanted soldiers who had no disciplinary problems in the company they were in.

I told him, "That leaves me out because I have an Article 104. The lieutenant said that he was sorry to hear that. Then he acted as if he was no longer interested in me. I spoke up and said, "Lieutenant, I would love to be part of an elite regiment honor guard, and if you would just put me on a thirty-day probation I'll prove that I can carry out the duties of the disciplined soldier you are looking for."

The lieutenant said that he would think about it. I didn't see the lieutenant for over two weeks. Then I was called into the company commander's office, old man Winters. He told me that I was being transferred to the honor guard platoon at regimental headquarters company and that it was to be a thirty-day probation. He said that if I didn't do well, in thirty days I would be sent back to his company.

This was the break that I had been waiting for, and I made up my mind that I was going to do my best at soldiering. I reported to the honor guard platoon just at the time it was getting started. My platoon sergeant's name was George, and he was a very sharp soldier. He had been trained in, and knew how to train, the platoon in fancy drill movements.

We were always on the parade field drilling, and we always had to look like we had just stepped out of a bandbox. We were expected to out-sharp and shine every soldier in the infantry regiment, and unconditional obedience was expected of us. All our equipment that was brass was to be highly shined, and if it was any other metal, that had to be chrome plated. Our boots and dress shoes were sent out to a shoemaker to have metal cleats put on the heels.

We were issued the Army's old rifle of World War I, the 30.06 Springfield. All the metal parts were chrome plated and the carrying sling was white. We used the bolt action 30.06 because it was a lightweight rifle and easy to do fancy tricks with. We did things like throwing the rifle straight up in the air and the rifle would do a complete turn, and when the rifle would come down the soldier would catch the rifle in his hands at the port arms position in front of him. Then we would throw our rifles at each other. This is called "Changing arms." We learned the technique of twirling the rifle like a baton. We put BBs in the bottom of the stock to make the rifle make sounds when doing manual of arms. Some of us learned these fancy moves with the rifle the hard way. I received a black eye. Some of the others in the platoon also got black eyes when the rifle came twirling around and their heads got in the way. It only takes one black eye before an honor guard soldier learns how to handle the rifle. I can just say they had us trained to do every fancy thing with rifle except "eat the rifle" during marching drill.

We were out on the drill field all day long. We all enjoyed doing fancy drill and forming different formations. We got so good that the drill sergeant didn't have to give any commands because we performed by silent counting by each soldier to himself, and knowing when to execute the next movement on a certain number. When we were first learning these movements we looked like a bunch of lost sheep, but by day after day of drilling we got good.

Whenever the whole regiment had a pass in review in a parade, the honor guard was called out in front of the reviewing stand where the general or the colonel of the regiment would be standing to review the parade. The honor guard would put on a thirty-minute fancy drill and formations, and executing fancy manual of arms with our rifles. When we were finished we would march back to where the regiment was waiting to march past the reviewing stand. The honor guard would position itself in front of the regiment so that the honor guard would be leading the parade, and also the honor guard carried the American flag and the flag of the regimental colors.

I served my thirty days' probation of being in the honor guard platoon, and then some. I was even promoted to corporal. That was a two striper, and at that time in the Army being a corporal was a good rank even if it was at the lowest rank of the non-commissioned officers' rank. This made me a squad leader.

Another duty of the honor guard was to provide security for the general and his family. The residence was located outside the military camp. There was a large fence around the house and a guard post at the front gate. Guards had to keep a record of who was permitted to enter the property. The general in Berlin at this time was General Maxwell Taylor. We were honor guards at formal officers' parties. I liked doing honor guard at the parties because when the party was over, and everybody was gone, we got a lot of the leftovers and maybe a bottle or two of good liquor, but we were expected to always have control over our actions. Sometimes we worked with the military police on downtown patrols checking soldiers in cafes and beer gardens.

I was in the honor guard around five months when the regiment at McNair Barracks got a new regimental commander by the name of Colonel P.D. Ginder. It wasn't long after the Colonel took command that things changed to the point that if a soldier saw the Colonel's sedan coming down the road of the camp, soldiers would take a quick detour. Soldiers did not want to be seen by the Colonel because Colonel Ginder wouldn't hesitate to have his driver come to a quick stop because a soldier might have given the Colonel a sloppy salute.

In response to more than one soldier the Colonel was known to have gotten out of his sedan with his aide, a lieutenant who always carried a note pad, and write down the soldier's name and his company. If the soldier had any rank, like a pfc or a corporal, and if he had given the Colonel a sloppy salute, or if the soldier's hat was cocked to one side, or if he had a button undone, that soldier would be reduced in rank on the spot.

Word went out through the camp, and everyone was on the alert. Suddenly there weren't many soldiers walking alone around the camp. There was a story around the camp that Colonel Ginder dropped by one of the infantry company's mess halls and asked to see one of the cook's fingernails. There was dirt under his nails. He was reduced on the spot from private first class back down to private.

I heard that the Colonel would also promote a soldier on the spot for being outstanding according to the Colonel's standards. To be on the safe side it was best to stay out of his way. The Colonel kept us all on the alert and on our toes. I know that I will never forget having had the privilege of serving under his command.

The regimental emblem on our unit's crest that all us soldiers wore on the shoulders of our uniforms was the symbol of an alligator. Colonel Ginder wanted a regimental mascot, so he had a live alligator sent from the United States to Berlin. One of the companies that had barracks near Tempelhof Airfield had the honor of housing and taking care of the three-foot alligator. The company made a large indoor pool for the reptile, so now every time there was a regimental parade, all the troops had to pass in review past the grandstand with the Colonel and his staff officers standing in the grandstand.

The alligator was also in the parade. A flat platform was made on the backseat of an open Jeep. The alligator was tied down on the platform and the Jeep was driven slowly past the reviewing stand. Since the alligator couldn't salute, the Colonel and his staff officers would salute the alligator.

Word went out that the Colonel wanted to have an organization day, which called for another regimental parade and other events. Since the organization day was about a month away, the Colonel wanted to find out how physically fit his troops were. The regiment staff officers set up a physical proficiency course that every soldier would have to go through and be tested.

When I was first told about the test, and that it was going to be a rough test, I started going over to the small gymnasium in the camp to get in shape for whatever they were going to put us through. No one seemed to know what the course was going to consist of. At the gymnasium I became friends with a soldier from another company who was also trying to get in shape for the upcoming physical test. We teamed up and worked out together.

When the day arrived and we marched out to a big physical training area, we could see that the regiment facility had the test area well organized. They had set up different staged stations that a soldier had to physically perform at. First we were told that there would be no talking to each other. At each testing station there was one officer and one non-commissioned officer from another company.

They would do the scoring and the soldier who was performing the test would not see his score until he had finished all the test areas. We were told there would be no resting between testing stations. We were to go from one station on the run to the next station. The first station was the three hundred yard dash, and we had to do six relays with five soldiers running at the same time staying in their clearly marked lanes.

There was a sit-up station where someone would hold your legs at the knees to keep you from bending your legs. One hundred sit-ups all the way down on your back and coming up to touching your elbow to your knee was the requirement.

The next station was push-ups. There they wanted your back straight with your arms straight. The tester put his hand flat on the ground, and the soldier's chest had to go down and touch the top of the tester's hand. Seventy push-ups were required with no stopping to rest. If the push-up was not done properly, it wasn't counted.

Next were the squat jumps. They wanted one hundred. Then the overhead chin-up bar. They wanted twenty-five chin-ups. The chin-up bar was high. A soldier had to jump way up to get his hands around the bar. All chin-ups had to be done without swinging your legs for momentum. They wanted arms straight, and when the person pulled himself up, they wanted the person's chin up over the top of the bar. Twenty-five were required. When I did my twenty-five I was told to stay on the bar, that I had to do more because one of the chin-ups wasn't going to count. My arms weren't straight on one of the chin-ups. I did the extra one and I was in a strain, but then I heard the tester tell me that the last one was good, and I was given credit for doing all twenty-five.

Next was hand-over-hand pulling your body up a thirty-foot, knotted rope without using your legs. It was required that a soldier come down from the rope the same way, using only his hands. Next was going up over a high wall and dropping down over the other side of the wall, and then, on the run, jumping over hurdles. All of this testing was done on a timed basis without resting. We were exhausted at the end of the testing. When it was over we were marched back to our barracks so that other companies could be tested.

None of us had any idea how we had performed during the physical testing until the next day when results were posted on the company's bulletin board. They posted every soldier's score. That's when I learned that I was the only soldier in the company with the highest score on the test. Before the day was over I was told that only two soldiers out of the regiment topped the possible score of 500 on the physical proficiency test.

During the next regimental parade the two of us with the highest scores were invited to stand with the regimental commander in the reviewing stand and watch the regiment parade by. Before the regiment marched by the reviewing stand, Colonel Ginder awarded each of us a trophy. Then the Colonel gave the standing troops a speech about the importance of infantry soldiers being physically fit.

After the parade the other soldier and I were ordered to report to the Colonel's office to receive a grade promotion. This was unexpected, but with Colonel Ginder, anything could happen. The other soldier was promoted to corporal and I was promoted to buck sergeant. When I returned to the honor guard platoon there were some who were resentful of my promotion. Some of them had been at the grade of corporal longer than I had been, and they were next in line to be promoted. Now Colonel Ginder had broken their bubble.

The first sergeant of this new company I was now in with the honor guard drill platoon was a big guy who wouldn't take any crap from anyone. One morning for reveille the order was given for everyone to fall out in formation in front of the company in our raincoats and with no underclothes under our raincoats. We were to wear boots on our feet. None of us knew what was going on. Had the company gone nuts? As strange as it seemed to us, we all complied with the order. We were standing in ranks that morning in the dark except for the lighting coming from the barracks, and there stood the first sergeant in front of the company holding a pump spray can.

Then he made the announcement that some soldiers in the company must have the crabs from going out and shacking up with German women. He said that it had to be some of us because he had not brought the crabs into the company. He said, "I've been in Germany over a year and I've never been out on pass." Then he said, "I have here in my hand a pump spray can of DDT." This is a powerful insecticide which was used widely by the Army during the forties and fifties to kill bugs.

The first sergeant said that when he comes down each rank of men he wanted us to open our raincoats wide and he would spray our front and under our armpits. Then we were to turn around and bend over, lift the raincoat, and he would spray our butts. The spray did burn some. As soon as each soldier was sprayed we were to break ranks and go into the barracks to shower. This spraying only happened once, so I guess the first sergeant was satisfied. He must have gotten rid of his crabs.

Another unspeakable thing the Army did at this time was to conduct a short arms inspection. This was always sprung on soldiers unexpectedly, at two or three o'clock in the morning. A team of medical corpsmen, and maybe a doctor, would come into our sleeping quarters and turn on the lights telling everyone to get out of bed and for all of us to stand at the end of our beds.

We would all be in our underwear. The medical corpsman would check each soldier for venereal disease. The soldier was asked to milk down his male organ. This is referred to as a "short arms inspection." At the same time each soldier is asked to open his clothing wall locker and his footlocker. They were looking for drugs. During one of these unexpected short arms inspections in another rifle company, the medical team found a half bottle of penicillin in a soldier's wall locker. The last I heard about that soldier was that he was going to be court-martialed for practicing medicine without a license.

A lot of time had passed since I'd seen the German girl, Helga. I was ready to settle down with a steady girlfriend who did not have a venereal disease. I didn't want to push my luck, and anyway, we were told that there were seven women to every man in Berlin. I'm pretty sure that I had had my seven in bed, and I think I even got someone else's seven as well. So far I was ahead. It was time to go steady with one girl.

I took the underground subway to Schmargendorf where Helga lived with her mother. I went bearing gifts, candy bars, cigarettes and coffee. After getting off the subway it was about a five block walk to the building where she lived. When I arrived Helga's Mutti wasn't at home, so I took that opportunity to get Helga in the sack. This was the first time I had been alone with Helga. Her mother was always watching over us like a mother hen.

When the mother did return, it didn't take Mutti long to realize that her young daughter had just been to bed with an American soldier. The bed was a mess. Mutti didn't say anything to me, but her attitude toward me changed. She would leave Helga and me alone more often. When I would get an overnight pass, Mutti would come into the bedroom and tuck her daughter and me in at night. Then she would sleep in the other room on a sofa.

I went steady with Helga for about a year. She was still going to high school. I learned later that before she met me she had a German boyfriend named Hans. He was a student at the high school she was attending. I also learned that Helga had a grandmother who lived in East Germany. Helga referred to her as her "Omi," which means "Grandmother."

At this time the Berlin Wall had not yet been erected. A lot of the East Germans were riding the underground subway to visit in West Berlin. I had one more year to serve in Berlin. That would be three years in Germany. I was a young and foolhardy soldier who was not really in love with the German girl, Helga, but I guess I felt sorry for her and the way she had to live in this war-torn country.

When I thought I knew what I was doing, I decided that I wanted to marry this German girl, Helga. I was talked to by the Army Chaplain. He told me that I should give this marriage a lot of thought, and be sure before I made the commitment. He also tried to tell me that a lot of German girls want to marry an American soldier just to get to the United States.

Well, I was young, and I thought I knew what I wanted, and what I was doing. I thought that the Army just did not want soldiers to marry German women. So I made up my mind that I was going to marry this German girl, no matter what. All the advice of the Army Chaplain went in one ear and out the other. Helga and I made plans to marry in a German church a short distance from Helga's house. So the date was set.

The Army in Berlin had regulations for soldiers who wanted to marry German women. The soldier couldn't get married until he was on his last six months left to serve in Berlin. So we got married, and that entitled me to an overnight pass every night. I did have to be back early in the morning for reveille.

After we were married we celebrated by having a small party at a small cafe. Helga invited her German friends, and even her high school boyfriend, Hans. My soldier friends came with their frauleins. We had beer and accordion music, all German songs of course.

After six months, which was early 1952, my three years in Berlin were over. I received orders sending me back to the United States for re-assignment. At this time the Army was still moving soldiers by troop ship. The Army's regulation at this time was soldiers returning to the states for re-assignment would be going by troop ship, and those who were going back to the States for discharge would get to fly. Another big disappointment was another of the Army's regulations. A married soldier could not travel on the same ship with his new wife. The soldier would go first, by ship, without his new wife. Then in three to four months the new wife would be given passage on a troop ship to join her husband in the States. The reasoning behind this stupid regulation was never revealed to me.

I could not understand why we wouldn't travel together on the same ship. Maybe they didn't want an enlisted man taking up private cabin space away from officers and their American wives. So Helga and I said our goodbyes. It took the ship eleven days to arrive in the States and I was seasick all the way.

At this time the Korean War was going hot and heavy. Most of us soldiers returning from Germany had no doubt that we would be sent to Korea as quickly as the Army could get us there. The draft was in full swing by this time, and soldiers were being sent to Korea right after basic training.

When I arrived back in the States, and the processing was done, I was given orders to report to Camp Indian-Town Gap in Pennsylvania, a basic training center. I was to be a drill sergeant. When I received my new assignment I didn't know what I was in for. I was given a fifteen-day leave to visit my mother and other relatives in Houston, Texas before reporting in for my new assignment in Pennsylvania.

It sure was nice to see my relatives again. I could tell that my mother was a little disappointed that I had married a German girl, because my mother had given me explicit orders, "Don't you marry any of those German girls. I don't want to be the grandmother of any little Nazis."

12

ACROSS THE PACIFIC BY TROOP SHIP

With my new assignment to Indian-Town Gap I thought maybe I was luckier than soldiers who had received orders for Korea. I reported to my duty station. I had to take a long bus ride from Harrisburg, Pennsylvania. As soon as I arrived at the camp I made up my mind that I didn't like it.

I reported to my new infantry company and was assigned to the training facility as a weapons instructor to new recruits. This sometimes included night and day firing on the range.

Saturdays were inspections of the recruits or parading. After four months of this duty I wished I were back in Berlin. Also, after four months I was informed by the Army that my German wife would be arriving on a troop ship and that I would be given leave time to meet her at the port of the ship's debarkation. After receiving this notice, on the weekend I went looking for an apartment in Harrisburg where a lot of German people lived. I thought that would be a good place to find an apartment.

After a lot of footwork I found an apartment and there were German-speaking people living close by. When the time came to meet her, and she got off the ship, I could see that she had made a lot of friends aboard the ship. She was hugging a lot of people and saying goodbye.

There were other German brides arriving in the States aboard this ship. After her baggage was unloaded we took a Greyhound bus to Harrisburg. When we arrived at our new apartment we spent some time together, then I showed her around the town. We met some German-speaking people.

Helga was away from home and away from her mother for the first time. After only a week in America I could see that she was starting to get homesick for her home in Berlin. I could only see her on weekends. I knew that could only make matters worse. During the training of recruits we worked late at night and early in the morning.

I had no car at this time. The landlady told me that she would look after Helga when I wasn't there. After about two months of being in the United States Helga made me make her a promise that I would help her get her mother to the United States. This was when she told me that while on board the ship she had met a nice Army officer, and he told her that if her husband couldn't do anything about getting her mother to the States, that maybe he could do something. Helga gave me a piece of paper that had the officer's name and his new duty station on it. I smelled a rat with this story. I've sailed on enough troop ships, and I've seen enough hanky-panky between officers and civilian dependents aboard the ship. They are together on the same deck and they eat in the same dining hall. These decks are off limits to enlisted men. They have to stay at the lowest level of the decks with no deck chairs. I asked Helga why this officer would want to help her get her mother to the United States. She said, "Because he was just a nice man." I did not trust this story but I kept it to myself.

Later I called the Immigration Office and asked about the process I would have to go through to sponsor getting my German mother-in-law to the United States. I was told that first I would have to show that I had $30,000 in the bank to prove that she wouldn't become a burden on the government.

Well, that left me out. I didn't have that much money. When the lady who owned the apartment learned that Helga needed a sponsor, she told us that she had heard of a rich man who had helped to sponsor some Germans to the States, and maybe we should talk to him. After Helga talked to some other Germans in the community, we were given his name and address. We called and made an appointment to see him. He had an office in his home. He was an older man.

My wife told him, in her broken English, about wanting a sponsor for getting her mother to the States. As she was talking I could see his eyes moving up and down my wife's body as if he were trying to undress her with his eyes. He showed us some pictures of some of the young German girls he had sponsored to the States. I noticed in the pictures that there were very few men. He asked me if I had seen duty in Korea yet.

I said, "No." Then he sat back in his chair with his eyes looking up and down my wife. He said, "Right now there is just nothing I can do for you." He was presently sponsoring a person from Germany. He also suggested that she not give up, and to keep checking with him. He said he would do all that he could at a later date. I thought to myself, "Sure, you dirty old man. I know what's on your mind from the way you're looking over my wife."

Since my wife was thinking she had reached a dead end on her chances of getting someone to be a sponsor for getting her mother to the United States, it wasn't long before Helga wanted me to write a letter to the Army officer she had met on the ship. I didn't believe it. Why would a complete stranger make a promise like that unless he wanted something in return. I wrote to the officer and I was not surprised when the letter came back marked, "No Such Address." I could see disappointment on Helga's face. Well, as it was, my luck ran out after being in Indian-Town Gap, Pennsylvania for six months.

I was given orders for Korea where a war was being fought. This meant that I would be leaving Helga in Harrisburg by herself. I was told that if my German wife didn't have her citizenship, and if she wanted to become an American citizen without waiting the allotted time that foreigners had to wait to become eligible for citizenship, she could. I had been given orders from the military to a country that my wife could not go to. I was told that she should take a copy of my overseas orders to the American Immigration Office and that she would be given American citizenship papers right away.

Now that my German bride was going to be left alone in America, I was beginning to understand why the Army tried to discourage soldiers from marrying German frauleins. I did feel sorry for Helga having to go it alone in a strange country, especially since she had always been with her mother. We said our goodbyes again and I left her in the apartment in Harrisburg.

The troop ship embarkation was sailing out of New York City to Korea. This was the trip that was known as "The Milk Run." The ship was to sail through the Panama Canal with a port of call in Puerto Rico, another in Hawaii, then on to Japan, and the last port was Korea.

We were told that the trip would take thirty days. The Army packed the troop ship as they usually did, like sardines, down in the bottom of the ship. The upper decks with cabins were for officers and civilian dependents. Some were going to join their husbands in the service and some were going to Japan.

The Army put a large group of soldiers from Puerto Rico aboard the ship and they were to disembark in their homeland. The Army was scheduled to pick up fresh troops from Puerto Rico who were, like the rest of us, destined for combat in Korea. There were a lot of non-commissioned officers aboard the ship, so I didn't have to worry about being singled out to be assigned a group of soldiers for a work detail aboard the ship.

I tried to keep a low profile. A sergeant friend of mine got stuck with forming a guard duty detail for security throughout the ship, including guarding the officers and civilian decks. They were to keep the enlisted soldiers from going up to the officers and civilian decks.

I was down in the bottom of the ship with the rest of them. I was lucky, in a way. I got a canvas cot second from the bottom. The cots were stacked five high. Trying to sleep wasn't easy. The lights in the compartments would be dimmed down at night and this was just enough for all the poker games and dice gambling games to go on all night.

Everyone was standing in line in the morning. There was a line of soldiers behind each wash basin to brush our teeth and shave, and a line to take a shower. Even to use the toilet, soldiers had to line up behind each commode. It sure was hard to use the toilet with fifty guys staring at you and their eyes telling you to "S_ _t or get off the pot."

After breakfast and clean up of the quarters, we were all sent up on the upper, open deck. There were troops sitting where they could, gambling was going on everywhere. I was no newcomer to troop ships, so I came up with a good system for getting ahead of the chow line. At every meal the line of soldiers would be so long that by the time people got to the galley to eat breakfast, troops were already lining up for dinner. So I took up with three soldiers of lower rank than I was, and I told them that I could get them ahead of the chow line at every meal if they would just follow me and go along with my system.

In my duffel bag I had a clipboard with a tablet on it. So I got out the clipboard and wrote in big letters, "Ship's Fan Tail Detail." The rear of the ship is where they throw the garbage over. I printed each of the three soldier's names as being on the detail. I learned that in the Army, when you see an officer or a sergeant walking around carrying a clipboard, the first thing a soldier would think was, "This person carrying a clipboard is either making an important inspection or he's taking names for some dirty detail." Most soldiers would stay out of the way of a person with a clipboard.

In the Army everyone hated a line bucker, and bucking a chow line is a good way to get your head knocked off. So we made a plan that we would all meet at a certain place on the ship, and then I would put them ahead of me. As we would go walking past the chow line I would keep saying so that all could hear me, "Make way, please. Ship's detail coming through. These three soldiers are on detail and have to get ahead of the line."

It worked like a charm. What was funny was that even other sergeants who outranked me didn't know they were being tricked by allowing us to buck the chow line. Most of the sergeants would step off to the side and say to my detail, "Go right ahead, Sergeant." I would hold my clipboard out in front of me to make sure the soldiers could see the big letters, "DETAIL."

The soldiers in the chow line wouldn't say anything for fear that they would be put on detail.

After bucking the chow line at each meal most of the soldiers got so used to seeing my men and me on the ship's detail coming to buck the chow line that I didn't have to say anything. The other soldiers in line would say, "Here comes that sergeant with his detail," and they would automatically move over to let us pass.

The chow line for the enlisted men's mess hall would take us past the officers and civilians' dining room. We could look in the porthole and see white tablecloths on each table that would seat six officers at a table eating from plates with waiters to serve them. They were given menus to order from. They weren't eating the same food the enlisted men were being served. The troops were eating out of metal trays.

The days passed and the weather got bad. There were a lot of seasick soldiers with their heads hanging over the rails throwing up, including me. I'll never forget the experience of being seasick and hanging my head over the side, then having the wind blow the vomit of someone on a higher deck right in my face. A lot of times there was vomit on the steps going down to our sleeping quarters.

As the ship got closer to the Panama Canal the sea got calmer and the sun got hotter. A lot of the soldiers took their shirts off to get a suntan. I found a clear spot on the deck where I could lie down on the deck with my shirt off. I put the shirt under me and fell asleep. The sun was nice and warm. I must have slept for about three hours.

The ship's loudspeaker woke me up. They were warning that all soldiers who took their shirts off and allowed themselves to get sunburned requiring treatment at the ship's first aid station would be facing a court martial. I looked at my arms. They were beet red and my back was on fire. I put my shirt back on. That night I really started to feel my arms and back burn. Wearing my shirt irritated the sunburn. The top of my arms and my back started to get blisters and I couldn't lie down on my canvas cot.

I sat up all night sitting on my pillow on the deck of the sleeping compartment. I had the company of all the soldiers who were gambling all night. One of the gamblers, who must have been an old country boy, gave me some bag balm cream to put on my sunburn. He told me his mother always made him carry bag balm in his duffel bag. It seemed to help some, but my burn was so warm the bag balm started crystallizing on my arms and back. After about four days the blisters started draining, and at times, I could peel the skin off my arms in big layers. When the blisters did start draining I could go to bed. Lying in the sun aboard ship was a hard learned lesson for me.

One day while I was sitting on the deck reading a book a sergeant friend I had served with while in Berlin, and who was the same sergeant who got stuck with setting up the security for the officers and civilians' deck, asked me if I would like to accompany him on his rounds. He said he would show me his office. I jumped at the invitation. He gave me a badge to wear showing that I was permitted to be walking on the deck with the officers and civilian dependents.

What I saw was that they had a lot of room on their deck. They had sun chairs. Some were in bathing suits tanning themselves with a cold drink in their hands. Some were playing games on the deck. They had a nice sitting room for reading and playing cards.

When we arrived at his office it was small but nice and had air conditioning. After we got to talking he said that he wanted to tell me something. He said that he had given it some thought, wondering whether telling me was a wise thing to do. But then he said that if what he was about to tell me had happened to him, he would be grateful if a friend told him. I didn't know what he was talking about, but then he told me the story. He said that he was on the same ship that brought my wife, Helga, to the United States. He knew my wife when he saw her. I had taken her into the camp to the movies and to the service club, but he had never met her personally.

He told me that on that ship he was one of the sergeants in charge of security of the officers and civilians' decks just as he was on this ship. He asked me if I would want to know from him what he had seen aboard that ship concerning my wife. I said, "Sure. Let's have it. I want to hear what you have to say." So he told me that my wife, Helga, had been seen going into and coming out of an officer's cabin and that sometimes she spent a lot of time in his cabin. He said they sat together on deck chairs close to one another. They even sat at the same table in the dining room and they were seen walking together on the deck in the evening.

He said that he hated telling me this about my new wife knowing that I was going into combat in Korea. Having this about my wife on my mind was not good, but he wanted to tell me now, because after we arrived in Korea we might not see each other again since we were going to Korea as replacements.

I thanked him for telling me what he had seen going on with my wife aboard the troop ship. I also told him that she had told me about the nice officer who gave her his name and new military address, which turned out to be a false address. I told him that when she told me about that officer I had my own picture in my mind about what had gone on aboard that ship. I told him that I wasn't the jealous type when it came to women. If a woman is going to cheat there's nothing a man can do about it, and then it's time to leave her.

After this conversation the sergeant said that he got to feed his detail of soldiers for security duty early in the enlisted men's mess galley, and that on his way out with his men, he had seen me coming to the front of the chow line with a work detail. He asked me, "What detail did they stick you with?" I told him that this was just between him and me, but that I was using the old Army clipboard trick and it was working. He though it was funny and said that I was using a good old military maneuver. My friend told me that anytime I wanted to get away from the rest of the troops for me to tell one of his security guards at the top of the stairs that I wanted to visit the sergeant in charge in his office. He said that he would be glad to have me come to shoot the bull with him any time. I thanked him for the invitation. As we were walking toward the stairs that led down to the deck where I came from we stood at the railing. We saw an Army captain and a good looking lady walk by looking at each other as if they were madly in love.

My friend told me that this was another one of the games of play when the mice are away. He told me, "The Captain is on his way to Korea, and the lady is going to Japan to join her husband who has duty there. Need I say more?" He said he knew enough dirt on many of the passengers that he could write a book. Before the trip was over I visited my friend many times when I felt that I needed more elbow room.

The ship's paper was printed every other day and was prepared by three or four enlisted soldiers. We received a copy of the ship's paper and that kept us up on the latest news and weather, the knots the ship was traveling at, the miles we had traveled, and the number of miles we had yet to go.

When the ship arrived in Puerto Rico, the soldiers from Puerto Rico got off the ship and new Puerto Rican soldiers got on the ship with their duffel bags. The ship stayed tied to the dock in Puerto Rico that evening and all night. That evening the Army let the ones who wanted to get off the ship go to the Post Exchange and beer hall that was inside the Army port area. Their orders were that no one was to leave the port area, and the ones who got off the ship had to sign out at the top of the gangway. We were to sign back in again when we came back aboard the ship. We were to be back that evening by eleven o'clock.

Well, the beer hall was crowded and a lot of the soldiers were getting drunk. How they ever got drunk on the low alcohol content beers they sold at the Army run clubs I'll never know. It's a good thing they weren't drinking German beer. It was about twelve to fourteen percent.

Before the evening was over there were soldiers staggering back to the ship and fights were breaking out between soldiers in the beer hall and those on the deck. At about ten o'clock that evening they had to close the beer hall. This angered the soldiers who were already drunk. A near revolt almost broke out. A company of military police from the port was called to the ship to get the soldiers aboard. All these soldiers were going to a war in Korea and they felt that they had nothing to lose by being defiant.

By midnight they had all the drunken soldiers aboard the ship. When we were about a day out from reaching Hawaii, they made an announcement over the ship's speaker system that the ship would be staying in Hawaii for two days, and that liberty would be given to all officers and the first three grades of non-commissioned officers. I was glad to hear that because that included me, but the announcement didn't go over very well with the lower enlisted rank. They started voicing their disapproval of having been left out of those permitted to go ashore in Hawaii. The open grumbling continued. All us who were looking forward to going ashore started going through our duffel bags to get out our summer dress uniforms. There was a pressing iron being passed around so that we could press our uniforms.

I teamed up with two other sergeants to go on liberty. We sure were looking forward to going ashore in Hawaii. The ship was to get into port early the next morning some time after breakfast. The weather was warm and sunny that day. Everyone wanted to be up on the deck to see the island as it came into view. At breakfast we were served oranges along with the S.O.S. which was beef and gravy over a piece of toasted bread.

By the time the ship was coming into the place to be docked, everyone on the troop ship was out on the deck. It was hard to find a place to stand. There was a crowd at the dock, and there was a stage set up on the dock with a welcome entertainment band and eight Hawaiian girls in grass skirts and flowers in their hair, barefoot and doing the Hawaiian hula dance.

The soldiers were like a pack of howling wolves as the bow of the ship was being docked and tied up, and the stern of the ship was coming into place to be tied up to the dock. Then someone in this crowd of soldiers threw an orange from the ship and made a direct hit on one of the dancing girl's head. She fell to the floor of the grandstand like a rock. The band stopped playing and the other girls left the grandstand. All the soldiers broke out in laughter when the orange hit the girl in the head. The ship's loud speakers ordered all military personnel to clear the deck and ordered everyone to go to their assigned compartments.

They kept repeating the order to clear the decks. After the decks were cleared, over the ship's speaker system they asked the person who had thrown the orange to report to the military control office. This was repeated for more than thirty minutes. When the guilty person did not turn himself in, they broadcasted over the speaker system that if anyone witnessed the person throwing the orange, that person should report to the military control office.

Two hours later the next announcement over the speaker system was that all liberty to shore was cancelled until the guilty person turned himself in. Well, no one admitted to throwing the orange. The enlisted men who were not going on liberty were happy that no one was going on liberty. They would make remarks about all us sergeants who had been pressing our uniforms to go on liberty. They would say things like, "Well Sarge, you can wear your nice pressed uniform on the front line in Korea." Everybody would laugh.

The officers and the civilians did get liberty to shore, so there we sat aboard a troop ship tied up to the port, and all the enlisted men could do was to stand at the ship's rail and look at workers working on the dock, or go to the other side of the ship and look at all the small tugboats and sailboats. After sitting for two days at the port in Hawaii we were out to sea again, and the morale of the soldiers aboard this troop ship was starting to go downhill, and not just because there had been no liberty in Hawaii.

The cause was the long trip, the rough seas, and the over-crowding. Everybody was starting to get on each other's nerves. Most of the gamblers had lost what money they had, and now, they couldn't even buy cigarettes for themselves. They went around bumming cigarettes from the ones who had them. The winning gamblers had their winnings locked up in the ship's safe that was used for those who had anything of value.

The long trip was also making the troops bored. Fights began breaking out. The non-commissioned officers were expected to break up the fights. We had to maintain discipline, and we would have to remind them that there was a lock-up brig in the bow of the ship. There were some who got out of hand and they were locked up in the ship's brig. When we were about half way from arriving in Japan, the food we were being served seemed to get worse. Some of the soldiers would only eat one meal a day. This made the mess line shorter to stand in for the chowhounds.

One evening the ship's newsletter was passed out to all the troops on the ship. When I read it I couldn't believe what they had written. The disgruntled enlisted men who were the editors of the ship's newsletter, which was about four or five pages long, had written two full pages blasting the negative things about this long trip, beginning with no liberty in Hawaii. They said it wasn't fair that the officers got to go ashore. Then they wrote about how the officers were traveling in luxury in their two and four-man cabins, plenty of room to move around on their decks, and lounging on their deck chairs while all the enlisted men were so crowded we couldn't even find a place to sit on the bare, hard steel deck.

The newsletter went on to say that the officers were eating in a nice dining room with tables with tablecloths, waiters to wait on them, and the officers weren't eating the same food the enlisted men were being served. The newsletter blasted everything about the trip. I sure was glad they didn't know anything about my clipboard maneuver to get ahead of the chow line, or I'm sure they would have printed that as well.

The ship's newsletter was the chaplain's responsibility. He was supposed to read and approve of the newsletter before it went to press and before it was distributed to the troops on the ship. I guess the chaplain was sleeping on this one. The newsletter could have incited a riot among the troops on the ship.

As soon as the newsletter came out and was passed out to the troops, an announcement came over the ship's speakers that all the newsletters were to be turned in to the ship's military office without delay. Any soldier caught with a newsletter would be subject to disciplinary action. Some of the soldiers who were reading the newsletter heard the announcement and dropped it over the side of the ship into the ocean. It was as if they had been holding something red hot in their hands.

About every hour this announcement came over the ship's speakers, "Turn in all of today's newsletters." I don't know what happened to the newsletter editors. I know that we never received another newsletter for the rest of the voyage. When our leaders wanted us to know anything from that point on they would inform us over the ship's loud speakers.

I could hear some of the soldiers who had read that last newsletter starting to grumble about what they had read and knew to be true. We were getting close to arriving in Japan to let all the civilians off. All of us soldiers were hoping they would let us go ashore. But I had already gotten the word through the grapevine that in no way were they going to let us go ashore. I had the feeling that they thought we couldn't be trusted. I also heard through the grapevine that the enlisted men of that newsletter were going to be court-martialed. I don't know whether any action was going to be taken against the chaplain.

As the ship got closer to Japan, and we could see the outline of the land, what stood out beautifully on the skyline was Mt. Fujiyama with its snow-capped peak. As always, when a ship is coming into a country's port, everybody is up on deck and leaning on the ship railings. In this case soldiers were everywhere on the deck. The ship came into the port of Yokohama. There was a big crowd on the dock. All that I saw were Americans. Everyone on the dock was waving to someone aboard the ship. The waving was for the civilians on our ship, mostly wives and children who were ready to join husbands and fathers in Japan.

I was thinking to myself, "I sure wish I could have duty in Japan." My friend who had the security on the deck with the officers invited me on that deck so I could get a good view of the gangway where people would disembark. I could look down and see everything. My friend told me to keep an eye out for that good looking lady who was more than just friendly with a captain aboard the ship. The captain was also standing at the ship's railing looking down at all the people on the dock.

When the unloading ramp was in place, Japanese dockworkers came aboard to help carry the baggage off the ship for those who were getting off. When the people started getting off, I saw the good looking lady fall into the arms of her captain husband who was standing at the end of the ramp.

When her baggage was loaded up into an Army staff car, and as her husband opened the rear door of the car for her, she turned around and gave a four-finger ripple wave and a wide smile to a captain on the ship. Of course everyone standing at the ship's railing waved back at her, including the captain.

We all knew who the smile and ripple-finger wave were really for. This dramatic scene we were all watching brought a flashback into my memory. This same thing had happened to me when I was standing at the dock waiting for my wife, Helga, and I also took her into my arms when she came down the gangway. I don't recall whether or not she waved at her lover, the man who had promised to get her mother from Germany to the United States. "Oh well," I thought, "There's a sucker born every day."

My sergeant friend came up to me smiling and said, "Well, Clark, does this bring back memories?" I said, "It sure does." I told my friend, "I'll bet the captain of this ship sure will be lonely now with no women to play with for the rest of the trip to Korea."

The ship stayed overnight at the port of Yokohama, Japan. That evening, standing on the deck with the rest of the troops, I struck up a conversation with a sergeant standing at the railing and staring at Mt. Fujiyama. I told him that I sure would like duty in Japan. The sergeant told me that he had spent two years in Japan, and that it was the best duty he had ever served, but now he was on his way to Korea. He also told me about a Japanese belief that if you look at Mt. Fujiyama on your departure from Japan, you are destined to return.

We stood there staring at the mountain and watching the sun go down behind it. We watched until dark and we couldn't see the mountain anymore. The sergeant told me not to forget to look at Mt. Fujiyama in the morning when the ship would leave port and head out for open seas. I told him, "I'll be there."

The next morning after breakfast I was up on the deck and the mountain was still there to be seen. As the ship left the dock, moved out of the harbor, and headed for open seas, I stared at the mountain and said to myself, "Mt. Fujiyama, if your powers are as I was told, I would love to return to Japan and feast my eyes upon your beauty again."

Now we were headed for Korea, "The Land of the Morning Calm," but with a war raging there I didn't think we would be getting much calm where most of us were going. During our trip from Japan to Korea they were announcing on the loudspeaker that this was the last chance for anyone who had a copy of the newsletter to turn it in or face a court martial.

During the trip from Japan to Korea the troops aboard the ship seemed to quiet down. I think it was now sinking in that a lot of us would be going into combat, and not everyone would be returning to see our homeland again. The ship finally arrived in Korean waters.

The day was hazy with rain and fog. The ship couldn't go into the port to dock because the Inchon port didn't have a dock for ships to come into, and tie up to, because of the tide drop at Inchon. There was a thirty-one or thirty-two foot drop tide every six hours. The Inchon channel had never been dredged. This made unloading troops difficult, so all ships had to drop anchor about three miles off the shore of Inchon. The ship had to be tied to a certain numbered floating buoy that the harbor master assigned to the ship by radio hours before the ship arrived in the channel of Inchon.

All the troops who boarded in New York had been on this ship twenty-nine days. We stayed aboard the ship that first night, and after breakfast we were all packed up and our duffel bags carried up and lined up on the open deck. Then everyone was put on details to clean the ship and sleeping compartments.

By the afternoon floating barges were towed by Army tugs out to the ship and placed and tied along the ship. Then Landing Craft Utility boats, LCUs, were brought out and they dropped down the front ramp even with the end of the barges. This enabled the troops to come down a ramp that was like steps with a railing to be lowered down from the side of the ship.

Troops were to go down the ramp from the ship with their duffel bags, step onto the floating barge, then onto an LCU boat which had room for two or three hundred soldiers and their baggage. All soldiers were accounted for when their names were called before leaving the ship. After the LCU was loaded, the ramp was lifted up and the LCU would back off clearing the loading barge. There would be another empty LCU boat standing by to take the place of the one leaving. Then the next LCU would load up with disembarking troops from the ship to take them ashore.

All this troop movement had to be done when the tide was high. The LCUs transported troops through the channel and unloaded the troops onto floating barges that were tied together and used as an unloading dock. The barges for unloading were tied up to the shore, and at the shore end of the barges was a walk-up ramp where there was a convoy of Army trucks to transport all of us to the places where we would be sent out for replacement.

As we were waiting to be loaded into trucks, I looked back at the harbor of Inchon and wondered how hard it must have been in 1950 when the Chinese and North Korean armies overran South Korea. Truman was sending American troops to Korea then to take back land for the South Koreans. I thought about General MacArthur's amphibious invasion of Inchon, and then, the taking back of the city of Seoul, Korea. We lost a lot of American soldiers taking back that land.

The ride in the trucks was rough because the roads were. All we could see were shacks, huts and rice paddies. After about a twenty-five minute drive we were taken to a small camp called, Ashcom. The buildings were Quonset hut barracks.

13

KOREA, THE FRONT LINE AND NO MAN'S LAND

Our stay at ASCOM was about three days. They took away all the clothing I came with and issued clothing that was being worn on the front line and in most of Korea. Since winter was on its way the clothing was warmer than what we came to Korea with. The clothing had been soaked and treated with DDT insecticide. This was to keep the lice and bugs off us for a while. We were issued a field-pack ammunition belt, rubber boots, and a mountain sleeping bag. The zipper had been taken off and the sleeping bag had also been treated with insecticide.

We were given a knife, fork and spoon, but no mess kit to eat out of. We were told after we left this camp it would be field rations out of a can from then on. We were given a can opener that soldiers called a P-38. Just about every soldier carried a P-38 around his neck on his dog tag chain. This little opener would be worth its weight in gold in the field.

The processing at this camp took about three days. We were told we would be receiving combat pay while on the front line. I had the Army send all my monthly pay, including my combat pay, home to a bank so my wife could live off it. I also had a $10,000 life insurance policy that the military would pay to my spouse if I were killed. At that time $10,000 was just about what a person would need for the down payment on a new house.

A soldier on the front line doesn't need money. He needs God's protection and good luck. After three days we were all given our new assignments as replacements for different infantry divisions who were already on the front line known as the 38th parallel. On the map of Korea this was the line that both the Americans and its allies, and the enemy, the North Koreans, agreed to stop carrying the fighting into an offensive, but to dig in and hold defensive positions. But the fighting would continue until the outcome of the talks between the Americans and the North Koreans at Panmunjom, Korea.

At this time in the war everyone was wishing for a peaceful settlement so the fighting and bloodshed would stop, and no one was wishing for an end to the fighting more than the soldiers on the front line. We were loaded aboard trucks and headed toward the front. The road was narrow, one dusty, bumpy road and nothing but abandoned rice paddies on both sides of the road.

The driver told us before we started that he would be driving in the middle of the road because there were land mines in some places on the side of the road that had been placed there when the enemy held all of South Korea. Not all of them had been found and disarmed. After leaving Seoul the roads were very narrow. When another military vehicle came from the other direction, each vehicle would almost come to a stop, and then pass each other with caution. Everyone in both vehicles would be holding his breath and praying that we didn't go up in a blast.

Now and then we could see what was left of a destroyed tank off the side of the road from the fighting that had taken place in this area. We rode a long way. Our first stop was an artillery company that had their big guns lined up, pointed toward the front, and sighted on the enemy's position. About eight of the soldiers in the truck got out. This was their new assignment. They were trained as artillery gunners.

We continued on up the road to a small unit of the Third Infantry Division. This is where the rest of us soldiers unloaded from the truck. We were given weapons and ammunition. I was issued a 45 caliber pistol and a carbine, 30 caliber, that can be fired semi-automatic or full automatic. I was given four 30-round magazines, called a Banana Magazine, for the carbine 30-caliber, and four magazines for the pistol.

We were told that we would not be going to the same company on the front line. We were going to be split up and sent to different companies. Only another sergeant, two privates, and I would be going to the same company. We had to wait for someone from the company on the line to come and guide us to the company.

From where we were we could hear small arms firing and mortar rounds exploding. When the guide came to get us we put our packs and sleeping bags on our backs and started walking toward the front line called the 38th parallel.

We walked up and down some of the most rugged hills and mountains that I have ever seen. We were huffing and puffing all the way. Sometimes we were up high, walking on the edges of the mountains, and looking down in the valley of rice paddies. There were mortar rounds hitting and exploding down in the valley. Our guide told us that those mortar rounds were gifts from the enemy's front lines and for us not to worry. He said that we were out of range. Then, in the same breath, he said if one did land on us we would never have to worry about anything again.

It was starting to get dark, and it was hard to see where we were stepping. We must have walked four miles up and down hills and mountains. The guide knew his way, so each of us just followed the man in front. Finally, after coming down from a steep hill, the guide told us the next big mountain was where the front line was. The sound of guns firing got louder. Then when we were almost to the top of that big mountain, we stopped. The guide pointed to a bunker that was dug out in the side of the hill facing away from the side of the mountain that was facing the enemy.

We could see the bunker had sandbags stacked up all around it. We were told that this was the command post where the company commander commanded the company from, and where his field office and quarters were. We all stayed outside while the guide went in and reported he had arrived with replacements. When he came out he said the company commander wanted to talk to the arriving sergeants first. So the other sergeant and I went into the bunker while the others waited outside.

The company commander was a captain. He started right in on what our mission was, to hold and defend the Third Infantry Division's position on the MLR, the Main Line of Resistance. He told us that there were no officers at the present in any of the platoons in the company, and if he had anything to say about it, he didn't want any young lieutenants being careless and taking risks and getting men killed.

He said that he had every confidence that his non-commissioned officers could do a good job of leading the men in the platoons of his company. He also told us that we never knew when a massive force from the enemy would attack us, and that we would just have to be alert and ready.

Then he assigned us to our duties at the front. I was given two squads of the heavy weapons platoon who were already in position. It was dark in the trenches when I arrived, so I didn't really get to scope out the whole situation and meet face to face with everyone in the platoon I was assigned to.

I was taken around to all the positions that were being manned in the trenches. At this time there were some enemy artillery rounds coming in on our position, but they seemed to be placing a heavier concentration further up the line of the trenches.

There was no lighting of any kind. Cigarette smoking was not allowed in the trenches at night except in the bunkers. There was a canvas cover over the door opening of the bunkers where they had been dug out. The walls of the bunkers were about six feet wide and six feet long with dirt floors. There were planks the size of railroad ties for sides, and overhead bracings were used. All bunkers, and at the top of the trenches were stacked sandbags. Since there was no sand, dirt was used in the sandbags. In the company, and in all the platoons and squads, we had South Korean soldiers. They were called KATUSA soldiers.

I had four Korean KATUSA soldiers under me. When daylight came, and I got to go out and meet each soldier in the company, I could see the fatigue and exhaustion in all the soldiers' bloodshot eyes. Some had been on the front line for months. One of them told me that after about three months on the line, a soldier gets the "just don't give a damn anymore" feeling.

As a newcomer on the line I could smell urine in some places in the trench. I was told where the slit trench was. This is where soldiers go to the toilet. It was on the slope of a hill behind the bunkers facing away from the enemy.

I was warned, "Don't get caught on the slit trench when the enemy's artillery starts coming in. They will catch you with your pants down." I asked, "Where do you go to the bathroom when the artillery rounds are coming in?" One soldier said, "In your pants." I was told, "You'll see and learn." There was a trench passageway leading to the slit trench toilet from the main trench. One thing I learned was in the Army a soldier should always have on his person toilet paper when out in the field.

At the time I was being shown around, we were receiving small arms fire with bullets kicking up dirt around the top of our trenches coming from the enemy's positions on top of their mountain. They had our range. I was shown where the field rations and the ammunitions were stored in bunkers behind our trench in the same direction as the slit toilet.

The sergeant who was telling me what to expect said, "Being up on the front line is like being sentenced to death. Each day you'll wonder if this is going to be your death day. Only here, you might get a chance to fight back."

After my first daylight time on the front line, and as dark was closing in, the small arms shooting onto our positions stopped, and I was led up on top of our defensive trenches by the same sergeant. We crouched and sometimes moved on our bellies to conceal ourselves behind sandbags. With field glasses I could see strands of barbed wire out in front of our positions. The general locations of land mines and the approximate locations of booby traps that had been put in place by our side were pointed out to me.

The foxhole out in front of our defensive position was about seventy-five yards away. I was told that this foxhole was what is known as the LP, Listening

Post. Each night one or two of our men were to man this foxhole after dark and all night. They were to give advance warning to the main line of resistance of an approaching enemy.

The soldier manning this LP was to have with him a sound-powered field telephone to call and give advance warning of approaching enemy, and after giving the warning he was to get back to the MLR as fast as he could. I was told that some don't make it back. They are killed or taken prisoner by the enemy. The route that should be taken when leading a patrol at night down in the valley that's called, No Man's Land, was shown to me. It was nothing but old rice paddies filled with dirty water. All this land was between the enemy's position and ours.

I got to know the soldiers under me and their positions. I remembered having been told by old soldiers in the past, "In combat don't make friends. Make acquaintances because if they get killed it won't be the hard trauma of losing a soldier you're serving with."

It was up to me to keep a schedule of who should be on guard duty at different positions in the trench, and who should, and at what time, be manning the machine guns in the bunkers. Each soldier pulled two hours of guard duty and four hours off. This included me. During the daylight hours all soldiers who weren't on guard duty would clean their weapons and dig and fill sandbags with dirt to repair the trenches. If the enemy's artillery made a direct hit and caved in the walls of the trench, some of the trench would be unrecognizable.

All of this repair work could only be done when the enemy was not shooting big shells at us during the day. We always received small arms fire. Sometimes we would take a stick, put a steel helmet on the end of it, and hold it up in the air to give them something to shoot at. Sometimes they got lucky and hit it.

We always had an extra helmet around from someone who had been killed or wounded. Just about every night the enemy would pound our position with heavy guns until the ground would tremble. Sometimes they would stop and broadcast over loud speakers that could be heard all over the valley of No Man's Land. The things they would broadcast were nothing but blatant propaganda. Speaking in good English they asked us to lay down our arms and come over to their side. They said that fighting was useless, and if we came over to their side, they would give us food and treat us well.

All of us in the trenches got a big kick out of all the things they were going to give us if we would just lay down our weapons. After the talking a female would talk to us in good English and play us Korean love songs. This would go on for about an hour, but when the music stopped, we all learned to brace ourselves because then the North Koreans would hit us with artillery and mortar fire all night. Nights seemed endless. Being in the trenches was not a safe haven. A lot of times their artillery or mortar rounds would make a direct hit on our trenches. This would cause a number of casualties and wounded.

We had sound-power phones in some of the bunkers that were connected to the company commander's command post. The first thing, when daylight would arrive and the enemy's artillery bombardment fire would stop or slow down, each of us section sergeants had to give a report of our dead and wounded to the command post so they could request replacements.

I learned to have respect and admiration for the men of the medical corps. They were right there after men got hit with fragments. They didn't worry about their own safety. They treated the wounded or evacuated them on stretchers. An all night shelling by the enemy is something a soldier never gets used to. It leaves a man's nerves on edge. When the enemy's artillery is coming in, soldiers on duty at lookout posts in the trench would have to stay at their posts and watch for a front line attack from the enemy, which could come at any time.

North Koreans, mixed with Chinese, send their soldiers out to attack under their own artillery fire. Their casualty rate was high, but they didn't seem to care how many of their soldiers died. We could always tell when things weren't going well at the Peace Talks at Panmunjom. The enemy would hit us hard with big artillery guns and send in an attacking probing force on our positions. When the enemy was assembling for a frontal attack, and we suspected an attack, we put on a 100% alert. Our spotter plane or our forward observer would let us know what the enemy was up to, and even that wasn't with 100% accuracy.

In bad weather we had to be ready for anything. The enemy's favorite time to attack was at two or three o'clock in the morning. They would take advantage of the darkness, and they knew this was the most vulnerable time for a soldier on watch. He would be at his sleepiest.

The times when we thought there wasn't going to be a frontal attack on our positions from the enemy, the soldiers who weren't on watch were in bunkers trying to get some sleep, crowded together on the ground in their sleeping bags. I was told by ones who had been on the front line awhile the reason why the zippers on the sleeping bag were taken off.

About two months before I arrived the enemy got in the trenches without anybody knowing. They cut the throats of the half-asleep trench guards, got to the openings of the bunkers, and catching men in the bunkers zipped up sleeping bags, shot them. Those who tried to get out of their sleeping bags were bayoneted before they could get out.

This happened to one of the platoons of another company on the front line. Incidents like this reached the ears of all the soldiers on the front line, and that's when the order was given that all zippers on sleeping bags were to be taken off.

The main events that would take place when things were a little quiet during the day were digging and filling of sandbags to better our trenches and repair the damage the enemy's artillery shelling had caused. The other event during the day was visiting with other soldiers within the company and trading field rations. The field rations came in different varieties, like cans of spaghetti, wieners and beans, chicken stew, corned beef hash and others.

My favorite was chicken stew until I found feathers in the stew. From then on I stayed with spaghetti. We had a small Coleman one-can burner that we passed around to heat up our cans on, or we could eat the contents of the can cold. The soldiers in the armored tank units attached to us heated their cans of rations by putting the cans on their tank engine exhaust manifold. Since we weren't allowed to have any fires, this was the best we could do. When we had a chance to shave we washed and shaved from our steel helmets with cold water. After about three weeks on the front line, I was starting to smell like those who had been in the trenches for months. I knew I was starting to get body lice. I was starting to scratch and I could feel them digging in. One soldier told me, "Just wait until you get the crabs. Then you'll be a full fledged member of us trench rats."

I was also told that sometimes Korean rats got in the trenches and in the bunkers looking for food. Also, the rats' fleas carry a deadly sickness they call, "Hemorrhagic Fever." It is a particularly dreadful, fatal disease which causes bleeding from the skin and eyeballs. This is caused by the fleas from the trench rats.

When it would rain the trenches got muddy, but it could have been worse. The soil was like slate rock. This was in our favor except when it came to digging, which we did every day.

I was on the front line when President Truman broke up black soldiers' units and Puerto Rican soldiers' units and integrated those soldiers into all white companies on the front line. Two blacks and two Puerto Ricans, and two more Korean soldiers were assigned to my section. The only thing I found hard was that one of the Puerto Ricans couldn't speak English or understand English. That didn't bother me because I had some Korean soldiers in my unit who couldn't speak English either.

I did notice that there was some rebellion coming from one of the new men. At first I overlooked it because I could understand his situation. I knew it would take them time to adjust to being in our company. After they got to know everyone, and when they knew that we were all in this war together, they would realize that the only enemies we had were those out in front of our position, the North Koreans and their Chinese advisors.

One day I had just made out a new schedule of who was to be sent out to the foxhole in front of the MLR to man the Listening Post. I took the schedule around for each man to see. I had my name on the list to show that I would take my turn out on the LP.

Since I was in charge I didn't have to go out on the LP. I could just stay and supervise, but since I had an assistant who would take my place in the trench, I was free to take a turn out on the LP. One of the rules I made for myself from the day I was made a non-commissioned officer and had soldiers under me, was that I would never ask or assign a soldier to do something that I wouldn't do myself, or something I had not already done.

One evening, just before dark, I went around showing the men in my section the LP schedule. The new soldiers who came from the 65th infantry regiment of the Third Division, the two black soldiers and the two new Puerto Rican soldiers, were shown the new schedule. I wanted them to understand their names and the times they were to man the LP. When there were no questions, I turned and walked away. Since it was starting to get dark and the enemy snipers didn't have enough light to get a good shot at our positions, their artillery hadn't started shooting at us.

I climbed over the top of the trench and started walking toward the company commander's bunker to turn in a copy of the LP schedule. I got about half way when a rifle was fired behind me and a bullet went whizzing by my ear. Right away I knew by the sound of the rifle shot that it came from our trench.

I went right back to the trench. When I got back in the trench, one of my men who was standing watch pointed to one of the bunkers. I went in and took each soldier's rifle, and after checking the rifles over, I found the one that had been fired. It belonged to one of the soldiers who couldn't speak English. When I confronted him about taking a shot at me of course he denied that he had.

I let him know that I could have him court-martialed, but if I did, that would take him off the front line and out of combat. I wanted him right there with me. I told him, "You missed my back. Now it's my turn. But I won't shoot you in the back. Just keep your eyes open."

I made sure from that time on that that soldier was always out in front of me, and when we would go on ambush patrols he would be my point man. That way he could let us know where the enemy's booby-traps and land mines were. When we were out on patrol in No Man's Land we never knew when we would be ambushed by the enemy. The point man's life is short lived, but somebody's got to do it.

The two South Korean KATUSA soldiers had been on the front line fighting the North Koreans for a long time. I had respect for their advice about what they thought the enemy was up to and when they thought the next attack was coming.

I will never forget the night when one of them was killed in front of me. That night some of us were looking over a map of No Man's Land planning for our next ambush patrol. We went into one of the machine gun bunkers where there was a small second room that had a wall separating it from the machine gun opening. We could light a candle without any light showing from the bunker. At that time one of the KATUSA soldiers was standing watch as the machine gunner. He had an ammo box to stand on to reach the gun. He was short. We weren't in the bunker long before the Korean soldier said, "Sargey," that's what the Korean soldiers called me, "They will be coming soon."

I came out from behind the wall to ask him how he knew this. He got in a good position behind the machine gun ready to fire. His next words to me were, "I can smell them," and in the next second a mortar round exploded right outside the front of the bunker where the opening was for the machine gunner to get a good field of fire. The explosion hit the Korean soldier right in the face. His head and blood splattered all over the bunker and he hit the floor of the bunker like a rock falling. I was knocked down by the explosion but not hurt. I had blood on me from the dead soldier, and his brains and head parts splattered and stuck to the flak vest I was wearing. The body was pushed out of the way, and the machine gun that had been blown off its tripod. Another machine gun was put in place and another soldier took over as gunner.

All soldiers in the trenches, bunkers, and at the command post were alerted that an attack might be imminent. From what the Korean soldier told me a 100% alert was called. The soldiers in the trench wanted to fix bayonets on their rifles and most said a prayer.

Our armor tanks moved up closer and right above our trench with their big guns pointed toward the enemy's mountain and down into No Man's Land. Parachute flares were fired in the air from our side to light up the valley below us. We could see about a company size number of North Koreans in quilted uniforms, armed with burp guns, and some with rifles, trying to cut a path through our strands of barbed wire.

As soon as the flares lit up the area all hell broke loose. Our big guns from the tanks started firing, and our machine guns opened up, and all of us in the trench laid down rifle fire on the advancing enemy. We could see they were taking a big loss in soldiers, but they just kept coming. The ones who got through the barbed wire and the booby-traps charged, shooting as they came, and throwing potato-masher grenades. None of them got in our trench, but they got close, and they were shooting in rapid succession.

Our soldiers in the trench were firing, and the tank firing was so heavy that you would wonder how a mouse could get through the rain of bullets and the hand grenades exploding. These enemy soldiers in quilted uniforms acted as if they were on dope and didn't care whether they lived or died. We heard a bugle being blown from the bottom of No Man's Land.

At the sound of the bugle the ones who were left retreated, dragging their dead and wounded. We didn't let up our firing and killing. This was war and the object was to let the enemy know that we were ready. This was my first big up-close engagement with the enemy. I had no problem with shooting to kill these soldiers in quilted uniforms. This was what the Army had long and hard trained me to do, to kill.

So I was more than ready. It was like all combat soldiers say, "It's them or us who die in war." Attacks from the enemy are uncertain, and when you're fighting for your life everybody is capable of brutality. It was a horrifying feeling during the attack by the enemy. We took care of our casualties. The medical corpsmen were right there taking care of the wounded. The wounded were letting out feeble groans and blood was all over. The Korean soldier who was my machine gunner and had warned us all that the enemy was coming because he could smell them was dead.

The medical men took the Korean soldier's body out of the bunker in a body bag while all the soldiers were getting their senses and emotions back in control from the attack. Other soldiers and I were splattered with blood and flesh parts from the wounded. I took a shovel and a burlap bag and went into the machine gun bunker and shoveled up parts of the brains and head of the Korean soldier who had told me they were coming.

I threw the burlap bag over the embankment of our trench. I remember going back in the bunker and sitting on the ground with my back to the wall. In my mind I was picturing that KATUSA soldier standing on that ammo box so he could reach the machine gun, and I could hear his last words to me. I always got a kick out of the Korean soldiers addressing me as "Sargey" because they couldn't get the English word out, "Sergeant." I sat there and said a small prayer for the KATUSA soldier and I thanked him for his advance warning. He saved a lot of lives.

The soldier who was now on duty behind the machine gun saw me sitting there in quietness. The soldier asked me, "What's wrong, Sergeant?" I said, "Nothing. Everything's just fine. Let's be ready if they decide to attack again." And I left the bunker. Everyone was getting ready in case another encounter and clash with the enemy was to come.

That evening the North Koreans hit us hard with their big artillery guns, and our own artillery was doing the same to their positions. There was one thing I learned quickly in war. I could take small arms fights with the enemy knowing that the enemy is aiming his rifle or burp gun at you. His bullet has your name on it, and it's up to you to take cover from that bullet. But when those big artillery shells and mortar shells are coming in at you, and they explode in thousands of big and little pieces, and they leave craters in the ground where you might have been standing, those shells have no one individual's name on them. What they do have is, "To Whom It May Concern."

They reach out in a big area, and the concussion from the blast can take your head or your limbs off. The enemy had what we called "air burst shells." They would explode in the air right over our positions, and the exploding metal would spray downward like an umbrella. Then there were the white phosphorus shells that would explode over our position. When a piece of that hits a person it burns a hole right through wherever it lands on you.

When I was home on leave at my mother's house she gave me a small King James Bible that fit in my shirt pocket. It had a metal cover on the front. I carried that Bible with me and I read it every chance I got. I even had soldiers ask me if they could read my Bible when I wasn't reading it. One thing I can say is I never met a soldier on the front line who would say he didn't believe in God. As I would walk down the trench checking soldiers at their posts, I would see some sitting, waiting, hoping, day-dreaming, and others would be praying.

During the day when soldiers wanted to talk, the conversation was mostly about the stalemate we were living in, and all the while, taking a beating and pounding from the enemy's artillery. Being in this position day after day, the enemy knew exactly the range of our position for their big guns and they could hit us with alarming precision.

All the soldiers would say that they would rather be on the offensive, attacking the enemy, and moving forward. There was a lot of talk about their disappointment that President Truman had relieved General MacArthur of his command of the troops in Korea in 1951 for insubordination. If MacArthur had still been in command of American soldiers, we would be moving forward and attacking the enemy. In my opinion, and a lot of the other soldiers in the trenches agreed, General MacArthur was an outstanding military leader and a brilliant strategic military genius. This might not be others' opinion, but it's mine.

Because of the way things were at this time, morale was low. We had little information in general about what was happening in the world, and even less about what was going on at the Panmunjom negotiations for a ceasefire. These talks were going to determine whether the war in Korea was going to continue or not. The talks had been going on for a long time. In the meantime, the enemy's big guns pounded us.

The only news we got about what was going on in the world around us came in the form of rumors that came down the trenches from one soldier to the next soldier. I heard one story from the soldiers from the country of Turkey who were also up on the front line with us and on the right flank of us in the trenches. The Turks were good fighters. I heard that when they took a North Korean soldier or a Chinese prisoner, and put that soldier under interrogation, if the Turks didn't get the information they wanted from the enemy soldier, the Turks would beat him with a 2 X 4 wrapped in barbed wire.

Another rumor that reached us was that Turks had cut off the heads of enemy soldiers, put the heads on sticks, and anchored the sticks with the heads on them out in front of their trenches facing the enemy position. It was said that one of our American chaplains went over to the Turks' position and asked them if they would, please, take the heads down from the sticks and bury them. The Turks didn't like having an American telling them what to do, so they ran the chaplain off.

One night, when things on the front line were quiet, I was sitting up in one of the bunkers with my back to the wall with five or six soldiers who were trying to get a little sleep before going on night watch. We were packed in this small bunker like sardines in a can. As I sat there trying to doze off with my loaded carbine on my lap, I put my head back against the wall where I was looking up, trying to doze off, when I noticed something in the ceiling rafters moving. I could see that it was a big trench rat that was looking for food.

I don't know how he got up on the ceiling rafters, but I knew that I didn't want that rat in the bunker. So I took aim with my carbine and with half a thirty-round magazine, I blasted that rat. I never saw sleeping soldiers move so fast. They all jumped up at the same time with their rifles in their hands, and they all tried to get out of the bunker opening at the same time. They thought the enemy was in the trench. The soldiers standing watch in the trench didn't know what was wrong with all these guys coming out of the bunker as they did.

When they got out of the bunker and saw that everything was okay in the trenches, they started asking each other, "Who the hell was firing in the bunker? At about this time I came out of the bunker holding the big, shot-up rat by its tail. One of the soldiers said, "Damn you, Sergeant. You scared the hell out of us. We thought the enemy was in the trench."

I said, "Well, I'm glad to see you're all on your toes even when you're sleeping." At this I got a smile out of some of them, "And anyway," I said, "This Korean rat was just about to jump down from the rafters looking for food." They all went back into the bunker telling me that the next time I was going to shoot a rat inside the bunker to let them know. I said, "Okay guys, I'll do that." After this incident I noticed that when a soldier came into the bunker he would look up towards the rafters in the ceiling looking for rats.

Each time a soldier was sent out to the LP in front of the MLR at night, none of us was sure if we would ever see that soldier again. When it came my turn to man the foxhole for two hours I took hand grenades and flares. These were not to be used unless we were sure that the enemy was approaching and there was no way to escape. We were not to make contact with the enemy. Our mission was to give advance warning to the MLR of an approaching enemy, either by the sound-power phone that we took with us, or to get back to the MLR quickly without being detected by the enemy.

I was told that if the foxhole had water in it from the rain that I should lie flat on the ground behind a stack of sandbags. Everyone on the line was alerted that a man would be sent out front so they wouldn't fire their weapons at me.

I went up and over the trench and took the route they told me to so that I wouldn't get caught up in the barbed wire or set off any booby traps. I was lucky in a way. It was a clear night and the enemy's artillery hadn't started yet. But our big artillery was hitting the enemy's position. I could hear our big shells cracking through the air headed toward the enemy's position.

I worked my way out to the LP foxhole on my belly, hands and knees at a slow pace stopping now and then to listen for any sounds of the enemy. I would be in a hell of a fix if I came across one of the enemy patrols that they send out into No Man's Land to kill any United Nations troops which I was a part of. Was I afraid? Yes, but I didn't let myself dwell on it. I just told myself that this was the same LP post that I had sent soldiers under me out to.

So now it was my turn. All I could do was to ask God to give me the will and the strength to do my duty just like the other soldiers. I made it out to the LP foxhole and found that the foxhole had a foot of water in it. So I just lay down behind some sandbags and positioned myself where I could see out in front of me. I couldn't see very far because it was getting dark as the night closed in.

I hooked up the field phone that I had brought with me. The wires for the phone were on the ground, and the end of the wire for the phone was hanging down into the foxhole. I pulled them up and attached them to the phone hoping they would work and stay in contact with the front line trench. They were waiting for my call. I turned the crank on the side of the phone about five or ten turns and made contact with the person on the other side.

I reported that I had made it out to the LP and everything seemed quiet. The ground was wet and cold and so was I. But that was another thing I didn't dwell on. I just lay there and listened for any sound and strained my eyes to see if anything was moving out in front of me or off to the side.

The LP foxhole was still on the hillside. What brush Korea had was on the hills and mountains. The brush was mostly like our sagebrush. As I strained my eyes, after about an hour the brush seemed to be moving, or I could see someone behind the brush. This was my imagination playing tricks on me.

After about two hours of lying on the ground, wet and cold, I received a call on the field phone telling me to withdraw from the LP and high-tail it back to the MLR, and that a 100% alert had been called down from headquarters. That meant the enemy was getting ready for another attack. One thing I knew for sure was I damn sure didn't want to get caught out there in No Man's Land all by myself when the enemy came this way for the attack.

It didn't take me long to get back to the trench. I went back on the run. I was lucky because the enemy's artillery hadn't started yet. When I got back everybody in the trench was ready with fixed bayonets and they had scrambled into positions. Soldiers had been alerted that I would be coming up from the forward LP. Orders had been given not to shoot.

As I was coming up the hill to get into the trench I was hoping and praying that none of our soldiers had a nervous trigger finger. When I got back I was informed that reports had been coming in that the enemy was attacking our MLR just two miles from us, and they were attacking in a large force. Our headquarters was expecting a large attack on our position. About a half hour after I got back in the trench, the enemy started pounding us with their big guns.

14

FROM THE TRENCHES IN KOREA TO SENDAI, JAPAN

Everyone was standing at his post in the trenches and we were starting to receive incoming shells from the enemy. As the minutes passed the bombardment on our position got heavier. The ground trembled beneath our feet and black smoke rose in the air. The suffocating smell of sulfur from exploding shells burned our nostrils and was overwhelming. Exploding incendiary bombs were falling over our trenches.

I could hear soldiers up and down the trench yelling, "I'm hit." They had been hit by shrapnel from exploding shells. The brave medic corpsmen were running in the trenches to treat the wounded giving them morphine to ease the pain and carrying the wounded out on stretchers. They would take some wounded into the bunkers to give them first aid.

We could hear the enemy attacking a company on our left flank. We knew that at any time they would be attacking our position. We just had to wait. It seemed like an eternity. At three in the morning the enemy troops had not attacked our position. The shelling from the enemy lightened up. By daybreak they stopped shelling. Rumors came down through the trenches that one of the companies on our far left flank got hit hard and had suffered a lot of casualties. We knew we were lucky, except for our casualties. At daybreak the enemy withdrew and we could say our prayers to ourselves. Thoughts ran through my mind during the enemy's shelling of our position. I thought we were all going to die at any time. But a soldier should never give up hope, and in this situation, it is, "Do battle when it comes and stay alive."

At full daylight we had the job of repairing our trenches from all the bombardment. One of the sergeants asked me if I had seen the graveyard. I said I hadn't. He said, "Follow me." As we went through the trench leading to our company's ammunition storage bunker, there was a big pile of skulls and bones.

He told me that all these skeletons came from the digging of the trenches. In Korea the dead are buried on high ground. They have done this for centuries, and the place where we had dug our trenches had been a graveyard. The soldiers who dug our trenches had brought the bones to this spot and put them in a pile so that maybe some day the bones could be put back in the ground.

Winter had started closing in on us. It was starting to get cold when our division commander couldn't stand the way his company's soldiers smelled. So one company at a time was relieved from the trenches on the MLR.

We hiked about two miles to the rear towards a road where there were trucks waiting to take us to shower tents set up about ten miles from the MLR. We were told that we would be given a five-day rest from the trenches. The shower tents were big tents that had big hot water tanks suspended from the top of the tents. The floors were plywood. Before we went into the showers, we were sprayed with an insecticide to kill the lice and crabs that all of us had. We had to step into a pan of a chemical to cure athlete's foot. We were given clean and insecticide treated clothing. This time it was heavier clothing because the weather was getting colder. After the showers we were feeling good.

We got back on the waiting trucks. After being driven a short distance we were unloaded to a place that looked like a tent city. This was where we were to spend five days of eating hot meals and getting some good sleep and rest on canvas cots. We were told that each of us would be given three cans of beer each day. After hearing that the beer drinkers started being buddies with the ones who didn't drink beer.

The company commander told some of us sergeants that while we were there at the rest camp, the company would be joined by four or five young O.C.S. 2nd lieutenants. I thought to myself, "What a burden the military has put on the backs of the sergeants." The company commander told us that he had held off for as long as he could by not having young lieutenants in his company. But division headquarters had sent him lieutenants and he wanted us to be patient while they learned about war. We were also told that headquarters sent word down that if our company should ever have to withdraw from the MLR, it would be called, "retrograde movement," and not retreat.

At the rest camp I learned that a million dollar wound was a broken bone. This was enough to get a soldier evacuated out of Korea and sent to a hospital in Japan. They told us that bones just didn't heal that well in Korea. When the soldiers heard that,everyone was wishing for a broken bone instead of having parts of one's body torn away by shrapnel, and that would be better than being carried out in a body bag. Everyone was hoping for a broken bone. When our five-day rest time was over, my company was moved back on the front line.

We relieved the company that had relieved us. They said they had had only one small probing attack on the position, but lots of shelling. The day we got back I showed the new lieutenant around the positions that I was responsible for, including the machine gun bunkers and emplacements for the mortars. My assistant went with us around to the positions. The lieutenant wanted to inspect the machine guns for cleanliness. I had to tell him that they were loaded, manned, and ready to go at any moment, and that he could take my word for it that they were clean and ready.

He didn't like this, so he started nit-picking. He saw that we had open boxes of ammunition and hand grenades at each post. My assistant and I couldn't believe what we were hearing. Before I could say anything the soldier behind the machine gun spoke up and said, "We've never had an enemy complain yet about getting blown up by a grenade with rust on it." My assistant and I just had to smile at that one.

I had to explain to the lieutenant that we did clean and oil the machines guns one at a time during the day when things were quiet and we weren't expecting an attack. The oiling of the ammunition, I explained to him, we didn't do because dirt would stick to the ammunition and then jam the chamber of the gun. I told him that we do keep our ammunition clean from dirt. I guess he was satisfied with that, so he went up the trench looking for something else to complain about. During this time in the Korean War, and also when I was soldiering in Berlin, I never heard of or saw marijuana or of any American soldier being on dope.

We didn't have women in our ranks, and it was a good thing we didn't. Most of the soldiers had been in the trenches for a long time without seeing a woman and they were hard up. If there had been any women in the trench, I'm sure there would have been a lot of hustle and restlessness among the soldiers in the trench.

During the time the enemy's artillery came in on our positions all night, and soldiers couldn't get to the slip trenches where we were supposed to relieve ourselves, it was nothing to see a soldier in the trench or in a bunk squatting over a small field ration box relieving himself with the other soldiers sitting around the bunker holding their noses from the smell. Then the soldier would throw the field ration box over the embankment of the trench hoping the attacking enemy would step in it just before we shot them.

After the new lieutenant made his rounds talking with each soldier in the trench, he came to me and asked me what I thought about taking enemy prisoners for interrogation when the opportunity arose. I told him I'd never seen one who wanted to surrender. The lieutenant told me that everyone he had asked had said, "Hell no. We don't take prisoners. We shoot them. If it wasn't for those S.O.B.s wanting to fight, we wouldn't be here."

I told the lieutenant that most of the soldiers on the front line had seen atrocities or had heard what the enemy had done to American soldiers who were taken prisoners by the North Koreans. Their hands were tied behind their backs and they were shot execution style.

After the first evening, back on the line and with night falling, the enemy's concentrations of artillery shells started in on our positions. I could see the new lieutenant in a crouching position with no place to hide. He was in the trenches with all of us. Our own artillery was firing back at the enemy with their 155 howitzers. Our tanks above our trench were firing their big guns.

The next day when things quieted down we were told that it was our company's turn to send out an ambush patrol of fifteen men to venture out into No Man's Land. After dark we were to take up a position where we thought the enemy might be sending out their patrols.

The K-9 dog, with his handler, came down to our trench to accompany us on the patrol. The K-9 dog was a German police dog. I could see the dog had white tape down the center of his ears. I was told that when it's dark the handler can see the white tape and can tell whether the dog is on the alert and knows that something is out in front of our patrol. That's when the German Shepherd's ears come straight up and move forward. We were also told that should the dog get killed or wounded, we were to make sure we brought the dog back. I don't know if this was because the Koreans eat dogs.

We ventured out. There was a certain route that we had to take from the MLR so we wouldn't walk on any booby traps. Our two point men had infrared scope devices mounted on their rifles, so we would stop now and then to scan what might be hiding in front of us. The infrared scope would allow us to see shadows in the dark. We would be crouching and crawling along on the ground to where we wanted to set up our ambush, making our way in the dark using military skill, just moving at short distances, then stopping and listening and searching the area in front of us with the infrared scope.

When we could see the area was clear, and after analyzing our best next move, we would advance again, creeping and sneaking forward. We were close to the bottom of the enemy's mountain. We were now on flat land which was an abandoned rice paddy field. Each one of us had foul smelling water and human waste the Koreans used for fertilizer on our clothes and in our boots.

We set up our position just at the edge of the rice paddies. It was cold and the paddies were starting to get a thin coat of ice on them. We could see about fifty yards in front of the outline of the land when lying on the ground. As we lay on the ground and listened for sound, I thought how lucky we had been to get this far without running into an enemy ambush ourselves, or walking into a full company of the enemy in preparation for an attack on our MLR. That would have been a terrifying encounter. We would never have made it back to our lines. We were lucky. After lying there for about an hour, the K-9 handler said in a low voice that the dog was showing signs of hearing something in the direction of the enemy's position.

We all trained our ears for sounds then. Our soldiers, using the infrared scope, spotted shadow figures of armed enemy soldiers walking slowly on the upper ridge of the rice paddies. We all got in a good firing position. We had no way of knowing whether it was point soldiers for an advancing company or a point for an enemy patrol. We knew we couldn't make a move. We had a radio that was carried on one of our soldier's back, so we had communications with the command post on the MLR.

We kept them informed of the situation. The command wanted to know if we wanted mortar fire placed at the bottom of the enemy's positions. We said, "Not yet." We wanted to see if there were any more enemy soldiers following the eight soldiers who were walking toward our left flank.

The order was given to hold our fire until the order was given to shoot to kill. As the enemy got closer, and we could make out their full image, we could see they were carrying their weapons in front of them and at the ready. They would stop now and then to look over the area like they were looking for something. Their voices were above a whisper and we could hear them. The two South Korean soldiers who were in our patrol passed the word that some of these soldiers were speaking Chinese.

We waited until the eight soldiers got to about fifteen yards from our positions. It was at about this time that they stopped to communicate with each other. Our patrol had them now in our weapons' sights. The word was given to fire. The enemy soldiers didn't know what hit them. A hell of a lot of bullets hit them. They went down, and they, and their weapons, were now a part of the bad smelling rice paddy.

There were no wounded among them. We made sure of that. In war the motto is, "Element of surprise, hit first and hit so hard your opponent will not rise." We had no sooner stopped firing our weapons when the enemy started dropping mortar rounds in our direction. We quickly started moving back toward our MLR, and we radioed back requesting artillery and mortar fire to be placed in the middle of No Man's Land and on the enemy's positions. This was to try to stop them from dropping mortar fire on us.

Our request was granted. We could hear the big rounds hitting the enemy's position. We made it back to our MLR without any casualties in our patrol. The new lieutenant didn't go with us on this patrol. He was ordered to stay in the trench and to be ready to go out on the next patrol.

As I passed the lieutenant in the trench when we got back, some of the men from our patrol made the remark so that all could hear, "None of the enemy wanted to surrender, so we went on a killing spree." The lieutenant was stone faced. I thought to myself, "This guy is going to learn the hard way about war, and I hope I'm not around while he's learning."

It wasn't long after we arrived back in the trench before the enemy put a heavy concentration of artillery on our position. The soldier with the K-9 dog couldn't get back to his unit because of the shelling. We had him and the dog stay all night in one of the machine gun bunkers until the shelling stopped, and that would be at daybreak if we were lucky.

After an all night bombardment on our position, we were expecting an attack. It didn't come that night. As the weeks went by our casualty rate went up, not just from small enemy attacks and going out on patrol, but also as a result of the enemy's shelling of our position. That caused a high number of casualties among our soldiers. After spending a winter on the front line in the trenches, I learned why the soldiers in Korea referred to this place as, "The Frozen Chosen."

I've never been so cold in my life as I was in the trenches, and we weren't allowed to have a fire. Some did get frostbite. We were hoping the body lice that we all had would freeze to death and fall off, but the lice just dug into our skin.

As we looked out of the trench, all we could see was snow-capped mountains. When we weren't in a bunker trying to keep our feet warm during the day, we would double-time in place trying to keep the blood moving and to flex our cramps.

Just about every morning we would see our fighter planes go over our positions headed for the enemy's mountain to bomb them. As they would go over our position they seemed to tip their wings at us. A lot of us would say, "Go get 'em Fly Boy." Then it wouldn't be long. We could hear the fighter planes dropping their bombs and missiles on them and we would all say, "It's payback time." That was an event that made us feel good, knowing they would be taking casualties and licking their wounds.

Our company started getting hot food. This helped morale some. The

Army drove vehicles up to our position as close as they could carry a field mess. The hot food was in thermos containers, and just a small number of us at a time would walk back to get fed. When one group returned, another group of us would take our turn. This didn't happen every day, but on the days when we got a hot meal it was good.

The worst, in any war, has to be fighting on the front line at Thanksgiving and on Christmas day. We all got three cans of beer each on Thanksgiving and Christmas.

When my time on the front was over and it was time for me to leave Korea and return to the states, I requested re-assignment to Japan. I felt that I wasn't ready to go back to civilization in the states. I knew in my heart that I had changed. I needed time to be at peace and think. I knew I had no loving wife waiting for me. I didn't receive very many letters from my German wife, and in the letters I did receive, there were unwritten things. There were things between the lines that I didn't understand that left me with a lot of doubt about returning after all that I'd been through on the front line.

My request was granted. Orders came down that I was to be re-assigned to Japan. All my fellow soldiers thought I was out of my head. Some of them would say, "This war has done something to you that you don't want to go back to the states."

So, after spending that miserable winter in the trenches of Korea, and after a number of times going out into No Man's Land on patrols, and after a number of frontal attacks by the North Koreans, two other soldiers and I were told that our time was up on the front line and our replacements had arrived. A Jeep was waiting on a road two miles back on the front line to take us back to civilization.

When my replacement arrived in the trench I wasted no time getting out of there. I didn't even say goodbye to anyone. I didn't want the soldiers who had a lot of time to spend on the front line still to feel disappointed and discouraged that they were not the ones who were getting out of that hell hole. I made a fast disappearance to the rear where the Jeep was waiting.

I sat up front with the Jeep driver. The other two soldiers got in the back seat. The driver said he had orders to drive us to Kim-po Airfield where we would be processed, reassigned, and flown out of Korea. I thought I would never hear those words. I just couldn't believe I had made it. The other two soldiers were thinking and saying the same thing. They couldn't believe they were still alive.

All I could say and give credit to for our survival was that it was by the grace of God that we made it. The driver of the Jeep told us it was a long way to the military airport of Kim-po. I told the driver I didn't care if it took days to get there, just as long as I put that front line of the MLR far behind me.

As we were on our way, and had put many miles behind us, we could see how the soldiers who were not in the infantry or armor tanks were living. They were living in big twenty-men tents, and they had tents for their mess halls. They got to sleep on Army cots and they didn't get any artillery shells thrown at them.

Seeing all this made me envious, but I had wanted to be an infantry soldier, and that meant being out front. I was always told in the Army that it takes twenty soldiers in the rear serving to supply and keep one infantry soldier on the front line. Knowing that, I didn't feel so bad, but I was beginning to see how lucky these soldiers were. They didn't have to live in a trench and they did not have someone shooting at them day and night.

It was a great feeling to be out in the open without having to worry that someone wanted to kill you. It was good to be able to flex my muscles and get the cramps out of my joints. After a long ride in the Jeep we reached the military airport at Kim-po.

We were directed to the showers, given a can of DDT to get rid of the lice and other bugs, and then we were served a good, hot meal at their mess hall and given a cot to sleep on in a big twenty-man tent. There were other soldiers in the tent who had been on the front line from other infantry units. They were also waiting to fly out of Korea for new reassignments. It was great to get a good night's sleep, and how nice it was to be in a warm tent. It felt good to be clean again. They gave us clothing that hadn't been soaked in DDT.

My stay at Kim-po Airfield was two days. When my new assignment orders were given to me saying I was being sent to Japan, I was feeling good. I got the assignment I wanted. Out of all the soldiers returning from the front line, there were only about ten of us going to Japan. When I got aboard that airplane and it took off, I felt good about leaving the living hell of war behind me. But I knew that the casualties of war that I had seen, and the way we had to live to survive, and the killings would always be with me. I told myself that now that I was going to Japan I had to forget everything that happened in combat.

As the military plane was flying over the coast of Japan, I looked out the window. The first thing I saw was the snowcapped mountain of Mt. Fujiyama. I now became a believer in the Japanese saying that a person leaving Japan would return to Japan if that person saw Mt. Fujiyama on his departure. This made a believer out of me.

When the plane landed at the military base outside of Tokyo, I felt that I was really alive and that I was one lucky soldier. It was like I was given a new life from the pits of hell, and I was thankful to God that I could walk out of that hell.

After landing at the air base we were put on buses and driven to Camp Drake, an Army base on the outskirts of Tokyo. When coming into the camp the first thing a soldier would see was a large smokestack, and painted on the top of the stack was the patch emblem of the U.S. Army's First Cavalry Division that was once stationed at this camp before being sent to Korea. When the war first broke out, and since they were one of the first divisions to enter the war in Korea, they suffered heavy casualties. Now that the First Cavalry Division was no longer here, there were just small Army units spread throughout the camp.

We were told that each of us would be assigned to units throughout Japan as part of an occupation force, and that our stay at Camp Drake would be about a week. It was a week I needed. I needed to catch up on my sleep. It sure felt good to be able to sleep in a bed again between two white sheets, to eat good food at the mess hall, and to know that nobody was trying to kill me. I felt that I had been given a new life by the grace of God.

At Camp Drake the Army didn't bother any of us soldiers who arrived from Korea. We were allowed to rest and get used to the peace and quiet. I didn't realize how shell-shocked I was, or how much post-traumatic stress I was experiencing as a result of the ordeal of war. I loved the quiet, but in my head and my remembering, I could still hear the exploding shells of artillery firing. My nerves were on edge, and without realizing it, I was in a hostile, explosive state of anger.

I knew and I hoped that I could get back to normal by working things out on my own. One evening I was sitting in the service club and half dozing off to sleep in the lounge chair. The soldier sitting next to me was reading the newspaper, and as he was going from page to page, and the paper was making a crackling sound, I became frightened. I was down on the floor on my face, thinking that I was back in Korea with an artillery shell cracking through the air and not knowing where it would explode. The soldier with the paper looked at me wondering what was wrong. I told him it was nothing, that I had just been in a trance and thought I was back in the war.

While at Camp Drake I had the Army set up my pay records so that I would receive $75.00 a month while I was in Japan, and the rest of my monthly pay would go to my German wife. I thought that when I did get back to the United States we would have money in the bank, and with all my combat pay from the time in Korea, I hoped to have enough money to buy a new car.

After being at Camp Drake for a week, I was issued orders assigning me to the A Regiment of the 24th Infantry Division stationed at Sendai which was up in the northern part of Japan. A soldier who was at the service club at Camp Drake had been stationed there for over a year. He told me that he loved the place.

We had a long conversation. He told me that I was going to a place of hot floors, sliding doors, slant-eyed prostitutes, and plenty of Japanese bars that cater to American soldiers. He also gave me some advice on how I should present myself to Japanese bar girls the first time I patronized one of the many bars.

Most of the bar girls are looking for a steady American soldier who will buy them out of bondage from a moma-san, and the bar owner, and provide them with a room of their own. He told me to let them know I had just arrived in Japan, and that the Army had not paid me yet. He said, "Whatever you do, don't speak any Japanese words to the girls." He said that the bar girls get to know a soldier's face after coming to the bar more than once. The soldier told me to act dumb and green about being in Japan, and then the bar girls would give me free sex hoping that I would become a steady boyfriend. He went on to tell me that it didn't cost that much to keep a steady girl. He said, "Pay about fifteen dollars a month for a room, buy her fifty pounds of rice a month and a fresh fish now and then, take her to the camp service club now and then for ice cream and dancing, and your stay in Sendai will be a happy one." He also advised me that pulling this dumb act in the bar full of girls could only be played one time. The girls get to know your face, and if they have seen you with another girl before, they spread the word about you and label you as a butterfly boy. That means that you go from one girl to the next wanting sex.

I thanked the soldier for all the good advice and felt that I was more than ready for my new adventure into the sex world that the city of Sendai had to offer. I was more than ready. There were about six of us soldiers from Korea who were being assigned to Sendai, Japan.

We were put on a Japanese passenger train that left from downtown Tokyo. We were given bag lunches for two meals because the trip would take all day. It would be late in the evening before we would arrive at Sendai where we would be met by Army personnel.

The seating on the train was hard, wooden seats, but considering what I had just left behind me in Korea, this was luxury. The only thing we really had to get used to were all the black haired Japanese who just kept staring at us round-eyed people. A lot of Japanese had never seen Americans up close and in the flesh. When we saw them staring we would just smile and bow our heads. This would usually get a smile out of them. The train was a slow train because it would stop at the end of every rice field.

I sat next to the window at first, and then I would change with the person I was sitting next to. All I ever saw was Japanese women and some men wearing straw hats working bent over in the rice paddies wading in water up to their ankles. We never did see a town of any size. It was all countryside and rice paddies. Most of the paddies were a lush green. Now and then we would see a man behind oxen pulling a wooden plow. The country houses all looked alike. They were made of mud and straw with a lot of layers of straw for roofs.

As I looked out the window of the train, and in deep thought with my mind going back to Korea, I just couldn't believe I made it out in one piece. One of the things that crossed my mind was that if the North Koreans and the Chinese had used a surprise gas attack on us Americans, and all the troops of the United Nations who were in the trenches on the 38th parallel demilitarized zone, we would have been wiped out. I didn't have, nor do I know of any soldier in my company who had a gas mask.

I kept telling myself to forget the war in Korea, that I was in Japan now. So I put my thoughts on the people on the train I was on. I watched the young Japanese children who were sitting next to their mothers, and I noticed how well behaved the children were, just sitting there hour after hour and not saying anything or acting out.

The Japanese mothers were wearing the Japanese kimono and wooden sandals that were held on their feet by a strap that went between the big toe and the toe next to it. I watched them as they got on and off the train. The Japanese women moved like flustered butterflies. They would take short, shuffling steps. When the train finally arrived at the Sendai station after dark, there were two American soldiers there with transportation to take us about two miles from the small town of Sendai.

The camp was located at the edge of a small Japanese village. When we first got into the vehicle at the train station, the driver told us that we had been assigned to an infantry regiment that had been alerted to pack up and ship out for duty in Korea. We were all in shock thinking of going back to the hell hole we had just left. I asked the driver, "You're kidding right?" He assured us he wasn't. I was sick in the stomach to think that we would have to return to the war in Korea.

When we arrived at the camp I could see soldiers moving around and packing things to make a move. We were taken to a barracks and assigned a bunk. We were told that the mess hall had been left open and that cooks were standing by to feed us if we wanted to eat.

I didn't have any appetite after having been told that this regiment was going to Korea. Not wanting to eat, I thought maybe I should go to the mess hall and maybe pick up some rumors from the cooks. I was told by the mess sergeant that the regiment was going to Korea to guard prisoners of war at a prison camp at Koje-Do, Korea which held captive North Korean and Chinese soldiers. The captives were causing uprisings within the camp, and the prisoners had killed American and United Nations guards. The mess sergeant said, "It's too bad you soldiers who just came from Korea will be going back. Don't unpack your bags." None of us slept well that night knowing we were going back to Korea. But that's part of being a professional soldier.

The next day after our arrival we were called into the company commander's office and told that a meeting was held with headquarters. They had said that all of the soldiers returning from Korea would not have to go back to Korea with the regiment, but if any of us wanted to, we could volunteer to go. So the company commander looked at each of us standing there in his office and said, "Well, I don't hear any of you saying that you want to volunteer to go back." Then he smiled and said, "I don't blame you." I thought to myself, "Thank God." I felt rejuvenated. We were told that the regiment was only going to be sent to Korea for six months' temporary duty. They were not taking any dress uniforms or any of their personal things. These would stay in their foot lockers at camp.

Knowing enough about the way the Army operates by now, when they plan on going anywhere and say it's just a short, temporary duty, it generally turns out to be a lot longer than they planned for. All the soldiers who weren't going with the regiment would be assigned to a small unit that was going to stay behind at the camp. The unit was the 16th Corps. There was another small unit at another camp about a mile down the road. They weren't going to Korea. This small unit was a tactical subdivision of the 16th Corps. They also had a small detachment of military police at their camp.

As this regiment was getting ready to leave for Korea I was told by some of the soldiers where the good Japanese bars were to go to just outside the gates of the camp. There were about thirty of them lined up on both sides of the dirt road just outside the camp's gates. I had seen them when we arrived at the camp. The bars outside the camp were all lit up with pretty lights and each one of them had their own outside speakers blasting away with American country music. The music could be heard all over the camp's grounds.

I was told which bar had the best girls and what the going price was for going to bed with one of the bar girls. In one of my conversations with a sergeant who was shipping out with the regiment, he told me that there were a lot of Japanese girls out there who were steady shacks of some of the soldiers who were leaving. They had a room or two in the village that was paid up in advance for six months or more by the GI steady boyfriend and he told me those were the ones I should be looking for.

He also said that just as soon as the boyfriend leaves, the girl would be back in the bars working. I asked this sergeant how come he and most of the other soldiers had zippers up the full length of the inside of their boots. He told me this was the mark of a "shack rat," which meant soldiers who had steady girlfriends. In a Japanese house you are expected to remove your footwear, and having zippers in your boots makes shacking a lot easier for getting in and out of the house. He also told me where to go in the village to get zippers in my boots.

After being in camp about three weeks the regiment moved out for Korea. Those of us who were left at the camp numbered about three hundred. These were mostly soldiers from the regiment left behind for some reason. Some were waiting to be sent home for discharge and some had medical reasons.

We were all transferred over to this one large wooden barracks that was two stories high. The building was old and the wood was very dry and gray. The barracks was a firetrap. There were no fire extinguishers anywhere in the building. What we did have was two large fifty-five gallon metal drums filled with water in case of a fire. These barracks belonged to the Japanese during the war. Next to our barracks was the mess hall.

We had a very small post exchange which employed Japanese counter girls. We had a laundry and dry cleaners, but if we used it we had to pay. We had a service club where soldiers could go to play Bingo and eat ice cream and cookies. There was a movie theatre where soldiers could bring their Japanese girl friends even though most of these girls couldn't understand English.

Soldiers who didn't go to or hang around the service club would call those who did go to the service club, "club commandos." The duty at this camp was the easiest I had ever had. There was nothing military about it. It was like a rest camp, so they got no complaining from me.

Back at the barracks I could smell an odor coming from the water in the drums to be used for fire. The water must have been in the drums for years. Some soldiers who smoked would throw their cigarette butts in the water. I told the company commander that I was going to get a detail of men and change the water in the drums. He approved.

Well, after emptying the drums of water, we found in the bottom of the drums hypodermic needles. At first I thought that maybe this barracks had been a medical aid station, but after checking, there was no record of this barracks ever having had anything to do with medical aid. About this time a private first class told me that if I would look at some of these soldiers real good in the face and watch their actions that I would see that a lot of them were on drugs or smoking marijuana. He went on to tell me that drugs and marijuana were plentiful outside the gate of this camp.

At this time, in 1953 and 1954, the Army didn't have the methods to test soldiers for drugs as they do now in the service. I was surprised and disappointed that some American soldiers would become drug addicts. I was put in the position of field first sergeant. I was responsible for holding all the formations and seeing to it that all the camp details got out on their jobs. Once a week we had to send a fifteen-man guard and a sergeant in charge of the guards to go by truck for about an hour's ride out in the countryside from camp. This detail was to guard and keep the Japanese farmers from tearing down and taking what they might want from the abandoned Army Stockade that the 24th Infantry Regiment used at one time. They would send soldiers that had time to serve for bad behavior to the stockade.

15

DUTY IN JAPAN

All that remained of the old stockade were broken down guard towers and two small, one-story barracks which were still in good shape. There was a lot of fencing in place around the old stockade. The guard detail would take their sleeping bags with them. There were already cots for beds in the barracks. The sergeant in charge would make sure that cases of field rations were loaded on the truck, and Coleman lamps and lamp oil because there was no electricity out there.

There was an Army field phone in the barracks that was in direct communication with our headquarters here at the camp, and the sergeant in charge was to report by field phone every two hours into headquarters to the duty officer on duty. That person would log the calls that everything was secure at the stockade.

The duty officer could go by Jeep and check on the guards any time he wanted to without letting the guard detail know he was coming out to check on them. Some duty officers would go out to check. Then there were some who would never go out to check because they didn't like the bumpy ride out on the dirt road all the way and the stinking rice paddies on both sides of the road. The stockade was in a small county called Ho-Jo Jahara near a place called Tagajo, Japan.

The guards would stay on this duty for five days and then be relieved by another guard detail. I had never been out to the old stockade up until this time. My time came to have duty at the camp headquarters. The duty was Duty Sergeant on the weekend along with the Duty Officer, usually some young lieutenant.

This is also the place that the calls from the guard duty at Ho-Jo Jahara would be received and logged. This one Sunday the lieutenant asked me if I could take his Jeep and go out and check the guards at the old stockade. He said, "The driver knows the way out there." I wanted to see what the place looked like, so I said, "Sure, I'll go." The duty officer told me that when I returned I should write my report on how things were going at the old stockade.

The Jeep driver and I started out after lunch on Saturday. All we saw after we drove out of Sendai were rice paddies on both sides of the dirt road. The guards at the old stockade were never inspected on any regular basis because of the time it took to get there. When we arrived and turned off the main dirt road onto a narrow dirt road, from a distance we could see the two buildings.

This road was part of the property of the stockade. As we got closer the Jeep driver and I could see Japanese women coming out the front and back doors, and running, while putting their clothes on, toward a small village on the other side of the rice paddies a short distance from the stockade. The Jeep driver started laughing and said to me, "Well, sergeant, it looks like we caught them with their pants down."

When we drove up to the door of the barracks the sergeant in charge of the guards came out to the Jeep. I could see that they were surprised to see that someone had come out to check on them. I said to him, "It looks like you guys had a lot of female company." He started getting defensive, telling me that the Japanese women had just walked in the barracks without anyone knowing they were there. He said, "They wanted to know if we would sell them some of our field rations."

I looked at him and said, "Do you expect me to believe that?" I told him the duty officer had sent me out here and told me to bring back a report of what I found. I could see the sergeant starting to get nervous. I said to him, "Let's go in the barracks." As soon as I walked in the door I could smell beer. Some of the guards were lying down and some were sitting on their cots. They all said, "Hi, sergeant," to me. As I walked around the barracks I made a head count. I counted eleven soldiers in the barracks out of a count of fifteen.

I asked the sergeant of the guards if he had men posted on and around the outside of the stockade. The sergeant asked me if he could speak to me in private outside. I agreed. We went outside together. We sat in the Jeep and that was when he told me that he was going to tell me everything. He said that he had been caught by surprise and he knew he was in big trouble, and that he would be in big trouble when I turned in my report.

Then he went on to tell me that he and his guards got bored and felt like fools standing guard duty all day and night when all there was outside the barracks was a falling down fence and falling down guard towers. The Japanese girls from the village started coming around, so the guards talked them into having sex for some field rations.

I said, "You're missing four guards. Where are they?" He told me they went to the village to get some beer to bring back. I let him know that this was putting his rank and his Army career on the line. I told him that he and the rest of the soldiers who were out here, supposedly doing their duty as guards,could all be court-martialed after my report was turned in to the duty officer who had sent me out to see whether the guards were doing their duty. I told him I wanted him to read and follow his guard duty instructions pertaining to the property, and for him to post his guards on their posts right then while I was still present.

I have never seen anyone move as fast as he did to get things organized. Before I left I told the sergeant that from that point on, he and all his men should read the guard duty instructions and carry them out. I told him that I would not report this incident back to the duty officer. The worried look left the sergeant's face. I'm sure he thanked me a thousand times over.

I told him not to tell the men under him until the day when they were to be relieved by the next guards because I wanted them to have a chance to think about the trouble they could have been in for their actions and for not doing their duty.

The Jeep driver and I drove off to return to the camp at Sendai. On the way back I told the Jeep driver to keep what he had seen to himself. He told me, "I didn't see anything," and he said that I could trust him to keep his mouth closed.

When we arrived back at the camp, and I walked into headquarters, the duty officer asked me how things were going out at the old stockade. I reported that everything was in order, that the sergeant was in charge of the guards and everything was under control. "That's good," said the duty officer. "Put that in the log book." As I wrote that in the log book I was hoping that this didn't come back to bite me in the butt. Then I would be in as much trouble as the sergeant and his guards. I thought, "What the hell. That's just the chance a person has to take."

On my first time on pass to go off the camp, I ventured out to where all the bars were. They were on both sides of the street, about fifteen bars on each side of the street with the names of the states. The first one I went into was the California bar. It was just a wooden shack. There was a small dance floor and some booths off to the side and some tables and chairs. I could see about twenty young Japanese girls standing and sitting around the bar. They were pretty and nicely shaped, wearing mini-skirts, nail polish, lipstick, and high-heeled shoes. There were already some soldiers in the bar sitting with girls.

As soon as I walked into the bar, Moma-San, who owned the place, came up to me, bowing and welcoming me to her bar. She showed me a booth to sit at and waved for one of her girls to come and sit with me. Moma-San told me in broken English that if I didn't like the girl she picked to sit with me, all I had to do was send her away and she would send me another girl.

I was satisfied because she was pretty and nicely dressed. Her English wasn't that good. They didn't serve hard drinks, just beer, and they had American beer they had bought on the black market and that had come from the Post Exchange on the Army camp. I saw that the other soldiers in the bar were drinking beer from a quart bottle, so I told the girl sitting with me that I would have the same kind of beer as the other soldiers were having. The girl told me that it was a Japanese beer called, "Kirin Beer." She went to the bar and brought back a large bottle of beer for me. She poured the glass with beer to the rim and put it in front of me. Then she sat close to me on the same side of the booth, and every time I would take a drink from the glass of beer, she would quickly take the bottle and fill the glass back up to the rim of the glass.

I was surprised that none of these bar girls ever asked us soldiers to buy them a drink. I guess Moma-San didn't permit them to drink. As the bar girl was convinced that I was pleased with her company she started out the conversation by asking me, "How long you be Japan?" Right then my mind went back to the advice I had been given and that was, "Act dumb and new," so that's what I did.

I told her, "I will be Japan now one week." I could see her face light up and she became more alert. The next question she asked was, "Do you have a girlfriend?" I said, "No, not yet. I just look around." I wanted to know where she lived.

She told me she lived upstairs over the bar in one big room, and that many of the bar girls stay upstairs and they all sleep on the floor. She said that some of the bar girls who had an American boyfriend had a room in the village, and that the American soldiers paid the rent for them. She told me that she had never had a steady boyfriend because she hadn't worked as a bar girl very long.

I had the feeling that she was handing me a line of bull just like I was handing her. After getting up on the dance floor with her as an American song was being played on the record player, other soldiers started coming onto the dance floor. It wasn't long before all the bar girls were sitting or dancing with soldiers who had come in. It sure was nice to hold a woman and dance again. It had been a long time since I had danced. It wasn't long before we were holding hands and hugging, and then a kiss now and then.

After more than about three bottles of Kirin beer, and I took my time drinking them, I noticed that Japanese beer is stronger than American beer. As the evening slipped by I was having fun for the first time in a long time. I was told that all bars had to start closing at 10:30 pm because of a twelve o'clock midnight curfew. Everyone in Sendai had to be off the streets and in their houses and all motor vehicles had to come to a stop. The American military personnel also obeyed this rule. To enforce it American military police patrolled the streets in Jeeps along with Japanese police.

I had an overnight pass from the camp. I asked her if she could leave the bar for the night. She said she would have to tell the bar Moma-San that she was leaving with a soldier. Then I asked one of the soldiers in the bar where was a good place to take a girl for a one night lay. I was told that the most favorite place was a Japanese hotel named Ta-Keyia. It was a nice clean place with good food, the price was five dollars a night, and it was a short distance from the camp.

So, after the bar girl and I left the bar, we hailed a taxicab. I told the driver, "Ta-Keyia Hotel." When we arrived at the hotel I could see it was a nice place. It had a nice Japanese flower garden at the entrance. As we walked up to the front, paper-sliding door, the hotel Moma-San met us with bows and welcomed us to her hotel. There was a small entrance where we took off our shoes. For me it was my boots. Now I understood why soldiers had zippers put in their boots.

I had to sit and take time to unlace my boots while the bar girl and Moma-San waited for me. After we were in, we were shown a room that also had a paper-sliding door. There was nothing in the room but a short-legged table and some small pillows to sit on. The floor had nice and neat straw mats. I asked Moma-San, "Where is the bed?" She and the bar girl started giggling, then Moma-San opened a small closet and took out two thick quilts and two long, round pillows that were filled with beans for our heads.

She laid all this on the floor and we had a bed. She took us down the hall and showed us a room with a large hot tub that was sunken to floor level for a Japanese bath. All this only cost me five dollars for the hotel room. We were asked if we wanted food or drinks. I ordered a bottle of beer and the girl I was with ordered a bowl of rice and tea. When she had finished eating we took off our clothes and she helped me put on a Japanese men's kimono. There were white, thick slippers to put on our feet that fit like mittens where the big toe is separated from the rest of the foot.

In kimonos we walked to the bathtub room. She asked me if I had ever had a Japanese bath. I said, "No." And she started giggling. I thought, "Boy, I must be in for a surprise." When we entered the tub room she took off her kimono, and then helped me off with my kimono. I could see hot steam coming from the big tub. I thought that all we would do was get in the tub, but I was wrong.

She took me over to a place in the room that had a tiled floor, a small tub of hot water, and a drain in the floor. She took a wooden dipper and dipped hot water from the small tub and poured it all over my body and head. Then she pulled me down on the floor to where I was on my hands and knees on the floor. She continued pouring hot water and soap on me with the dipper. Then she climbed up on my back like she was riding piggyback, and using a rough kind of scrub cloth went over my shoulders and down my arms and legs. Every now and then she would pull off the first layer of my dirty skin. At first I thought maybe she was trying to skin me alive. She would put all this dirty skin in one pile.

I never realized how dirty my skin was until this little woman scrubbed me down. After she freshly skinned me, she poured more hot water all over me. Then she took me by the hand and motioned for me to get in the steaming hot wooden tub. I put in my big toe first and found that the water in the tub was boiling hot. I backed off and told her, "Water too hot. No can do." She kept saying, "You do. You do." Finally I inched my way into the hot tub like a small child getting into a swimming pool for the first time.

As I was inching my way into the boiling water, she was outside the tub giving herself a taking off the first layer of skin bath as she must have been doing since childhood. Finally I made it all the way into the hot tub, all of my body except my head. I noticed the water was clean, and soap is never permitted in the hot tub that was for soaking.

I could see that my arms were turning red. I thought I was getting boiled alive. When she finished washing with soap and skinning herself, she got into this steaming hot water tub like she was lowering herself into a nice cool swimming pool.

After soaking for about twenty minutes, and after playing Hanky-Panky with each other in the tub, we got out. I was feeling like a boiled lobster and I was as red as one. She dried herself and me off. I thought that now we would go to the room. I was getting overly anxious to go to bed, but she surprised me again.

She had me lie down on a short-legged long bench that was in this room. She wanted me on my stomach. Then she started giving me a massage that I will never forget. She got up on my back standing up. She walked up and down my back, from my buttocks to my shoulders and massaged me with her feet, with her toes working like fingers up and down my back. It was a great feeling.

Then she flipped me over and worked me over on my head down to my toes. I thought I was the luckiest man in the world. I sure was glad she was a small person running up and down my back. I wanted to give her a massage, but all she would do was shake her head, no, and giggle and point toward the door to leave the tub room. We put on our kimonos. I was beginning to feel like a child. She would not let me put the kimono on myself. She would put it on me. When we came out of the hot tub room, and back out into the fresh air, I felt like a newborn baby with new skin.

It wasn't long before we were in each other's arms embracing and having the experience of male and female physical sensations that made us feel that we were the only two people in the world at this time. I found that lying on the floor on a Japanese bed was great. I was even able to get a good toehold in our embrace. This was my first love making since leaving the United States and Korea.

The two of us didn't get any sleep all night with all the embracing we did. Before I knew it, it was time for me to get back to camp. She wanted me to take her back to the bar where she worked. Up to this time she never asked me for any money. She told me she wanted me to come back to the bar where she worked. I told her I would. When we were in the taxicab I slipped fifteen dollars in her hand. She thanked me many times for the money.

At this time in Japan this was a lot of money for a bar girl, but I'm sure Moma-San at the bar took some of the money I gave her. After being in Japan a while I learned that most of the bar girls were sent out into Japanese society to be on their own by their parents. Girls in a Japanese family are not their favorite. So a Japanese girl is more or less on her own. With Japan recovering from the war there were no jobs for young Japanese girls except working in a bar or learning to become a geisha girl. But not all Japanese girls want to become a geisha.

When bar owners, who are Moma-Sans, take girls in to work in the bars, she gives them a place to sleep and food. She buys them nice western-style clothing for work in the bar to attract American soldiers, and Moma-San keeps a log on each girl day by day so that she will know how much each girl has cost her in food, clothing and shelter.

If a soldier wants to take one of the bar girls for a steady girlfriend, and he wants to take her out of the bar to get a room, he has to bargain with Mom-San. He would have to pay Moma-San to take the girl out of the bar to live with him. Then the girl becomes the soldier's responsibility.

Japan was a charming and thrilling place to have occupation duty. From day to day their customs seemed a mystery to me. I saw no aggression from any of the Japanese people. All I saw were smiles, bows and politeness.

When I was young and we were at war with Japan, I was led to believe that the Japanese were a sneaky and treacherous people. I never lost sight of the fact that their soldiers in wars were barbarous, savage and cruel warriors who delighted in cutting people's heads off with swords, and I never forgot the inhumane way they treated American soldier prisoners of war.

I read a book when I was younger about wars between the Japanese and Chinese. The Japanese executed Chinese civilians, raped the women and conducted bayonet practice on the children. They also destroyed hospitals. This was not just in China. The same atrocities were carried out by the Japanese against the Filipino people.

I didn't let my emotional feelings show, nor did I blame the women or the young girls for what their Army did in war. My duty in Japan was great, but I started having trouble sleeping. I had nightmares about the war in the trenches of Korea. Sometimes I thought I could almost feel the exploding shells in my sleep. I think the duty in Japan helped me begin to forget, and helped the stress caused by the trauma of war.

I tried not to care about anything. I did my Army duties, and when I was on pass from the camp, I would booze it up, dance and play with the Japanese girls. They made me forget everything from the past. I just wish I had gotten to Japan sooner.

I know that some who read my life story in this book will be thinking, "This soldier was a womanizer." And I would say to them, "I surely was, and I loved it." I could never have had such a good time in the United States as I was having here in Japan.

I patronized all the bars, and during my first time in each bar I acted like a dumb soldier who had just arrived in Japan who was looking for a steady girl. It worked every time. I would get a free lay. But it only works one time in each bar because the bar girls had a good memory for soldiers' faces, and after that the freebies are over. I paid fifteen or twenty dollars for the hotel and the girl.

The thing that surprised me about the bars was that they had only one toilet, and both men and women used that one. There were no locks on the doors. It was nothing for a male to be standing urinating, and a bar girl would walk in to use the cut-out slit in the floor. And as they walked by, they liked to goose the men while they were trying to urinate. But I got used to it. There was no modesty.

After I got tired of barhopping I told this sergeant buddy of mine that I was going to start looking for a steady girl. He already had a steady girl. The next day he told me that his girl friend knew of a nice girl who was not a bar girl, and if I wanted to meet her I was invited to his place to have some drinks and meet this girl.

I took the invite. After duty we took a taxi to his shack. By this time I had had zippers put on my boots which made it easier going into and out of Japanese houses. I noticed that he lived a long distance from the camp.

The girl they wanted me to meet was already there. She was pretty but she couldn't speak a word of English, or understand anything in English. So my other sergeant's girlfriend had to be the translator. I found out that she was a nurse in a Japanese hospital and that she lived in the nurses' dormitory. But she wasn't happy living there. From that I got the point that she was looking for a steady boyfriend and to have her own room.

So, that evening we all ate and had drinks, and it just so happened that I had an overnight pass. The sergeant's girl made a bed on the floor for the nurse and me. When we got in the bed she acted like a high school girl in her first class of rape, or maybe it was the fast way I was coming on to her. There was nothing aggressive about her when it came to having sex, but I had to admit it was good, and I thought I could break this girl in myself. I knew for sure that I was the first American soldier she had ever been with.

The hospital where she worked was in downtown Sendai, which was a long distance from the Army camp. The next morning I told her, through the translator, that I would like to have her for a steady girl. I told her that if she would get us a nice room close to the Army camp that I would pay for the room and live with her.

She agreed. She said she wanted to continue to work as a nurse. I agreed. She also told me through a translator that she and I must never be seen together by anyone from the hospital or she would lose her job for going with an American. So, getting a room close to the camp was good because she didn't know anyone who worked at the hospital who lived in that area.

So it was all set up. She would find us a room, and in two days, at a certain time, I would meet her at the camp's personnel gate and she would show me where she had found a room. On the second day, she was right there to meet me. We took a taxi. The room was a short way from the camp.

When she showed me the room I liked it. It was in something like a small villa. There was a small entrance where we took off our shoes, and it was big enough for her to cook in with her small charcoal stove. What I liked most about the room was that someone had made a wooden bed. They had done a good job. It was strongly made. The toilet was just a short distance outside. There was also a big wooden barrel that was always steaming for anyone who wanted to take a bath, which we did.

The first thing I wanted to do after trying the wooden bed was love making. Then I wanted to teach my new girlfriend some words in English and for her to teach me some words in Japanese. I was starting to run out of hand movements trying to talk with my hands. There was one thing that was on my side. She was willing. She wanted to learn English. Her name was Takako. She became a loving person.

When I arrived at the room after work she was always there waiting for me at the entrance. She insisted that I sit and she would take off my boots. Then she would want me to stand so she could take off my clothes. Then she would put a Japanese kimono on me, the kimono she had bought me.

She would even surprise me by having a cold bottle of Japanese beer waiting for me. I would bring a can of boot polish to the room so that I would have shining boots when I went back to camp. After she watched me shining my boots in the mornings she started to shine my boots for me while I was shaving and brushing my teeth.

We were happy together, and I could spend more time with her after I volunteered to be assigned to a military police unit at the camp. I was now in the 16th Corps military police. I thought it was about time I got out of the infantry for a while. My duty was from three in the afternoon until eleven at night.

I had no other duty, so I could spend every night with my girlfriend. She got off work at the hospital at about four o'clock in the evening. On my days off she would cook for me. I was feeling like a king living in a shack. I felt great, even though all of the other soldiers who didn't have a steady girl referred to those of us who did as "Shack Rats."

Each evening my girl would learn a few new words in English. I wasn't as good at learning Japanese as she was at learning English. After about three months we could understand each other pretty well. It wasn't long before I wished I had never volunteered to be a military M.P.

The Provost Marshal was a captain who had always been in the military police and had never served a day in a combat unit. His interest was never for the men under him. He was too occupied in trying to please all the higher rank around him so he wouldn't be overlooked for the next promotion in rank. He was the type who didn't care who he walked on to achieve his goal.

He would put orders out to us military police to start writing and giving out more delinquency reports to soldiers who were out on passes at the bars. I didn't like giving out delinquency reports when out on patrol. I would give verbal warnings if a soldier was out of line in a bar or fighting outside a bar.

I didn't like giving out delinquency reports because when the delinquency report reached the soldier's company, disciplinary action would be taken against the soldier. I've seen some good soldiers lose their hard earned rank just for getting in a fight over a bar girl.

I was in the military police about four months when I was provoked into giving a private first class a delinquency report. It was during daylight hours. I was driving a military Jeep from another camp in Sendai back to our base camp. There was another M.P. soldier with me in the Jeep at the time.

The speed limit through that part of Sendai was fifteen miles an hour because the streets were very narrow, and the Japanese people and children walked in the streets because they had no sidewalks. We had just stopped to check out a bar that had a bunch of soldiers in it. When we started to enter the bar, a military Jeep with a private first class as the driver went by. My M.P. partner and I stopped the driver and Jeep just before he was getting ready to go into our camp.

I told the driver he was speeding. Right away he told me that he was in a hurry and that he was the driver for the Regional Commander who was a colonel. I told him that the next time I would have to write him up for speeding. All of a sudden this private first class showed anger and got very irritated toward me, telling me he didn't give a damn if I did write him up for speeding. He said that a speeding report didn't mean anything to him, and again he reminded me that he was the colonel's driver.

To me now this became a challenge, so I wrote my first delinquency report. A week later I was called into the Provost Marshal's office. The captain showed me the delinquency report I had written. He said, "Do you know who this driver drives for?" I told him I did know, but that the driver was breaking the speed limit and that we, the military police, were enforcing the speed limit when it involved a military vehicle.

The captain then told me he was going to revoke the delinquency report that I had written and that I owed the driver an apology. I told the captain that he could do what he wanted to with the delinquency report, but that I would not apologize to the Jeep driver or anybody else for the delinquency report I had written.

The captain then said that he would have to put a delinquency report in my military records. I said, "Do what you want, but I will not apologize." When I left his office I had made up my mind that this was the first and last delinquency report that I would ever write as a military policeman.

Later, through the military grapevine, I found out that the captain was being considered for promotion to the next higher rank of major, and he was the type of officer who wasn't going to let anything or anybody get in his way. He didn't care who he stepped on to get to that higher rank.

Since I left the combat arms of the infantry I could clearly distinguish between the leadership of an officer from a combat unit and the leadership of an officer of non-combat units such as the military police. An officer who had been in combat shows more respect for the soldiers under his command. They have been there, and they've seen the killings and the wounded.

This was at about the time in my Army career when I was not going to give officers the respect or courtesy of addressing them as, "Sir." From now on I would address them by their rank, such as, "Yes, Lieutenant," or "No, Lieutenant," or "Yes, Captain," or "No, Captain." I was in my military right as long as I addressed them by their rank. If I saw the officer had been in combat by the distinguishing decorations he was wearing on his uniform, then I showed him respect and would address him as, "Sir."

I did this all through my Army career. In the units that were left here in Sendai, there was no military training or discipline since the 24th Infantry departed for Korea. This might have been due to the fact that the officers who were left behind at the camp had as their main interest officers' parties and shacking up with Japanese girls. Almost daily it was nothing to see the camp commander coming into or going out of the camp sitting in the back seat of his military staff car with his Japanese girlfriend.

Seeing this day after day, those of us who weren't on drugs and liked women rather than dope, we decided to shack up also. I wasn't privileged to have a staff car to haul my Japanese girlfriend around town in, so I bought, from another soldier, an old Chuhman-style motor scooter that had been rebuilt. It had a Briggs and Stratton motor and ran on gas. It would get up to speeds of thirty miles an hour. I liked it because it had a seat long enough for two people to sit on and ride, and it had foot pedals for the passenger.

When I bought the scooter I was told to keep the chain tight that drives the sprocket that drove the back wheel. My Japanese girlfriend, Takako, liked riding on the scooter, but she didn't want anyone from the hospital where she worked to see her with an American soldier. So we never went to the part of town where the hospital was. When we did go someplace she would put a scarf on her head and wear dark sunglasses.

One weekend Takako wanted to show me a little town by the sea north of Sendai called Shiogama, between Sendai and Hokkaioo. Shiogama was about twenty miles from our camp, so we thought that no one in that small town would know her. We rode on the motor scooter since it was a nice day. The road, most of the way, was a dirt road with potholes and stinking rice paddies on both sides of the road. The only traffic we saw was an ox pulling a cart now and then. Shiogama, near Mastsushima Bay, was a pretty little town. It looked as if it had escaped the destruction of war.

The main thing Takako wanted me to see were two large rocks that rose out of the water like two small mountains. There was a large rope that reached from the top of one rock to the top of the other. Takako pointed out to me that the two rocks were married. There was a small boat that would take people out to the rocks and there was a small boat dock. People would get off the boat and there was a path that people would walk on that would wind around the large rock. People would take flowers out and place them at the base of the two married rocks. After visiting the married rocks we ate Japanese Soba, steaming hot noodles.

On our way back to Sendai I was trying to miss all the potholes in the road, and when were about a mile from Sendai, all of a sudden the chain that drives the back wheel came flying off and got tangled up in the sprocket. It happened so suddenly that when the back wheel locked up, the motor scooter came to a sudden stop throwing Takako and me off the scooter.

I went over an embankment and landed in a wet rice paddy. Takako was thrown onto the dirt road with cuts on her arms and knees. I didn't have any cuts, but I smelled like I had just fallen down the hole of an outhouse. When I picked myself up from the rice paddy to see how she was, she was standing up by then.

When she saw me and saw that I wasn't hurt, she and I thought it was funny and we started laughing. She tried cleaning off my wet face with her scarf. The motor scooter was lying at the edge of the road. The handlebars were bent a little. Other than that it was in good running condition. It took me awhile to pull the wadded chain from between the sprocket and the wheel, but I got the chain back on the sprocket and off we went at a slow speed.

As soon as we got to our room Takako removed my clothes, and both of us, wearing kimonos and native wooden sandals, were off to use the house Moma-Sans's bath house. Takako washed my khaki uniform. She even cleaned my boots and shined them.

It wasn't until the next day that we learned that someone who worked at the same hospital as Takako had seen us together. She was fired for being out with an American soldier. She cried for two days. There was a small American Army hospital in Sendai. I told her that I would see what I could do to get her a job there. I went to the American hospital and talked to the chief nurse in charge. I told them that Takako was a nurse and why she got fired from her job.

I was told that they couldn't hire her as a nurse because she wasn't an American, but that they would give her a nurse's aide job. When I told Takako about the nurse's aid job she was happy. But after working at the American Hospital for about four months she became depressed because the nurses at the hospital used her to do all the dirty work. But Takako told me she would work at the hospital until it was time for me to leave Japan and go back to America. Then she would leave the city of Sendai and go to the big city of Tokyo and find work there as a nurse.

My time spent in Sendai with Takako seemed to pass by quickly and I knew my stay in Japan would be cut short. The Armistice Agreement was signed by North Korea and the United Nations with General Mark Clark signing for our side to stop the fighting. It was reported that at the time of the signing General Clark made the remark that it was with a heavy heart that he was signing the Armistice Agreement. I knew in my own heart that all the soldiers I served with who were still alive would sure be happy to get out of the trenches and live like human beings again.

I thought that maybe the 24th Infantry Division would be coming back to Sendai, Japan, and I would rather not be there if they did return. It wasn't long after the Armistice was signed in Korea when I received my orders to go back to the United States. Takako became very sad. I was a little sad, but from the start of our relationship of living together, I had known that some day I would be leaving and might never see her again. She also understood this.

Being sent to Sendai, Japan and meeting Takako was the best thing that could have happened to me coming out of a war zone, being shell-shocked, and being in a state of post-traumatic stress. Takako understood my situation. She had seen the disaster and trauma of war when our planes bombed Japan. Our last night together Takako prepared my favorite Japanese food, Yakitori, white chicken meat, and beer to drink with it.

We didn't sleep much during our last night together. The next morning she gave me a big hug and it seemed that she didn't want me to go. She had tears streaming down her face. I told her that she would always be in my heart and memories. We said our goodbyes. In all my time in Japan I never saw any animosity toward any of us American soldiers from the Japanese people.

16

ARLINGTON NATIONAL CEMETERY

Some other soldiers who were going back to the states for reassignment and I were loaded up on Army trucks and taken to the port of Yokohama, then back onto a troop ship. As we walked up the ship's gangway each of us had to sound off with our rank and full name so that the officer in charge of troop movement could check the names on his ship's passenger list.

When I stepped aboard with my duffel bag on my shoulder and called out my name, I was told to step out of line from the rest of the troops who were coming aboard the ship. Some other sergeants were also separated from the larger group. A captain asked us sergeants if any of us had had any experience with prisoners. I thought to myself, "This captain is looking for someone to be in charge of a detail that I don't want any part of."

One sergeant spoke up and said he had worked with American soldiers in the stockade in Japan. The captain said that there were forty-one hard-core military prisoners going back to the states, and all of them were going back to serve time in prisons. They would be locked up in the ship's brig for the trip back to the states, and there would be prison guards selected from the troops coming aboard the ship.

About this time the sergeant who said he had worked with prisoners spoke up and volunteered to be in charge of the prisoners. That sure was a relief to me, and I could tell it was a relief to the other sergeants as well. But then the captain told the sergeant he would need an assistant.

At this all our chins dropped and some sergeants tried to step behind the others so they wouldn't be picked out to be the assistant to the sergeant. The captain asked if any of us wanted to volunteer. Each of us looked at each other and no one spoke up. So the captain told the sergeant who was going to be in charge of the prisoners to pick another sergeant from our group.

I was in luck. He picked the sergeant who was standing next to me. I said to myself, "I think luck is with me," but then the captain told the rest of us

sergeants that we would each be assigned to detail aboard the ship. Then he
started calling names from his roster.

My name was called to be in charge of a ship's troop compartment. There
were compartments that were broken down so that each compartment would
sleep about two hundred men, and there were many compartments. Being
in charge of it meant that it was my responsibility to maintain discipline
within the compartment among the troops and to supervise the clean up of the
compartment each morning for inspection.

There was one good thing about this trip. All of us sergeants who were
assigned to these duties were given first-class cabins, two sergeants to a cabin.
These cabins were to be given to military dependents, but on this trip there
weren't many dependents. So we lucked out.

This was the only trip by troop ship when I didn't feel like a sardine in a
can, and we got to eat in the first-class dining room. I didn't know what or
where my new assignment would be in the states. The ship was to dock at the
port of San Francisco, California. It was a good trip. I was only seasick two
days.

The ship sailed under the Golden Gate Bridge. All the troops were up on
deck to see the Golden Gate. As we went under the bridge, all the troops let
out a cheer. They were happy to be back. Most of the troops were Korean War
returnees. The ship docked at the port of San Francisco. There were civilian
chartered buses to take us to Fort Ord Army Base for re-assignment.

The prisoners were the last to leave the ship. They were brought up on the
deck and handcuffed to one of the ship's railings where they could watch all
the troops disembarking. They were told to keep their mouths shut. I saw about
thirty military police coming aboard the ship to take charge of the prisoners.
It took about a week for the processing. It took me longer. The processing
personnel said they had read my records and had a special assignment for me.
But they wouldn't tell me what they had for me, only that it would be special.
They said I would be one of the last ones to be assigned. That meant I would
have to stay at the processing center a day or two longer than the others being
processed.

The food was good at the camp and I had my own room in the barracks.
I went to a movie every night at the camp. I didn't let my wife Helga know
I was coming home because I wanted to surprise her. I wanted to buy a car
just as soon as I got home with all the money that was coming out of my pay
in allotment to her and my combat pay. Helga had told me she was putting
the money in the bank, so I thought I would have a nice nest egg by now. I
was also thinking that I could help Helga bring her mother to the states from

Germany.

The processing personnel called for me. They had my new assignment. They told me that I was going to the Presidential Honor Guard at Fort Meyer, Virginia, and that it was an honor to be selected for this assignment. They had seen in my records that I served in the Berlin Honor Guard and my records were clean from any court martials.

I was given my new orders for assignment and a fifteen-day furlough. I took a plane to Pennsylvania. When I arrived in Harrisburg it was after dark. I took a taxi to the address where Helga had moved to. It was an apartment house and I had to go up two flights of stairs to her apartment. I was all ready to give her a surprise by not letting her know I was coming home. I got to the door and knocked. Helga opened the door. Her mouth fell open and she threw her arms around me. As we embraced Helga's mother came to the door. The last time I had seen her was in Germany. I could see out of the corner of my eye that there was a man sitting in the living room in a big chair.

When the embracing was over with Helga there was silence. I asked her, pointing to her mother, "How did she get to America?" Helga said that she would tell me everything. At about that time, Omi, the grandmother, came out from another room in the apartment. I asked, "Who is this guy?" Helga told me he was Hans from Berlin. At that instant I knew who that fellow was, Helga's high school boyfriend, Hans. At that moment anger came over me. I grabbed Hans by the back of the shirt and shoved him out the apartment door. I told him to get out, and if he didn't start down the stairs I was going to throw him down.

He looked at me like he thought I wasn't serious. I told Helga, "Tell Hans in German what I just said." At about this time Mutti, the mother, came out of the kitchen waving a butcher knife and coming at me. Helga stopped her and said something to her in German that calmed her down and made her put the knife down.

Hans got half-way down the stairs and asked Helga for his jacket. She threw it down to him. Now I was beginning to understand what my mother had written to me when I was in the trenches in Korea. She wrote and told me, "Son, I don't want to worry you, but when I call Helga, a man who doesn't speak good English answers the phone." I told Helga, "Let's sit down and talk, but before we talk, bring me the bank book." I wanted to see how much of my money was in savings.

I had to ask to see the bank book three times before she went to the other room to get the book. She came back and handed it to me. I couldn't believe my eyes. The balance was twenty-five dollars. I asked her, "Where's the bank book showing all the money I sent you?" She assured me that this was the only bank book. Then she started explaining what all the money had been spent for. There were boat tickets to bring Mutti, her mother, Omi, her grandmother, and Hans to the United States. She said that I didn't have to worry; they were all going to pay me back for using my money to come to the United States. Then Helga told me that Mutti already had a job as a housekeeper, and that Hans had a job repairing clocks and watches, and that old Omi was looking for work.

So everyone was happy, and they thanked me for helping them. I sat there and couldn't believe what I was hearing, but seeing them all there, and looking at my bank book, I knew I had been taken for one big sucker.

Helga kept telling me that everyone was going to pay me back. Then she would translate what she had said to Mutti and Omi, emphasizing paying me back. Mutti and Omi quickly responded by shaking their heads, yes, and smiling. I failed to see the humor. This was not a laughing matter to me. I didn't even ask who it was who had sponsored Mutti, Omi, and Hans to come to the United States. I was so mad and disgusted that Helga would use my money that I was having the Army take out of my pay, and my combat pay, like this without my permission. And now I was supposed to be happy that they were all going to pay me back.

I told Helga, "I want out of this marriage right now." I told her that she could use the twenty-five dollars that was left in the bank to buy Hans some beer and cigarettes. I told her that I was going to call a taxi and go to a hotel to stay for the night. I also told her that I was going to make an appointment with a divorce attorney the next day, and that I would be coming to pick her up by taxi to take her to the attorney's office.

Helga wanted me to stay the night. She said that we could talk. I told her that things had gone beyond talking. I called a taxi and checked into a hotel in the city of Harrisburg.

The next morning I found a divorce attorney who would give Helga and me an appointment that day. So I took a taxi to the apartment and picked up Helga. When we arrived at the attorney's office the attorney separated Helga and me at my request. I was in one room of the attorney's office and Helga in another. I told the attorney the true story and why I wanted out of the marriage as soon as possible. I said that I wanted nothing and that there were no children involved in the marriage.

The attorney could see that I was in the service. He told me that I would have to continue to support Helga until the divorce was final, which would be in about six months. After the attorney and I talked, he went into the next room to talk to Helga. After about fifteen minutes of talking with her, the attorney came back to talk to me again. He told me that Helga had said that she would like to try to make the marriage work.

I told the attorney, "It's all over. Get out the papers I need to get the divorce started." He did. I gave him my new military address at Ft. Meyer, Virginia. I left the attorney's office without Helga. I walked back to the hotel, picked up my duffel bag, and caught a plane to Texas to spend my furlough with my mother and my family. That was the last time I ever saw Helga, in the attorney's office. I'm thankful there were no children involved in this marriage.

Those who gained from this divorce were Helga's German boyfriend, Hans, her mother, and her grandmother. They all hit the jackpot by getting their boat passage to the United States paid by me, which I knew nothing about. And I knew that now, with the divorce, I would never see a dime of my money that brought them to the United States. I would just have to mark it up as the hard knocks of experience.

When I arrived home at my mother's house in Houston, Texas, everybody was happy to see me. I had an enjoyable visit with all my relatives, although there was never a day that went by that I didn't think of all the soldiers I served with, and those who went to war in Korea before me, and those who would never come back to visit their relatives again. And now, to this day, the Korean War is referred to as the "Forgotten War," even though approximately 40,000 American servicemen lost their lives. And to this day, many of the soldiers and marines who were taken prisoner will never be accounted for. They will just be accounted for as soldiers and marine combatants of misfortune.

When my furlough was over and it was time to report to my new assignment, I looked upon the assignment as being an honor to serve in the Presidential Honor Guard. I had no idea what my new duties would be. I thought since I was in a drill platoon in Berlin, that more than likely that was what I would be doing at my new duty station.

When I arrived at Fort Meyer I could see that they were wearing the new uniform, not the olive brown that I was wearing with the Eisenhower Jacket. When I reported to headquarters, I was informed that I would have to turn in all my uniforms for new ones.

I was told that this was the first Army unit to have the honor of wearing the new uniform, and that later all the Army would be issued the new uniform. I was also told that all my boots and dress shoes were to be taken to the shoe repair to have horseshoe metal cleats that go all around the bottom of the heels of the shoes and boots attached. This was because they wanted us to be sharp when marching.

When I reported to my new company, the company commander called me into his office to welcome me and give me my new assignment. His first words to me after welcoming me were, "What kind of sergeant are you? One of those who are easy and let lower rank disobey, or are you hard and demanding when it comes to military discipline?" My answer was that I was a career soldier, and as long as the Army demands discipline from me and leadership, then I expect discipline from the men under me. I also told him that a lot depends on the backing us sergeants get from our commanding officers.

At this time the company commander stood up from his chair and slammed his fist on his desk and said, "My non-commissioned officers get 100% backing from me." Then he proceeded to tell me about this old guard outfit at Ft. Meyer, Virginia. He said that all the men who were assigned to this duty at Ft. Meyer were hand picked from other Army units with no bad records and they had to be sharp at all times. He let me know what platoons his company consisted of. One was a fancy drill platoon, another was guards for the Tomb of the Unknown Soldier, and there was a unit to perform military funeral services at the gravesites in Arlington National Cemetery.

At that time that sounded like something I wouldn't mind doing. Little did I know just how sad this duty would be. I spent most of my time, day after day, in the cemetery with my detail of pallbearers, rifle firing squad, and two buglers. There would also be one of the Army chaplains there to give the last benediction.

Some days we would perform two or three a day. A lot of the time was spent waiting for the casket to be delivered to the gravesite, and waiting for all the people who were attending the service to arrive. I know that being in charge of military funerals at Arlington was an honor, but day after day, and after almost a year of military funerals, it was starting to get to me emotionally.

There was one funeral at Arlington that I will always remember. I picked up the manifest at headquarters that informed me of the name of the deceased, rank, religion, the number of the gravesite, and the approximate number of people who would be attending the service.

I would send the bus carrying my firing squad, pallbearers, and buglers to the gravesite number, and they would wait for me to arrive with the chaplain. The manifest read that about twenty people, including the wife of the deceased, would be attending the funeral. The report I had on the manifest called for a casket burial.

We were all at the gravesite. We had been waiting a long time when an Army staff car pulled up. An Army major got out, came over to me and said that things had changed. The deceased soldier had been cremated at the request of his wife. His wife would not be attending the service, and all those who had been scheduled to attend the funeral service would not be present. I asked who we should give the flag to. The Army major told me that the wife of the deceased wanted the flag sent to her.

The cremated remains of the deceased were in a box on the back seat of the Army staff car with the folded flag on top. The chaplain said, "Let's give this soldier a military funeral and pretend that there are a hundred people attending this service." And that's what we did, with full military honors. That was the saddest funeral service at Arlington Cemetery that the honor guard and I ever attended.

I got to the point that I wanted to change my duty station. I went to the personnel office and asked what they had open for overseas. They said the only thing open was undesirable duty in Korea near the front line and living in squad tents. I volunteered to go back to Korea. This time the duty was for sixteen months. My duty station was Camp Casey, near the front line that was still manned by American soldiers. I was assigned to the 24th Infantry Division as platoon sergeant. We lived in big squad tents, about twenty soldiers to a tent. We slept on old Army canvas folding cots with sleeping bags. Each tent had two oil-burning, potbelly stoves, a stove at each end of the tent. We did have electric lights because of a large outside generator that supplied electricity to the entire company.

During my first winter at Camp Casey the snow was heavy and it was cold. I'll never forget one snowy night. It was so cold that in the middle of the night the copper line carrying the oil from the oil drums to our tent stoves froze up. The oil drums were outside. Heavy snow built up on the top of the tent. I was awakened with something heavy on top of me. The snow had caused the tent to cave in. Those of us in the tent couldn't get out of our sleeping bags.

Soldiers from other tents that hadn't caved in came to dig us out. Not long after this the company commander had Quonset huts delivered to all the company for the soldiers to sleep in. When the Quonset huts arrived it didn't take long for us soldiers to put them together. We didn't have to worry that they would cave in. Korea wasn't so bad this time. At least I didn't have the North Koreans shooting at me. This duty was good and we had a company commander who was a good military officer. He was firm, and he believed that non-commissioned officers were the backbone of the Army. All of us non-commissioned officers had respect for him.

Soldiers at Camp Casey were not permitted to go into any of the nearby villages. About every six weeks some of us from the company would get a weekend pass to visit the city of Seoul. To get there required a long, dusty, choking ride on a narrow, rough road riding in the back of an Army truck.

I made sure I got to ride up front with the driver. Even then it was a dusty ride and there were stinking rice paddies on both sides of the narrow road. The smell from the rice paddies was sometimes so overwhelming that it would almost make us sick to our stomachs.

When we arrived at the city of Seoul, and in front of the USO club, the men in the back of the truck would be covered with dust. They would get out of the truck trying to dust themselves off and complaining about the stinking dust. I made it a point to inform them that this was not just dust, but centuries of human excretion on their clothes. The USO in Seoul had a staff that came out to greet us. They said they had beds, showers, and food for all of us, and that we were free to visit and explore the city of Seoul on our own.

We knew what time we were expected to be on the truck the next day for our return back to our camp. We took showers and the USO fed us. Before we left the USO we were given a map of the city that showed areas that were off limits to all military personnel. Well, we knew that any area that the military had declared off limits to soldiers had to be a place where a soldier could have a good time, and a place where he would find all the good things a soldier was looking for, women. We also knew that we had to be careful and only go into an off limits area after dark because the military police would be patrolling the area. The map showed one of the areas was only two blocks from the USO. We all split up.

Three of my friends and I strolled through downtown Seoul, took pictures, and visited some bars that wanted American soldiers' money. The bars were lined up on both sides of the street. Most of the bars were named after an American state. We ended up in the New York Bar, which was blaring out American music through outside loudspeakers. The bar girls were plentiful. As soon as we sat down at a table the girls would sit next to us. The bar Moma-San came to our table and welcomed us to the bar.

We all ordered a beer. The Korean girls at our sides would pour our beer in our glass, and just as soon as one of us would take a sip of beer from the glass, the girl would fill the glass back up to the rim. Never before had I seen this kind of service since I left Japan. We all made small talk with the girls as well as we could. They did not know English, and we did not know Korean, but we all had a good time. We danced and we would get a good feel. The girls didn't seem to mind our roving hands. We spent a long time at the bar dancing with the girls.

We left the bar at dark. We hadn't been out of the bar very long when a small, young Korean boy came up to us and wanted to know if we wanted good-time girls. We all knew he was a pimpboy, so we showed him our map of the city and pointed to one of the off limits areas. The pimpboy kept saying, "Can-do, Can-do." So off we went following this Korean kid. We all kept a lookout for military MP Jeeps. We didn't see any, but we did see signs that said, "This Area Is Off Limits to All Military Personnel."

We went down some alleyways. I could see on the map that we were about three blocks from the USO. We came up to an old, two-story house with a tall, locked wooden gate. The pimp boy called out for Moma-San. She came to the gate and looked out the crack of the gate to see who was there before unlocking the gate. The little pimp boy talked to her in Korean and pointed at us. Moma-San broke out into a big smile and unlocked the gate to let us soldiers in. She kept bowing all the way to the door of the house, and saying, "Welcome to my house." She showed us a table. The pimp boy came in with his hand held out wanting a tip for escorting us to the house.

We didn't see any girls, but we could hear them giggling upstairs. Moma-San said she had American beer, but we had already had all the beer we wanted. What we wanted now was to see the girls, so Moma-San called for them to come down from upstairs. They followed each other down the stairs. There were about nine of them. They kept giggling all the way down the stairs. Then they stopped and stood in front of us. They all had nice robes on. By this time my buddies and I were standing. Moma-San said something to them, and they all completely opened their robes, still giggling. They were all completely naked. I think all of us soldiers were thinking, the same thing, "What a sight."

Each of us went down the line of girls and picked out the one we wanted, and then went up the stairs, and we were taken by the girls to each of their rooms. The girl I was with had a room with a window looking out to the road at the front of the house where my friends and I had come in.

The Korean girl and I weren't in the room one minute before I heard talking in English. I looked out the room window and saw a military police Jeep and three military police getting out of the Jeep and going into the house across from the one my friends and I were in.

Being an ex-military policeman myself, I knew they were pulling a surprise raid on all known houses of prostitution, known by the Koreans as "yellow houses." We Americans knew that in a red-light area the military raid is to catch servicemen in a district that's off limits. It didn't take me long to alert my two friends about the military police, and we knew this house would be next on their list to raid.

All three of us gathered in the hallway to plan the best way out. We went down the hallway and looked out the window at the back of the house. We saw that it led to a back alley. I asked Moma-San if there was a back door. She said, "No have." Going out the window from the second floor would be about a fifteen-foot drop to the ground. So out the window we went, one at a time. This led up the back alley where we couldn't be seen by the military police. We ran down the alley until we reached the back side of the USO. Then we walked to the front door.

Now we knew we were out of the off limits area and we began thinking, "What a dumb thing that was to do." We would have been in a lot of trouble being caught in a raid in a house of prostitution. So for the rest of our stay in the city of Seoul we stayed in the areas and bars that were on limits.

The next day we all showed up to get on the truck that would take us back to Camp Casey. When I got back I was given a message from a buddy of mine who was in another camp down the road from our camp. He was a member of a K-9 dog platoon. I went to see him. He told me that the K-9 unit was getting rid of all the female German police dogs, that they were just keeping male dogs. He said that if I wanted one of the female dogs I could have one. He said the dogs were not attack dogs, but trained for patrol dogs.

I went back to camp and talked it over with my commanding officer. He gave his permission for me to have the dog, but only under the stipulation that the dog would be the company's mascot, and it would be my responsibility to feed and take care of the dog. I agreed. I went back to the K-9 dog company and they let me take my choice of the female dogs. My friend, who knew the dogs, helped me, and I chose a dog named, "Lady." She was about four years old and had a good disposition. I took her back to my unit at Camp Casey.

All the soldiers in the company liked her. Lady had the free run of the company area, and it didn't take her long to know where the mess hall was. There was no place for me to buy dog food, so the mess sergeant let me set up a bucket where the soldiers would dump their scraps.

They all knew that what I wanted in the bucket was scrap meat or bones. Lady slept on the floor next to my cot. When my company was scheduled to go out of camp on military maneuvers, Lady would go too. She would sit in the front of the truck with the driver and me. She was good company. I found myself always talking to her as if she were another person. I took a ribbing from the other soldiers for talking to Lady. I had Lady for about a year when one weekend I was approved for a three-day pass to the city of Seoul for rest and recreation.

Lady couldn't go with me so I made arrangements for a sergeant friend of mine to look after Lady. When I got back to Camp Casey I was given the news that Lady was nowhere to be found, and no one had seen her for two days.

I looked up and down the road for her and inquired at other companies within the Army Division. No one had seen her. After about a week one of the Korean civilian house-boys who worked within the company called me aside and made me promise to not tell the other house-boys that he told me what happened to my dog, Lady.

He told me some of the other house-boys had put rope around her, tied her up and carried her to the village of Tong du ch'on-ne, about four miles down the road from our camp. This was a military off limits area. I asked the house-boy why they would want my dog. The house-boy hung his head down and told me in broken English that some Koreans eat dogs, and my dog was a big dog which Koreans didn't get to see around in Korea.

I asked if he knew where in the village my dog was taken. He said he didn't know because he didn't live in the village, and he said he didn't know which house-boys had been involved in taking Lady.

I went to the company commander and told him what the house-boy had told me and I asked, "Is there some way I could go into the village of Tong du ch'on-ne and look for Lady. The company commander told me he would have to go through higher headquarters and get their permission.

The next day I was given permission to enter the village of Tong du ch'on-ne. I was to be in the company of two sergeants, and I was given orders that I was not permitted to go into Korean homes. I was just to look around and ask the Koreans if they had seen a large dog.

I had a picture of Lady and I showed it around. I went to the small Korean police station in the village. I asked them and showed them some Korean money I had. I was hoping it would refresh their memory. They told me they hadn't seen the dog.

I could see that I was getting nowhere. I told the Korean police that I would pay a big reward if someone would bring my dog back to my company at Camp Casey. I left my name with them. After we left the village one of the sergeants said to me, "Clark, how many cows or horses or cats have you seen in Korea?" I said, "I have never seen any." "Well," the sergeant said, "They have eaten them all. That should tell you what the people in the village have done, or are going to do with your dog."

At that time I didn't have any liking for Koreans who would eat dogs, so there was nothing I could do about finding Lady. I've kept her picture all these years to remind me of the past and of what a good companion she was. She left a paw-print on my heart. I spent the rest of my sixteen months in Korea without her. The company commander also told me that Lady would be missed.

After my second tour of duty in Korea, I went back to the states. My new duty station was Fort Lewis, Washington. In 1957 I went to Houston, Texas on leave to visit my mother and sisters and to get married for the second time to a girl I met when I had Honor Guard duty at Fort Meyer.

We were married in Houston and honeymooned at Galveston, Texas. My duty at Fort Lewis was training recruits for infantry basic training. This was not a duty I liked. I liked serving in units in which everyone had his Army basic training behind him.

After about six months of training recruits I volunteered for duty with an armored tank company with the 4th Infantry Division. I started out as a tank commander, then as tank section commander, which made me in charge of more than just one tank.

17

THE WINDING RIVERS OF VIETNAM

It was something different, getting to ride instead of walking as an infantry soldier for so many years. Part of my tank training was done at Yakima, Washington and Fort Erwin in the Mojave Desert near the town of Barstow, California.

My new wife went with me to Barstow while I was taking tank training. We rented a small apartment in Barstow. She was pregnant at the time with our first child, Micki, who is now grown up and happily married to John. And now they have their own daughter, Evan.

After training at Fort Erwin we went back to Fort Lewis. After tank training I transferred to a new outfit that was getting started at Fort Lewis' 4th Infantry Division, 2nd Engineer Amphibious Support Command, known as armored troop carriers, LVTP5s. These track vehicles will go on land or water.

At Fort Lewis we took a lot of our training at Nisqually Reach water inlet. The amphibious unit sent all of us soldiers to train with the Marines at Camp Pendleton, California. The marines had battalions of LVTP5 track vehicles. We didn't have to take our track vehicles from Fort Lewis. We used the Marines' track vehicles.

Our training was to drive the LVTP5s off the beach and out into the surf of the sea, then go out into the bay and drive up on to an LST ship that had its forward ramp down so that we could drive the LVTP5 up the ramp and into the belly of the LST. The next day we would drive off the LST and head back to the beach for a simulated troop assault from ship to shore. I was lucky on the weekends at Camp Pendleton.

My sister, Jane, was married to a Marine officer and lived right outside of Camp Pendleton. At Oceanside she invited me to visit her and her family on the weekends, which I enjoyed. And I was lucky that I didn't have to stay in the barracks at Camp Pendleton on the weekends.

After training at Pendleton, and after we got back to Fort Lewis, my enlistment was up in the Army. I wanted to re-enlist, but I wanted to get into something where I could learn a trade that would help me when I got back to civilian life. It was lucky for me that the Army came out with a re-enlistment "School Catalog Book." I looked through the book and chose training at the Chief Marine Engineer School at Fort Eustis, Virginia.

This was a school to learn about shipboard diesel engines and all auxiliary equipment aboard Army seagoing vessels. In 1964 I enlisted for this school and was approved. I was sent to Fort Eustis, and I was more than pleased with the school there. Most of the classes were conducted in nice buildings. We even had students from other countries in our classes. The diesel engines were in the building classroom. I took the basic course and the advanced course of Marine engine operations. I graduated from the sixteen-week school in December, 1964.

My next new duty station was Louisiana, outside of New Orleans. The duty station was at Camp Leroy Johnson. This was a small Army camp that was right alongside of Lake Pontchartrain. I was assigned to a small boat company. My wife and our new baby daughter, Micki, lived outside the camp. First we rented a house, then, after a while, I bought a large house trailer and we lived in a nice trailer park.

While at this new duty station our second baby was born, a son we named Jimmie. He was born at Camp Leroy Johnson. My duty at this new station was Chief Marine Engineer aboard a large landing craft mike eight. The other boats that were in our unit were one small seagoing freight ship and about two T-boats, one of which had a small cargo compartment. There were many landing crafts mike eight.

Some of us would make trips with our landing craft up the Mississippi to Baton Rouge, and we took trips down to the Gulf of Mexico to Biloxi, Mississippi. At Biloxi we docked at an Air Force base that had rescue crash boats. We would stay overnight at this base and then continue on down to Pensacola Naval Air Station at Jacksonville, Florida.

They too had nice boat docks with crash boats. We stayed there about two weeks. We did get some liberty in Jacksonville, Florida. The boat unit I was in made this trip down to Mississippi and Florida many times. I enjoyed these trips and never did have any engine trouble. Our diesel engines were the gray Marine 671s that I found to be good running engines.

After my duty in Louisiana at Camp Leroy Johnson, my next assignment was back to Korea. This would be my third time to serve in Korea. My duty station was at Inchon, Korea, a small camp on a small island called Wolmi-Doe. A road was built joining the mainland of Inchon to the island of Wolmi-Doe. This was a military base with Quonset huts for buildings. The island is no longer a military base. It is now a large Korean civilian airport.

When I arrived at the port of Inchon, I was assigned to a J-boat, which was a small cabin boat with 671 engines inboard. I had a crew of three Korean civilians. This boat was used to accommodate the Port Commander for troop movement from troop ships and for fishing trips and parties for his invited friends. These included other officers and women nurses from the military hospital in Seoul.

My job was to pilot the boat while my crew served mixed drinks. Also, when fishing for sea bass, the crew's job was to tie hooks on the fishing lines and keep bait on the fishing lines for those who were fishing. Their other job was to serve food that the mess sergeant supplied for the boat before we departed for the trip.

The Port of Inchon had about a thirty-two foot drop tide every six hours, and the mudflat stretched way out into the bay from our boat docks. The tide had to be watched closely to determine when boats could be moved for trips. When the tide was out, our boats tied to the docks would be sitting down in the mud.

All large navigating ships bringing in cargo, including troop ships, had to anchor and tie up to an assigned buoy out in the bay. The Army Harbor Master would send Army tugboats out pushing flat barges to the ships. Then the barges would be placed and tied up alongside the ships and the ships' cargo would be unloaded onto the barges. When full, the tugboats would push the loaded barges back to the port, into a waterway, and into a lock that lets the seawater rise or fall. From there the barges were unloaded and the cargo was placed in warehouses.

On troop movement day, which was about once a month, the Army would send out large LCUs, (landing craft utilities), alongside the troop ships to bring in new replacements of soldiers from the ship to shore. LCUs were also used to carry troops who were going back to the United States out to the ship.

My duty this time was much different than during other times I served in Korea. This time all us soldiers got to work with the Korean civilians and we got to know them. There was nothing off limits to soldiers at Inchon, and the Korean people seemed to like Americans. I found the Korean people hard workers and they have a good sense of humor. They are eagerly ready to learn new ways of doing things, and they like having parties.

I remember one evening, as I was walking down a street in Inchon, I heard

Korean music coming from a Korean house. As I started to walk by a Korean came out and said, "Come. You are welcome." The next thing I knew they were pulling me into the house to join the rest of the party. I didn't know anyone at the party, and I was the only American present. Before I knew it I had a bottle of beer in my hand and food in front of me. The Koreans were singing Korean songs and just having a good time. I don't like Korean food because it's so hot, especially Korean Kimchee, but this time I was not in a position to be choosey. I was their guest and not to eat was an insult to the householder. But there was one thing I refused to eat, and that was meat. I got by with what I did eat because I had the beer to wash it down with.

I liked Inchon. The Port of Inchon had a very large statue of General MacArthur high up on a hill, above the town, and overlooking the Port. This was a tribute to General MacArthur from the Koreans. His Army, and the Marines under his command, took back Inchon from the Communist North Koreans, and they pushed them back north to the 38th parallel where they are to this day.

The duty at Inchon, Korea was like duty in Japan, lots of bar girls to draw the soldiers in. The Army at Inchon had nice clubs for the soldiers, plenty of scheduled floorshows from the United States, and nice dance floors. Soldiers would bring girls to the club. When the Navy and the merchant ships were in port, the sailors would visit our clubs at Inchon.

I was in Korea when the South Koreans demonstrated in angry mobs against their president, Syngman Rhee. There were demonstrators in the city of Seoul who wanted to overthrow Syngman Rhee because of the way he was handling the economy and the government of South Korea. Word was out that these demonstrations were going to take place. For the safety of President Syngman Rhee and his wife, they were flown out of the country to another country, and a new president of South Korea was put in office.

My next duty station was back to the United States at Fort Eustis, Virginia. This time I was assigned as Chief Engineer aboard an LCU. After serving aboard about six months, the pistol marksmanship team at the camp asked me if I would join their team of about nine expert pistol shooters. They did a lot of traveling on pistol matches.

The pistol team captain told me that he had learned that I had done some team pistol shooting at Fort Lewis, Washington. So I was given a tryout at the pistol range and then accepted on the pistol team. We fired three pistols, the 22 caliber, the 38 caliber, and the 45 caliber. We spent a lot of time on the pistol range practicing. Everyone on the team was an expert shooter with all three. All our shooting was done one handed, not two-handed. Our team traveled in Virginia and to other states to participate in pistol matches.

We were sent out on matches to represent the Army at Fort Eustis. We traveled using our own vehicles. A lot of pistol matches were fired on civilian ranges as well as on military ranges. We fired the 45 caliber, 38 caliber, and the 22 caliber pistols. We were all expert, and some were master shooters in classification. We were a good pistol team of nine shooters. I enjoyed this duty.

We were all members of the National Rifle Association, and we traveled to shooting matches in Pennsylvania, West Virginia, Maryland, North Carolina, South Carolina, and to Jacksonville, Florida all the way down to Coral Gables, Florida. All our matches were sponsored by the NRA, and as long as we brought back the winning team trophy to give to the commanding general of Fort Eustis, he was more than willing to send our team out to pistol matches.

While at Fort Eustis in 1964 I received word from my sister, Maxine, who lived in Houston, Texas, that my father, Charles Dayton Clark, aged 65, had died at the Veteran's Hospital. Before his death he had requested to be laid to rest in West Virginia, a place called, Ten Mile, which is an old cemetery back in the hills outside of Buckcannon. My sister, Maxine, and my sister, Marguerite, who also lives in Houston, Texas, called me and said that they would be the only ones from our family who would be flying to West Virginia to attend our father's funeral. They wanted to know if I would come to the funeral.

I said that I would drive to West Virginia with my wife and two babies. I was thinking to myself, "Why should I go to his funeral after the way he treated me?" But he was my father and I didn't hate him. I felt sorry that this man had wasted his life on alcohol.

I drove to West Virginia and met my two sisters. I found out that my father had died from complications of cirrhosis of the liver, which didn't come as a surprise to any of us. My father died as a poor man. The money he had made in the Merchant Marines had been spent on alcohol. There wasn't even enough money for a headstone. He was laid to rest back in the hills of Ten Mile, West Virginia, the same cemetery where his mother was laid to rest.

After my duty at Fort Eustis, I was sent to Vietnam. The war was raging. I will never forget the day our plane landed at the airport in Saigon, at TanSon Nhut Air Base. The plane door opened and it was like a heat wave going through the plane. It was so hot that the air seemed to have no oxygen, and our clothes started sticking to us.

By the time we unloaded the plane, picked up our duffel bags, and walked to the airport terminal and went through customs, the uniforms we were wearing were soaking wet. At the airport we were loaded up on Army trucks and taken to a small camp on the outskirts of Saigon.

The next day some of us were driven to Phan-Rang. This was another replacement center. I stayed at this camp about a week. My new assignment was to Cam-Ranh Bay to the 97th Transportation Heavy Boat Company, and my assignment was as Chief Engineer aboard a landing craft utility. It was a large flat bottom barge with a large ramp in front that could be let down to take on cargo. We could carry a large number of troops or armored tanks. The flat bottom on this boat would allow us to go up on the beach as far as we could to let our ramp down to let off our cargo.

We had living quarters and a galley, and usually eight or nine crewmembers counting the cook on board the boat. We had all the navigation equipment required for navigating by day or by night. For protection we had fifty caliber machine guns mounted on the deck and each soldier crewmember was armed with his military weapon. We traveled all along the coast of South Vietnam in the South China Sea from Qui Nhon to Phan Rang with the Army equipment and ammunition.

The one cargo I was leery about hauling was big rubber containers that reached the full length of our cargo deck. The containers were full of jet fuel that was very flammable. There was no smoking on deck when we were hauling this jet fuel. When sailing along the coast of Vietnam there was always the chance of coming under fire from the shore because it was known that the Vietcong were active all along the coastline.

We could hear the thunder of big artillery guns firing and the bombing of fighter planes hitting their targets. We all knew that if we should be fired on from an artillery gun on shore by the Vietcong, and if they got a direct hit on a cargo of jet fuel in long rubber containers almost half the length of the boat, we would be blown up in a fireball.

So we kept reminding the person who was steering the boat to keep a good distance from the shoreline. We also had to stay alert and on the lookout for the Vietnamese large boats they called, sampans. Vietnamese families lived aboard them, but the Vietcong had also been using sampans to attack American boats. At night the sampans were hard to see. They used no navigating lights. On one of our trips from Cam Ranh Bay we had moved up to the beach to unload the cargo. We had our front ramp down and had just secured the boat. Our cook stepped from the boat onto the shore when he was killed. Another unforgettable event was when an Air Force plane carrying about thirty American servicemen from Vietnam overshot the runway and crashed into the ocean killing all aboard.

These were men whose tour of duty was over and they were on their way home to the United States. The boat I was on and another boat were dispatched to the crash site with underwater divers and their equipment. When we got to the spot where the plane went down, the divers started bringing up bodies and their luggage. This was such a sad event. After all those servicemen had endured and survived in Vietnam, and now, on their way home, they all ended up drowning in the South China Sea.

Another unforgettable event was when our boat was on another trip to go pick up cargo. It was during one of Vietnam's monsoon seasons and we ran into a strong storm. The sea was so strong it would lift the bow of the boat up out of the water. It was at this time that we were having trouble with our front ramp. It wouldn't close all the way shut to where we could dog the ramp down into a locking position so it would be secure.

The way it was the ramp would stop to a position of being about ten inches from being completely closed. The ramp had large chains on each side that helped lower and raise the ramp. The chain's links are very large, almost like a big ship's anchor chain. The wind was blowing strong.

We were taking big waves over the bow, and each time a wave would hit, the ramp would drop down to the open position. And each time the bow would be lifted up and then slammed down. Our position was between Phan Rang and Cam Ranh Bay, our homeport. We were taking on water in the cargo deck. It wasn't long before our front ramp started dropping down to the half-open position. Then when a very large wave hit us hard at the bow, the ramp jolted wide open at the same time, and both sides of the chains suddenly snapped and broke. Ramp and chains went to the floor of the sea. We were in trouble.

The boat would not respond to where the skipper wanted to go. The skipper called our home base on the radio for assistance. They said assistance would be on the way. They would send a large Army seagoing tugboat. We had no idea how long it would take for the tugboat to arrive to assist us.

The skipper came up with the idea of running the boat backwards so that he would have better control over steering the boat in the direction he wanted. That didn't work. No sooner had we gotten the boat turned around when seawater went into the engine's exhaust and stopped all engines from running. Some LCU's engine exhausts have metal flappers that let exhaust out, but keep water from backing into the engine's exhaust. This particular boat had not had these flappers installed. By this time we had our life jackets on. We were like a piece of driftwood. We had to go where the sea wanted us to go.

We maintained radio contact with home base and with the rescue tugboat. They would let us know their position. We were thrown around almost one and a half hours before we heard the captain of the tugboat come over the radio saying he had us in sight and for us to be ready for their tug to come up alongside our LCU.

That sounded good to all of us. By this time we were all getting seasick. The tugboat arrived and secured a large steel cable to our stern and pulled us backward to Cam Ranh Bay. The LCU was pushed up onto the beach as far as the tug could push us up on the shore. A crew was on the beach to survey the damage to our LCU. I could see some of them laughing. They had never seen an LCU lose its ramp and chain.

We were told that we would be up on the beach and on dead time for over a month because the Army had to order the ramp and chain from the United States. There were none in stock in Vietnam. This would give my two assistants and me a lot of time to work on all the engines that seawater had gotten into. The days passed. Each morning the monkeys from the woods had less fear of us, and they would come up on our deck hoping someone would give them some food. We did, and that turned out to be a big mistake. Every day there were more and more monkeys. Finally we had to stop feeding them and start running them off. Other critters we had to be on the alert for were large sea snakes. They liked coming up on the warm deck of the boat at night, and they would still be there in the morning. They would be all coiled up taking in the heat of the deck and the hot sun. They were very big, long snakes and very poisonous.

In Vietnam it can get very hot in the mornings before noon. It can reach 110 degrees. One of the monkeys started getting people-friendly and would take things out of our hands. He would spend more time with our boat's crew than with his own kind. Before long the monkey wanted to sit on someone's shoulder.

A stray dog came by and also wanted to stay on our boat. The monkey got a little jealous of the dog and would torment the dog by jumping on the dog's back. The dog didn't like that.

Our boat's new ramp and chain arrived, and after a month and a half of being non-operational, we were now ready to be back on schedule for trips. Our first trip was to go out alongside a Navy ship that had anchored off shore. We had to pick up some cargo. By this time the monkey was almost part of the crew. To some of us he was a pain in the neck, always into something. And when any one of us tried to take something away from him that he shouldn't have, he would resist by showing his teeth at you and he would get ready to pounce.

While our boat was alongside the Navy ship, some of the sailors took an interest in our monkey and asked us what we would take for him. We told them that we would have to talk it over among us. It didn't take long to agree. The monkey had to go. So we told the sailors that we would like to have a big box of beef steaks. The sailors called it a deal.

The sailors gave us two big boxes of steaks, so we handed over the monkey to the sailors. When we left the Navy ship and headed back to our port, we were all laughing and relieved to be rid of that pesky monkey. Someone in the crew said he would give the sailors five days with that monkey and then they would be ready to throw him overboard. We all agreed.

All of us serving in Vietnam were hearing about the Vietnam anti-war demonstrations in the United States, and about young men burning their draft cards, and others running to Canada to avoid the draft. This did lower our morale some, but we all knew that there were cowards in every country. When my tour of duty was over in Vietnam I had twenty-two years in the Army, and I wanted to return to the United States and retire.

Another part of me wanted to stay on for thirty-years retirement, but after a lot of thinking it over, and after realizing how the Army was changing from the way it was when I first joined the Army, I thought it was time to leave. The Army now wanted young soldiers. I was among a large group of soldiers returning from Vietnam in 1969. When we arrived at the airport in Seattle, Washington, we were met by anti-war demonstrators carrying signs reading, "American Soldiers Are Fighting an Immoral War and Committing Pointless Murder, Killing Babies." Some of the soldiers were spat at. I thought to myself, "What a change in public attitude from the way the patriotism was shown, and the appreciation for the returning servicemen of World War II and the Korean War. I was shocked at what I was seeing.

After loading onto Army buses and being taken to Fort Lewis, I received my retirement orders. I was now a civilian, and living with my wife and children in Washington. I often wondered to myself how I had made it this far in my life when so many times death had been all around me. There were soldiers standing next to me or with me in the trenches who were getting killed, and I was not. It's hard to understand that I'm still alive. I'm grateful for every day to be among the living, but every day I think of the ones who didn't make it back from the war. They will always be in my thoughts and memories.

Back in civilian life, I went job hunting. During my first interview for a job I told an interviewer that I had just gotten out of the military after having served twenty-two years. His response to me was, "Well, you're now out here in a society where it's dog-eat-dog." I said, "I think I'll make it. I just came out of a place where people want to kill Americans." I didn't get that particular job, but after some looking and patience I found a job working for Lockheed Shipbuilding in Seattle. It was a good paying job, but there was something wrong within me.

The war was still raging in Vietnam. I guess I missed being in or around the military. One thing I remembered seeing while serving in Vietnam was Americans working for big American construction companies. I found out their addresses and sent out resumes to construction companies. After working for about six months at the Lockheed Shipyard in Seattle, I received an offer for a job in Vietnam with Morrison Knudsen, a company that was with Brown, Root and Jones doing construction work in Vietnam while the war was going on.

I had some misgivings about going back to Vietnam, but I also knew the wages were good and tax-free. Morrison Knudsen hired me. The job would be working under a sub-contract that the U.S. Navy had with Morrison Knudsen. The job was to survey rivers in Vietnam. Most of Vietnam's rivers had never been surveyed.

I was assigned as Chief Marine Engineer aboard a 65-foot T-boat, a boat the Army must have sold to Morrison Knudsen. The Army has some of these boats. They have a steel hull and one up-front cargo hold. On this T-boat the forward cargo hold had been converted into living quarters for a crew of eight. A steel plate had been welded down to cover the cargo hold. A spring-loaded steel hatch was put in place for entry into the living quarters. By turning a steel, round wheel the hatch would open. There was a wheel inside the hatch as well as on the outside. Then there was a steel ladder a person had to go down.

This would lead down into the galley which was to the forward of the boat. In this compartment was the shower and toilet. Then there was a steel door that would lead into the sleeping quarters. The sleeping bunks were up against the boat's hull which was below the water line. A person could hear the ripple of the water. There were three and four bunks high. In the middle of the sleeping quarters we had a long table for us to eat at and to play card games, poker and blackjack.

All eight of the civilian crew members slept and we cooked our meals in these compartments. Each one had to do his own cooking and supply his own food. Most of us teamed up with another person. The skipper, Captain Dan, who was the ninth crew member, had living quarters for himself.

High up in the pilot house, Dan the skipper was very much an alcoholic. He drank hard whiskey all the time. I will never know why the home office let him skipper a sixty-five foot vessel. When I arrived in Saigon, Vietnam I was taken to the main office of Morrison and Knudsen, and while I was waiting for my assignment, I noticed in the hallway of the office pictures of about twenty civilians and a sign saying, "In memory of those who lost their lives."

I found out later that when the American military fought and took the city of Hue from the Vietcong, Morrison Knudsen sent some of their employees in to do construction work in this city. The American military held the city long enough for a lot of the Vietnamese people to become friends with the Americans. But this didn't last long. The Vietcong reorganized and took the city back from the American military.

This is when a lot of Americans and other foreign civilians got trapped in the city. They were taken prisoner by the Vietcong. Most of them were lined up and shot for all the city of Hue to see. Also, the Vietcong carried out a massacre of their own people, those who had been friendly with and worked with the Americans. This is why there were pictures of the twenty construction workers hanging in the hallway of the main office in Saigon.

When I came aboard the vessel named, "Tudor," as Chief Engineer, and the vessel's skipper welcomed me aboard, I could tell he had been drinking. I could smell whiskey on his breath. I could tell that Skipper Dan didn't like me, but I wasn't going to let that bother me. The makeup of the crew was just Skipper Dan and me. The other seven aboard the vessel were civilian surveyors. They bunked down below, in the same compartment I did. The survey crew chief was a nice person named Ken. Two of his crew members were Vietnamese.

Being civilians we were not allowed to be armed personally, nor were we allowed to have any armaments on board the vessel. We were to survey rivers, and we were on our own. We usually fueled up at a port in Saigon. Then we headed out to survey rivers. Some of the rivers flowed through narrow Vietnam jungles with jungle grass on both sides of the vessel. The grass was almost as high as the vessel itself.

One day I was standing out on the deck drinking a cup of coffee. I was wearing a white t-shirt, and I noticed the grass was tall and the river wound around like a snake. As I was standing out on the deck rifle fire was coming from somewhere in the grass, and the bullets were hitting the side of the skipper's quarters and knocking the paint off the steel hull. It didn't take me long to realize that I was being shot at. Quickly I went into the skipper's quarters. There were steps in the skipper's quarters going up to the wheelhouse. I let him know we were being shot at. He picked up speed to get us out of that area.

After months of sailing many rivers in Vietnam I had the feeling that our luck would run out, and that we would all be killed or taken as prisoners then shot as spies. Sometimes on these rivers we would meet American Navy gunboats called swift boats patrolling the rivers. They would stop us even when we were flying the American flag.

They would come aboard and want to know where we were headed. After being shown on the map our destination, and after hearing that we would be surveying a certain place on the river, they would become flabbergasted, especially when they found out we had no armament of any kind. They would shake their heads and say that we were really asking to be blown out of the water and killed. We could see that these swift military riverboats were well armed with various weapons, mounted machine guns, quad 50 caliber, rocket launchers, mortars, and personal weapons.

They told us that some of their own swift boats had been attacked, and their men killed on these rivers by the Vietcong. We did have a powerful radio with which we could communicate with our headquarters in Saigon, but a lot of good that would do if we came under attack by the Vietcong. We would be lucky if we had time to radio headquarters. I remember one swift boat skipper told us we were vulnerable as Vietcong bait, and he said that we needed all the luck we could get. As they pulled away from our boat, the skipper stood on the bow of his gun boat and said, in a lowered voice, "I salute you guys."

When we needed food supplies we would drop anchor near a village and drop over the motorboat we had on board. Then one of us would take the two Vietnamese who were part of the survey team ashore to buy food from the Vietnamese market. The market was nothing but an outside, fly-infested place. We told the two Vietnamese what we wanted them to bring back. It was safer to send them because those villages did harbor Vietcong. When they were done shopping they would wave to us from shore and we would pick them up.

I remember the first time we sent them out for food supplies. They came back with a headless, skinned monkey, pork that looked like it had been pulled apart, French bread, and stinking, pungent fish sauce. When the Vietnamese cooked, it would stink so bad the Americans would have to go up on the deck of the boat to get fresh air. The Vietnamese ate the monkey.

We could always tell when either of the two Vietnamese used the toilet. Their rubber shower shoes, the only thing they ever wore on their feet, would leave shoe prints on the toilet seat. This was because they never used a toilet that a person would sit upright on. They were used to squatting over a big hole. They would also forget to flush. They had been shown how to do this.

One day while going up the river we were moving at a good speed with a strong current. I was up on the bow of the boat working on the anchor motor. I could see Skipper Dan up in the pilot house steering the boat. He always left the doors on the pilot house open for fresh air. I could see him drinking from the bottle of whiskey, but that was not an unusual thing to see him do by now.

It wasn't long before I heard my name being called repeatedly. I looked up at the window of the pilot house, and I didn't see the skipper. I looked at our boat's heading and it was headed toward shore through tall grass. I ran to the empty pilot house, turned the wheel to get the boat back on course, and cut the engines down. The skipper was lying outside the pilot house, on the deck, asking me to help him. He kept telling me he was all right and for me to put him back into the pilot house so he could take over the wheel and steer the boat. I had my doubts, but he was the skipper of the boat, so I helped him get back on the wheel to steer the boat. I made some coffee and encouraged him to drink that instead of the whiskey. I think that falling out of the pilot house and onto the hard, steel deck sobered him up some.

Traveling those winding rivers we never knew what was waiting for us around the next bend. I was amazed at some of the Vietnamese villages. We would come to their shacks which were built over the water on wooden pillars. They had a small boat to row to shore. I remember one time when we were coming up the river toward one of these villages, we saw a small bamboo raft that had a small dead baby tied to the raft floating down the river. I was told later that that's the way the river people discarded their dead babies.

18

SAIGON AND A SINKING VESSEL

When we were back in Saigon sometimes we would dock our boat at the Vietnamese Navy docks. This was next to the International Hotel. They had security. We would go uptown to our main office headquarters where we could buy food supplies down in the building's basement. They had a commissary stocked with canned foods and frozen meats from the United States. We would buy these for our next trip. Sometimes we would stay in Saigon a week before being sent out on our next survey assignment.

I got somewhat familiar with the city. I have never seen so many Japanese Honda motorcycles. It seemed that everyone had one. Sometimes I would see a whole family on a motorcycle at one time. They didn't know about wearing helmets.

I was told not to wear my wristwatch in town, to keep it in my pocket, because the men double up on one bike, and when they come to a red light they keep an eye out for Americans standing on the curb waiting for the light to change. The second guy on the motorcycle reaches out and grabs the unsuspecting person's wristwatch off his arm, and most of the time in this grabbing act, the band breaks and the watch is gone.

One morning when I was walking from our boat at the Saigon port uptown to Morrison Knudsen's main office, I took a short cut through some alleyways so I would miss a lot of traffic on the main streets. As I was walking two motorcycles came up the same alley behind me. I looked back and I could see there were two Vietnamese men on each motorcycle. I didn't think much about it because each man on the motorcycle had the South Vietnamese soldier's uniform on. They slowed down just before getting to where I was. They passed me just a little way and the two men riding on the back jumped off the motorcycles, rushed up to me, and each man had in his hand a 45 caliber pistol.

I know a standard United States sidearm semi-automatic pistol when I see one. They each pulled the slide back on the pistol and the slide slammed forward. That puts a bullet in the chamber. One of the Vietnamese got behind me with the pistol pressed on the back of my head. The other one stood in front of me with a pistol held to my forehead. The other two Vietnamese stayed with the motorcycles. The one behind me took my wallet and the money that was in it. It was only forty dollars.

He threw my wallet to the ground. The Vietnamese in front of me ripped my watch off my arm. After they got what they wanted, the two Vietnamese men walked backwards to the motorcycle all the time keeping the pistol pointed at me. They mounted the waiting motorcycle sitting backwards of the driver with their pistols still pointed at me.

They went up the alley and out into the main street and traffic. I thought to myself that I was lucky they didn't shoot me because they could have gotten away with shooting me. I came to the realization that I wasn't taking a shortcut through Mr. Roger's neighborhood.

Vietnam at this time came under martial law. The Vietnamese Army had the same authority as the Vietnamese police, and they were a corrupt force. When I got to the office I told them what happened to me and asked what I could do about it. I was told, "Nothing. Americans over here are good targets." They said there was no point in going to the American Embassy which was just a few blocks away. "They won't help you. You're an American civilian in Vietnam. They will tell you what the Embassy has been telling other Americans who have suffered at the hands of the Vietnamese police. And that is, 'You're a civilian. You don't have to be here. You can get on the big silver bird and fly back to America any time you want.'"

I learned fast that in South Vietnam there were a lot of Vietcong not wearing uniforms. The Vietcong could melt into the population and hide in the homes of Vietcong sympathizers. Another tactic they used to kill Americans was to drive by a popular restaurant or bar where American soldiers and civilians were. Most of these places would have their front doors open because of the heat. As the Vietcong terrorists would go by on motorcycles they would toss a satchel of explosives or a hand grenade into the establishment. I tried to avoid places where Americans would hang out. I would look inside and if I saw no Americans and all Vietnamese in the establishment, then that was where I would go.

One day I got into a Vietnamese taxi. Their taxis were small French cars with not much room in the back seat, so I sat up front with the driver. It was a blistering hot day, so I rolled down the window to get fresh air. The driver reached over and rolled the window back up saying, "No, no. Window not open." Then he told me as well as he could in English that "Vietcong see American in taxi, they throw in open window hand grenade."

I could see and understand what the driver was saying. In the traffic there were Vietnamese on motorcycles all around us. Also, there were reports of Americans being kidnapped or gunned down on the streets of Saigon. There was a curfew in place in the city of Saigon.

The curfew began at twelve o'clock midnight and went on until five-thirty in the morning. During this time everything stopped. Establishments would close and all traffic would be gone. This is when martial law really took over. The Vietnamese Army and their police patrolled the streets armed, and they were quick to shoot anyone moving on the streets after curfew.

Every night we would hear from our boat shootings going on in uptown Saigon. And every night we would hear American artillery and machine guns being fired on the outside of the city limits. We would see flares being fired to light up the area. The war was raging and the Vietcong wanted to invade Saigon.

While I was in Vietnam I visited Tan-Son Nhut Airport, American controlled, in Saigon. They had a good servicemen's club which I could go to. Every now and then the airport would receive an artillery round that the Vietcong fired at the base. This was nothing new.

I remember that my sister, Jean, and her husband, Ralph Wyke, told me that when they were in Vietnam with their two children, Betty Jane and Buzz, they had housing and their children attended school on the base of Tan-Son Nhut. At that time they were receiving terrorist attacks. Ralph was working for a big contracting company. Jean and Ralph and their children got out of Saigon just in time before the full-blown war started with Vietcong and Americans.

While I was in Vietnam as a civilian I received word from home in 1970 that Ralph, Jean and their children, Betty Jane and Buzz, were in Tehran, Iran on another contracting job for the Iranian government.

Our next survey trip was back up another river. On this trip we sailed past an island that was set off by itself. I was told in broken English by one of the Vietnamese on board our boat that this island, flying a black flag, was a leprosy colony. When we arrived at the place on the river to be surveyed, the seven member survey crew would get into aluminum boats with an outboard motor with all their survey equipment and disappear around the winding river. Our vessel, The Tudor, was anchored in the middle of the river. The skipper, Dan, and I would stay aboard the vessel. On this survey mission the survey took longer than it usually would have and we had no communication with the survey crew. The skipper and I were beginning to worry about them.

We were in an area where the Vietcong was active. It was late when they got back and each one of them was covered with blood-sucking leeches. In order to do their job, the survey crew sometimes had to get in the river to chart the river banks. Dan and I had the job of getting them off the crew.

Our next survey mission was more up north near the city of Hue, a city where fierce fighting took place when the American military took the city back from the Vietcong. When we arrived and anchored off shore, I told the skipper I wanted someone to take me ashore with the motorboat. I wanted to see the city of Hue and visit the temples and museums I had heard so much about. The skipper and our Vietnamese crew members thought I was crazy to want to go ashore in this city.

The city of Hue was now in the hands of our military, so I didn't think I would have to worry. I was taken ashore. I walked a long distance to get to the center of town. I spent most of the day taking pictures. I did notice that I didn't see any other Americans, and I did notice how cold the people were toward me.

They would steadily stare at me. I was walking past a street vendor selling cold drinks to Vietnamese children. There were a lot of children crowded around the vendor. As I walked past I saw kids pointing at me and saying things in Vietnamese. I smiled at them but it didn't do any good.

I was almost past all of them when a small number of them started throwing rocks in my direction. I turned around and pointed my finger at them and I was saying, "No, no, not good." Then the grownups started laughing at what the children were doing, and then the grownups started throwing rocks at me.

I started running in the direction of the city center. I thought that if I ran two or three blocks they would give up and stop running after me. I was wrong. Each time I looked back I could see the crowd was getting larger and there were more grownups than kids.

The rocks were starting to reach me, hitting my back and legs, and sometimes I would get one to the head. I had a long way to run to get to the place where the boat was anchored. I knew too that I would have to stop at the shore and get the crew's attention to come with the small motorboat to pick me up. I knew the crowd would catch up with me. As I was running I was thinking I would have to swim out to the vessel. I knew I was running in the right direction. I remembered seeing a small military building fortified with sandbags in front of it and two machine gun positions.

I made up my mind as I was running that this was where I was going. I looked behind me. The mob was bigger and they were yelling things in

Vietnamese. I reached the military fortified position. There was a military policeman looking out between the sandbags. I told him I was an American and I was coming in because the whole town of Hue was after me.

He could hear the crowd yelling and he saw the rocks being thrown. "Hurry," he said, "Come in." As I got behind the sandbags about six military police stood out onto the sidewalk and pointed their weapons at the crowd. They stopped in their tracks and went back towards town. The MPs wanted to know what in hell I did to get the whole town mad enough to want to stone me to death. All I could say was, "Nothing. I was just walking around taking pictures." One of the military police asked me to follow him into the building to see his commanding officer. I showed my identification to the commanding officer and explained why and how I got there and what I was doing uptown.

The commander told me that this was a very dangerous town for an American to be in, that the Vietnamese don't want to be friends with Americans because they had seen what happened to some of them. When the Vietcong re-took the city from the Americans, many of their people were executed. The commander said that I could eat with them and later that evening they would take me by Jeep with armed guards back down to where I could get on my vessel.

All I could think of was how lucky I was that this American outpost was there when I needed a safe place to run to. I thanked them and told them how grateful I was. I got back to the vessel and I told everyone what had happened to me. And I told them that this was the last time I would ever want to go to a town while we were on these survey missions.

On completion of this mission we went to Da-Nang which had a big harbor and a place where we could dock our vessel and wait for word from the main office in Saigon for our next mission. The city of Da-Nang also was a big city, but I had no desire to walk around in it.

After about two days in Da-Nang we were radioed to go on our next mission to Dong-Ha and survey their river, and that we would go by sea until we reached the river to be surveyed. We were also told that this would be just a short distance from North Vietnam, and that it was a very hostile area. We were told not to worry, that those at the main office of Morrison Knudsen had made arrangements with the U.S. Navy, and that the Navy would have gunboats there to protect us. They were to be there when we arrived.

Knowing this I didn't have anything to worry about. The reason the military wanted these rivers surveyed was because the Vietcong were blowing up most of all the ammunition being transported to our troops. Ammunition was transported by trucks, and there were many of them on the roads. Because of this problem there was an interest in using the rivers and hauling ammunition by boats and barges. But a lot of these rivers had high spots in them and needed to be dredged. It was our job to find the high spots and the narrowness, and then map this information so that Morrison Knudsen and our military could be informed.

After we received this new survey assignment, and while we were still in the port of Da-Nang, the crew and I talked and thought about the mission. We heard from some of the servicemen at Da-Nang that this was a very hostile place and infested with Vietcong. All of us on board the vessel knew that as civilians we could refuse the mission and go back to the United States. But after being told that the U.S. Navy promised to provide armed protection for our vessel and crew, and after being informed by radio from our home base, Morrison Knudsen in Saigon, that the armed protection would be there in the river when we arrived, we decided to go on the mission to survey the Qua-Viet River in Don-Ha. When we departed Da-Nang the weather was nice and hot, but it didn't last long.

The sea started getting rough, and before we knew it, we were in a big storm. The waves were washing over our deck and everything on the deck that wasn't tied down was washed overboard. The bow of the boat would shoot straight up and then slam down. Then the stern would lift up out of the water and the vessel would rock from one side to the other.

We could see large boulders along the shoreline. Skipper Dan kept saying to me, "Clark, don't let the engine die or we'll be slammed up on those boulders." We only had one engine. If it had quit there wasn't much I could have done because we would have been pushed into the boulders before I could have gotten the engine started again.

I was seasick like I've never been before. I had to go down into the hot engine room to check and make sure the vessel wasn't sinking. The fumes from the diesel engine finally got to me. I couldn't go out on the deck to throw up or I would have been washed over the side of the vessel.

Skipper Dan was having a hard time steering the vessel. I came out of the engine room and went into his living quarters and started throwing up in his toilet. I threw up so much the toilet got plugged up and wouldn't take any more. Then I started throwing up in his wash sink, and it wasn't long before the sink was plugged up. Then I found a bucket and I had no more throw-up in me. I lay down on his bunk and that seemed to help me. All this time the skipper thought I was down in the engine room. All the members of the survey team were lying down on their bunks down in the living quarters. After a long time the sea and storm started to calm down.

I got up and went into the wheel-house to tell the skipper that I had plugged up his sink and toilet, and that I was going to fix and clean up the mess. Survey crew members started coming up on deck to get some fresh air. I could see that they were all green in the face and hanging their heads over the side of the boat's railing. They all said they got seasick, even those who, in the past, said that they never got seasick. As I look back in my memory, if our engine had quit running we would have slammed into the boulders that were rising out of the water. We were a long way from shore and none of us were wearing life jackets.

We would more than likely have had a sinking vessel. We found the opening of the Qua-Viet River at Don-Ha and we started up the river looking for the Navy gunboats. We found none. All that we did see was a small South Vietnamese boat dock with two or three small boats tied up to the dock. There was no way we could tie up to their dock because it was so small and it looked as if it wasn't strong enough to support our vessel. The skipper thought we should drop anchor out in the middle of the river, which we did.

The skipper radioed back to Morrison Knudsen in Saigon and reported that we had arrived at the river and there were no Navy gunboats in sight. He told them we had gone a good way up the river and had seen nothing in the way of security for the vessel and crew.

Their reply to us was to stay there, that security was on its way. This was at about one o'clock in the afternoon on the 24th of February, 1971. We were all up on deck looking over the area. One side of the bank of the river was thick with jungle. The other side was cleared with a small beach. We could see small wooden Vietnamese fishing boats going past our vessel. They were headed up river. We did see a small Vietnamese village when we went up the river.

As the Vietnamese boats were going by I noticed that there were no men in the boats. They were all old women dressed in their usual black-looking pajamas and round straw hats. I mentioned to the skipper and to the rest of the crew that it seemed strange that there were no men in the small boats with the women. Skipper Dan said, "The missing men are probably in the Vietcong Army." That was a good probability considering that we were only about seven to ten miles from the demilitarized zone separating South Vietnam from the north. Later in the afternoon a large tugboat came up the river towing a large floating barge which they called, "The Sand Caster."

It was a small dredge that had about a three man crew, all civilians. The Sand Caster could operate in rivers, but not in the open sea. It was used to dig out the high spots our vessel would find. We had depth radar to determine the location of high spots in the rivers, and the Sand Caster would follow up behind us.

After the tugboat placed the Sand Caster close to shore, the tugboat left to go back to Da-Nang. After the Sand Caster was secured to the shore we picked up anchor and moved over and tied up alongside the Sand Caster. The Sand Caster did have small living quarters for the crew. Later that day, just before it started getting dark, Skipper Dan called by radio again and reported that the protection from the Navy still had not arrived. We were told again that they would be there.

When night came we were in enemy waters with all our running lights on both sides of our vessel, port and starboard, looking like we were sitting in San Francisco Bay. The skipper did his usual thing, drinking from his bottle of whiskey. We never had anyone stand watch, so after we cooked our meals and the skipper went to his cabin hugging his bottle of whiskey, the eight of us went down to our sleeping quarters closing the spring-loaded hatch behind us.

We went through the kitchen, then through a heavy steel door to our quarters where there was a long table and chairs and footlockers along the walls. We all sat around the table playing blackjack. Five of us were at the table playing cards and the other three men lay on their bunks reading books. There was a lot of money on the table.

It was about two o'clock in the morning. I was sitting next to the chief survey boss. He had just nudged me showing me his cards. I looked and he had two queens. At that instant there was a big explosion that came inward from the outside of our living quarters bringing with it the steel hull of our vessel as shrapnel. The explosion knocked out our generator.

It was pitch black. I was blown backward on my back. River water came rushing into our compartment. I could hear groaning and moaning from the men in the compartment. I stood up and I could feel the water coming up fast around my body. I waved my arms around to see if I could grab hold of anyone. I couldn't, so I knew I had to move fast. After being blown off the chair onto my back I had to get my sense of direction. The water was now above my waist. I pushed myself toward the steel door that would take me through the kitchen where the hatch was to get out.

I found the steel door. I was lucky that whoever had closed the door only latched it with one top latch. The water carried me through the kitchen. Not being able to see I had to move by feel. I was desperately trying to find the ladder that led up to the hatch. The water was now up to my chin and rising fast.

I tried turning the wheel. It wouldn't turn. I didn't know it at the time, but the explosion had bent the steel rod that locked the hatch into the round grooves. By turning the wheel this lets the hatch spring open. As I was trying to turn the wheel a hand grabbed me by the ankle and tried to pull me off the ladder. I thought this was one of the men fighting for his life, but I wasn't going to let him pull me away from the ladder. So I held onto the ladder with one hand and leaned down into the water. I was going to grab his hand, but just as I filled my lungs with air to dive and grab the person who had his hand on my ankle, he let go.

I tried waving my hand down by my ankle, but I couldn't find him. The water was now up to my nose. I had to keep my head held back to get air to breathe. I used all the strength I had to make the wheel turn on the hatch. I really did some praying. I was asking God to help me. The air pocket was getting smaller as the water was rising.

I could feel the bow of the boat going down. It got to the point that I knew I was going to drown, but I also knew I had to control myself and not panic. My air pocket was filling up with water, so I told myself to take one big intake of air in my lungs and try one last time to open the escape hatch, and if it didn't open, I would be ready to give up my life.

So I filled my lungs with air and I used all the strength in me to turn the steel wheel on the hatch. I could feel the wheel starting to turn and suddenly the hatch flew open and my body shot out of the hatch and I floated to the surface.

The skipper was already out of the boat and was standing on the Sand Caster barge. He bent down and reached out his hand. I swam over to him and he pulled me out of the river. As he did he asked me where the rest of the seven men were. I told him that I thought they were all dead. As I was standing on the Sand Caster barge I had blood coming from my right eye and my leg and shoulder.

All I had on was a t-shirt and pants. I had no shoes on. Standing there on the deck I could see that the bow of the boat was completely underwater. The stern of the sinking boat was straining on the stern rope that had been used to tie our boat to the barge, and the barge was being pulled down.

At about this time two explosions came from underneath the Sand Caster barge. The Vietcong were trying to sink it along with our boat. We could see that no more of our crew were coming out of the hatch that I came out of. The skipper and one of the crew members of the Sand Caster took an axe and cut the stern rope off our boat to let it sink because it was pulling the barge down. I was losing a lot of blood. The skipper said he was going to run up the beach and get medical help for me.

That's all I can remember. I went unconscious and the next thing I faintly remember was being tied down on a stretcher and put into a helicopter, and then an Army nurse giving me morphine. She told me that I would be OK and that they were taking me to a field hospital.

I wanted to talk but I couldn't. My tongue was swollen. A piece of shrapnel had entered the side of my jaw and embedded itself in the side of my tongue. The next thing I remember was being in a small hospital in Da-Nang. I could only see out of one eye. They had a bandage on my right eye.

The first thing that ran through my mind was, "I lost my right eye." A nurse came over to my bed and told me that I still had my right eye, but that it had some shrapnel in it. The doctors were sure that they could get the shrapnel out, and my other wounds would be taken care of. I looked around and could see about thirty wounded military personnel in the ward. No one was talking. I was only there about two days. While I was there Skipper Dan came to visit me. He told me that I was the only one who got out alive, and that American divers were brought in to bring up the bodies of the others. He said the divers couldn't get into the compartment hatch that I had come out of. He said that as the boat went down in the river, bow first, all the foot and wall lockers shifted forward and blocked the hatch that I got out of. He told me that I had gotten out of the hatch just in time before everything shifted to block it. The divers had to burn their way in through the steel side of the boat.

They brought up the bodies and put them in body bags. A lot of Vietnamese village people came out to the riverbank to watch what was going on, and most of them were pointing at the body bags and laughing. The skipper said that if he had had a gun he would have shot them all.

The skipper also told me that when he went up to the beach toward the South Vietnamese Navy boat dock to use their radio to call for medical help, he was being shot at. I could see on the skipper's face that he was taking all that had happened very hard. We had lost our boat and all seven men of the survey crew. Dan told me that the next night after the sinking of our boat, South Vietnamese had shot and killed the North Vietnamese underwater frogman known as a "Sapper." He was trying to blow up their boats. The report said he was the frogman who sank our boat.

I thought to myself that what happened, the sinking of our boat and losing all our friends, might drive the skipper to being sober, or it might make him hit the whiskey bottle that much more. That was the last time I saw him. The hospital people wheeled me into the examination room. They had me half doped up with medicine. I heard the examining doctor tell someone in the room, "Put this man on the evacuating list to Guam." I wanted to say, "No. I don't want to be evacuated to Guam," but I couldn't talk or move.

I must have passed out right after hearing that. The next thing I remember I was being carried aboard a plane with a lot of military wounded, and a nurse was giving me more medicine. I think she wanted to knock me out again for the flight to Guam.

My next memory is of a big ward with a lot of beds with wounded military personnel in them. I asked the guy in the next bed who was looking at me, "Where am I?" He said, "Naval hospital in Guam." I asked him how long he had been there in the hospital. He said, "Three days."

I asked him if he had been wounded in Vietnam. He said, "Yes," and that everyone in the ward had been wounded in Vietnam. He told me that it would be about two days before they would wheel me into the operating room to close my wounds. It wasn't long before I found out why they wait two days. Each morning and each evening two medical personnel would come into the ward pushing a wheeled cart with containers of brown-looking liquid. They had very small looking mops that they would use to swab this brown medicine on our wounds, and this brown liquid would sting in the wound.

We all hated seeing this silver cart come wheeling down the ward. There was one wounded soldier in the ward I had sympathy for. I was told that he had been standing next to an ammunition bunker when the Vietcong hit the bunker with a direct mortar shell blowing up the bunker. He was lucky to be alive. I have never seen as many wounds on a body as this soldier had, big open wounds up his back and on the front of his body and face. When the brown medicine was swabbed on him there was screaming. I just gritted my teeth.

While I was in the hospital I received a letter from the main office of Morrison Knudsen telling me they were sorry that our boat was blown up and that we had lost seven men. They told me that all of the men in the boat compartment with me died instantly at the time of the explosion, and that the military divers brought up the bodies out of the boat in pieces, so they didn't suffer. I thought to myself, "What a lie." I was there when the explosion happened, and I know damn well that not all of them died instantly. Right after the explosion I had heard men moaning, and when I reached the ladder to the hatch, the only way out, someone grabbed my ankle, but let go before I could reach him.

This will be in my memory for the rest of my life. I keep thinking that if only I could have been a little quicker in diving down in the water to grab hold of the person, he might be alive today. I will always feel that hand pulling on my ankle. Those men were fighting for their lives.

While I was in the hospital I had a lot of time to think about the sinking of our boat and about the seven men who died. I had a lot of time to wonder why I was the only one to survive. And I would wonder why I had made the decision to volunteer to go back to Vietnam as a civilian when a war was going on.

As I was lying there a soldier on crutches came up to my bed and asked me what outfit I was with, and where in Vietnam I was when I got wounded. I was the only civilian in the ward. I told him that I was not in any military outfit, that I was a civilian in Vietnam. The soldier didn't know about civilian contractors in Vietnam. When I told him he said, "You must be nuts to be in Vietnam as a civilian." At the time, when I did decide to go back to Vietnam, I had a feeling of being indestructible. I no longer have that feeling. I feel that I have died and come back. I am very thankful that God heard my prayers asking for his helping hand out of a sinking boat.

I stayed in the hospital about thirty days. The doctors picked most of the shrapnel out of my body and closed my wounds. They couldn't get some of the shrapnel out because it was embedded in my bones. My right eye had small pieces of shrapnel in the nerves. They didn't want to remove it because that would cause more damage to the eye. I would just have to live with it.

I'm lucky and thankful to be alive. When the hospital discharged me they gave me a belt and a wristwatch, a Timex. The crystal was broken on the watch and there was dried blood on the face of it, but the watch would still work.

When I was taken to the first aid station when I first got wounded, they cut all my clothes off me, so now I was lucky that Morrison Knudsen sent me some of my pay while I was in the hospital. There was a small store on the first floor of the hospital where I bought some clothes so that I could walk out with clothes on.

All the while I was working in Vietnam as a civilian there was a strong saying among all the workers that President Lyndon B. Johnson owned stock with MK and BRJ, Morrison Knudsen and Brown, Root and Jones contracting companies while the Vietnam War was raging.

My going back to Vietnam as a civilian was a very foolish thing to do. Back home I found myself consuming a lot of alcohol and fighting a lot of war flashbacks and nightmares. This is called Post-Traumatic Stress syndrome. Booze would make the terrifying memories fade, but after a long while I had to get off alcohol, which I did.

I felt anger toward Morrison Knudsen and anger toward the U.S. Navy for their failure to provide the promised security for our crew members and our vessel, the Tudor. If the Navy had provided security all seven men who lost their lives by enemy action would more than likely be alive today.

Through all these years Navy officials have not even attempted to offer an apology, but I will not let anger overtake me. I once heard it said that, "After anger when the spitting fire is calm, when the intense danger is past, when the flaming fury is spent, how wide the trail of ashes."

My travels through life's rocky roads have taught me the value of hard work, personal achievement, pursuing my dreams and knowing that the Lord was with me every step of the way in my life.

RECOMMENDED MILITARY BOOKS TO READ

1. <u>Vietnam Military Lore Legends, Shadows and Heroes</u>, by M/Sgt. Roy Bows, U.S. Army Retired.
2. <u>This Kind of War</u>, (The Classic Korean War History), by T.R. Fehrenbach, Books, Brassey's, Washington and London.
3. <u>Soldiers of Misfortune</u>, by James D. Sanders and Mark A. Sauter, R. Cort Kirkwood.
4. <u>The Lost Ships of Guadalcanal</u>, by Robert Ballard with Rick Archbold.
5. <u>The Siege at Hue</u>, by George W. Smith.
6. <u>Why Didn't You Get Me Out?</u>, by Frank Anton with Tommy Denton.
7. <u>The Execution of Private Slovik</u>, by William Bradford Huie.
8. <u>No Name on the Bullet</u>, <u>Autobiography of Audie Murphy</u>, by Don Graham.

ISBN 141205938-0